AUTHORSHIP, COMMERCE, AND GENDER IN EARLY EIGHTEENTH-CENTURY ENGLAND

A CULTURE OF PAPER CREDIT

Speculative investment and the popular novel can be seen as analogous in the early eighteenth century in offering new forms of "paper credit"; and in both, women – who invested enthusiastically in financial schemes, and were significant producers and consumers of novels – played an essential role. Examining women's participation in the South Sea Bubble and the representations of investors and stockbrokers as "feminized," Catherine Ingrassia discusses the connection between the cultural resistance to speculative finance and hostility to the similarly "feminized" professional writers that Alexander Pope depicts in the *Dunciad*. Focusing on Eliza Haywood, and also on her male contemporaries Pope and Samuel Richardson, Ingrassia goes on to illustrate how new financial and fictional models were important for women's social, sexual, and economic interaction.

Catherine Ingrassia is Assistant Professor of English at Virginia Commonwealth University.

AUTHORSHIP, COMMERCE, AND GENDER IN EARLY EIGHTEENTH-CENTURY ENGLAND

A Culture of Paper Credit

CATHERINE INGRASSIA

CAMBRIDGE
UNIVERSITY PRESS

CAMBRIDGE UNIVERSITY PRESS
Cambridge, New York, Melbourne, Madrid, Cape Town, Singapore, São Paulo

Cambridge University Press
The Edinburgh Building, Cambridge CB2 2RU, UK

Published in the United States of America by Cambridge University Press, New York

www.cambridge.org
Information on this title: www.cambridge.org/9780521630634

First published 1998
This digitally printed first paperback version 2005

A catalogue record for this publication is available from the British Library

Library of Congress Cataloguing in Publication data
Ingrassia, Catherine.
Authorship, commerce, and gender in early eighteenth-century
England: a culture of paper credit/Catherine Ingrassia.
p.   cm.
Includes bibliographical references and index.
ISBN 0 521 63063 0 (hb)
1. English literature – 18th century–History and criticism.
2. Authorship–Economic aspects – England – History – 18th century.
3. Women and literature – England – History – 18th century.
4. Speculation – England – History – 18th century.   5. England –
Economic conditions – 18th century.   6. Commerce – England –
History – 18th century.   7. Economics in literature.   8. Sex role in
literature.   I. Title.
PR468.E36I54 1998
820.9'005–dc21   97-35276   CIP

ISBN-13 978-0-521-63063-4 hardback
ISBN-10 0-521-63063-0 hardback

ISBN-13 978-0-521-02301-6 paperback
ISBN-10 0-521-02301-7 paperback

For Miles, of course

Contents

Figures

Acknowledgments

The Dow Jones industrial average that serves as the index for the New York Stock Exchange has shattered 8,000 in a record-breaking bull market that some think has no end in sight. As one financial analyst observes, "Wall Street isn't too concerned about the economy," suggesting the sort of fictional, alternative reality in which "high finance" operates. I recently received a brochure from a financial firm that claims it has elevated investment to "an *art form*" with "passion, energy, and creative thinking" (the same impulses viewed with suspicion in the eighteenth century). Speculative investment as artistic creation. We no longer call middle Americans who participate in the market "speculators," yet they display a credulity reminiscent of British investors of the early eighteenth century, gripped with the excitement about paper credit. They want to believe that the climate of financial prosperity and rising stock prices will continue indefinitely. Investors now must be gently reminded that shares in a mutual fund "are not deposits or obligations, not endorsed or guaranteed by any bank." Despite appearances to the contrary, such investment does not ensure wealth; the market correction will inevitably occur and the bubble of the 1990s, like the South Sea Bubble of 1720, will ultimately burst (or at least deflate a little). While speculative investment operated in a somewhat less sophisticated fashion during the early eighteenth century, then as now it was driven by the same willingness to believe a fiction about the future. This book looks at the development of different types of narratives – fictional and financial – that individuals create in an attempt to improve or change their lives. Though it focuses on early eighteenth-century England, that culture's enthusiasm for creating and sustaining fictional narratives, its desire to acquire "wealth" (no matter how imaginary), and its fascination with the stories of others who do, make those issues and concerns resonate within our time as well.

Many individuals and institutions invested speculatively in the future of my book (begun when the Dow was considerably lower). Virginia Commonwealth University provided research funding in the form of a Grants-in-Aid Award and a Faculty Development Award. My department chair, Richard Fine, as well as Vice-Provost David Hiley, enabled me to take advantage of opportunities for leave and course reduction. The National Endowment for the Humanities 1994 summer seminar at the Public Record Office, Chancery Lane, proved central to my work. I profited tremendously from the knowledge, kindness, and intellectual rigor of its director, Paula Backscheider, and from the invaluable material I located at the PRO. The William Andrews Clark Memorial Library and the University of Texas at Austin provided essential fellowships during the early stages of this project.

I had the good fortune to spend time at the Newberry Library twice: once as a graduate student and then, more recently and extensively, as the Monticello College Foundation Fellow (1995/96). That fellowship and the intellectual home of the Newberry provided the ideal environment to complete this book. During my time there, I benefited from interaction with the following scholars and "fellow" fellows who asked challenging questions that helped me refine my project: Cristelle Baskins, Henry Binford, Toni Bowers, Margaret Ferguson, Fred Hoxie, Susan Manning, Meredith Magill, Jeff Ravel, and Mary Beth Rose. David Lowenstein offered sage advice at just the right moment. I am especially grateful to Theresa Toulouse (the most generous scholar I know) who taught by example and who pushed me to be less "tidy" in my thinking.

Other individuals have read, commented on, or otherwise supported this project at various stages: Joe Anne Brabham, Boyd Berry, Vincent Carretta, Glen Coburn, R. C. Emerson, Paul J. and Vita C. Ingrassia, Marguerite Harkness, Theresa Kelley, Devoney Looser, Sarah J. Marsh, Charlotte Morse, Melinda Reed, Judy Slagle, and Denise Sechelski. The responses from the anonymous readers for Cambridge improved the manuscript tremendously. The members of the Folger Institute Colloquium (1992–95) "Women in the Eighteenth Century" offered keen criticism and good friendship. Early on, Lance Bertelsen helped me see how discrete parts could become a whole.

Finally, I need to acknowledge debts of a more personal nature. My fellowship at the Newberry put me in geographic proximity to my parents, Paul R. and Roberta E. Ingrassia. They graciously allowed their only child to commandeer their home, their laser printer, and their laundry room. As with all things in my life, they made this project more enjoyable and attainable. Most profoundly, I thank Miles Scott McCrimmon – best friend, best editor, and best possible partner in life. His patience, insight, and understanding are unrivaled, and his enthusiasm is on every page.

Abbreviations

Corr. *The Correspondence of Alexander Pope*, in 5 vols., edited by George Sherburn (Oxford: Clarendon Press, 1956).

Spectator *The Spectator*, in 5 vols., edited by Donald Bond (Oxford at the Clarendon Press, 1965).

TE *The Twickenham Edition of the Poems of Alexander Pope*, in 11 vols. General editor John Butt (London: Methuen, 1938–68).

Introduction: paper credit

I began this project by asking a deceptively simple question about Alexander Pope's 1728 edition of the *Dunciad*: why was the figure of Dulness, who embodies his worst fears about the deterioration of culture, a woman? While critics had written extensively on how the satire depicts the commercialization of literature, no one had ever focused on the woman in the center of the poem – the goddess Dulness with her monstrous femininity.[1] Prolifically reproducing, Dulness populates the "new Saturnian Age of Lead" with energetic yet misdirected dunces whose absolute submission to the goddess bespeaks her dangerous power. In exploring Pope's representation of Dulness, I realized that his anxiety, while focusing on the activities of the literary marketplace or "Grub Street," also expresses cultural ambivalence about the increasing centrality of speculative investment and the mechanisms of the new financial marketplace, or "Exchange Alley." As Pope subsequently indicates in *Epistle to Bathurst* (1733) and the 1743 edition of the *Dunciad*, the commercialization of literature and the growth of speculative investment, and the participants in each phenomenon, hacks and stock-jobbers, were both for him symptomatic of a larger cultural problem. His representation of the intertwined activities of the literary and financial spheres emphasizes what he regards as the absence of masculinity, indeed the feminization of a new breed of economic, literary, and political subject. Gendering the participants and their practices, Pope attempts to diminish them by highlighting the stereotypically feminized characteristics that he feels influenced their actions and the direction of culture as a whole.

This pattern of representation is not unique to Pope but appears in numerous other texts relating to the emergent financial and literary activities. Although Pope wrote from a very specific (and to his mind embattled) cultural position, his anxieties and the connections he made between the new literary and financial practices are consistent with other discursive attempts to deal with these innovations and their destabilizing effect on constructions of gender. My book explores the relationship between the development of speculative investment and the emergence of the novel in early eighteenth-century England. I'm concerned with the ways activities in the new economic system and pursuits in the literary marketplace were constructed as culturally analogous and can be read as historically contingent symbolic practices that changed individuals' understanding of their opportunities for "improvement." The social, ideological, discursive, and, I argue, even emotional possibilities introduced by speculative investment inform actions within the literary marketplace and come to manifest themselves in the genre and discourse of the novel. Reading a novel, like investing in a speculative financial venture, demanded readers' imaginative participation in a narrative that could potentially be a vehicle with which early modern subjects could reinvent themselves and envisage their lives differently. At the same time, the development of popular fiction and the acceptance of various narrative conventions naturalized the demands speculative investment made on participants' imaginations. Not only did both these cultural innovations alter the way individuals considered the possibilities and limitations of eighteenth-century culture, they also created a significant new space for women to act with some agency. The interplay between the material participation of women in financial and literary milieus and the symbolic characterization of certain subjects and activities as "feminized" is central to the construction of gender and the representation of and cultural attitude toward these rapid changes.

The reasons for the feminized characterization of these practices and their participants are multiple. This feminization is not absolute nor can the term be applied uncritically; nevertheless it is a consistent, albeit shifting, pattern of representation that stems, in part, from an older practice of gendering feminine that which is devalued. The discourse also draws on traditional iconographic associations with the unstable female figures such as Credit, Fortune, and Luxury, that symbolically control the marketplace (literary and financial). Furthermore, as I noted above, such symbolic prominence is not without material precedents. Women of the middle and upper classes had a marked and culturally significant presence in Grub Street and Exchange Alley. Within these undefined and penetrable cultural spaces women with the financial capital or literary ambition exploited the opportunity to act. Between 1690 and 1740, women consistently accounted for approximately 20 percent of the investors in major stock and bank funds.[2] Their production of popular fiction was similarly impressive and women, for a time, were emerging as important participants in these new literary and financial venues.[3] Peter Stallybrass and Allon White observe that one might occupy a "powerful symbolic domain despite and because of . . . actual social marginalization."[4] The participation of women, while seemingly peripheral, actually fueled the gendered characterization placed on the commercialization of the literary marketplace, the proliferation of speculative investment, and the readers and writers of the novel.

A complex series of (often antagonistic) class relationships also contributed to this persistent representation of different segments of the population as increasingly "feminized." Depending on one's subject position, almost any other group was, at one time, figured as somehow "feminine," for a failure to meet the accepted standards of masculinity. While these characterizations manifested themselves at various points in the century, most significant for my discussion is the persistent feminized characterization of the so-called "new economic man" who deals in stocks or invests speculatively. J. G. A. Pocock has asserted the economic man was perceived as a feminized or even an "effeminate" being "still wrestling with his own passions and hysterias and with interior and exterior forces let loose by his fantasies and appetites." He was seen relying on the imaginative forces necessary for financial investment in a fluctuating market where "production and exchange are regularly equated with the ascendancy of the passions and the female principles."[5] Pocock's assertions, which have drawn reconsiderations most notably from Joyce Appleby and most recently from Michael McKeon, reconstruct what he perceives as the neo-Harringtonian model of citizenship that emerged in the late seventeenth century in response to various political, social, and economic changes.[6] A landed aristocracy (or those who allied themselves with such), concerned with the potential erosion of its cultural dominance, resurrected a classical construction of citizenship to bolster the claims to superiority it already possessed (legally and ideologically).

England had been wedded to the idealized concept of land as the most important form of property in which the individual located his political subjectivity, his civic responsibility, and his public personality. The "moneyed" or economic subjects, in contrast to the paternal, stable, and rational figure of the landed citizen, were perceived as symbolically indulging their desires and displaying their "feminized" tendencies. Though intended as an assertion of cultural dominance by a specific social group, the potent pattern of gendered representation continued into the middle decades of the eighteenth century and became increasingly widespread. While some of this language (such as the image of the bubble to signify the financial revolution) originated in the Opposition, other tropes, rhetorical techniques, and symbols (such as the female figure of Credit) originated with the Whigs and were used by multiple groups to various effects.[7]

The pervasive imagery also developed, in part, because of the financial and literary world's dependence on paper credit and the new intangible forms of property which were thought to require and stimulate characteristics culturally constructed as feminine. Both Exchange Alley and Grub Street demanded an ability to participate in a symbolic imaginative economy or value system based on paper, the so-called "paper credit" to which my title refers. The term "paper credit" has been closely associated with Pope's representation in *Epistle to Bathurst* of the insubstantial and intangible forms of property circulating in society. He laments the "invention of money" and the increasing facility with which individuals have access to funds. "Blest paper-credit! last and best supply! / That lends Corruption lighter wings to fly."[8] In this context, Pope refers quite specifically and disparagingly to a growing paper economy ushered in by England's financial revolution of the 1690s. He resists the "lightness" (indeed near weightlessness) and immateriality of money and its increased efficiency to bribe, barter, or borrow: "A single leaf shall waft an Army o'er, / Or ship off Senates to a distant Shore; / A leaf, like Sibyl's, scatter to and fro / Our fates and fortunes, as the winds shall blow: / Pregnant with thousands flits the Scrap unseen, / And silent sells a King, or buys a Queen" (73–78). "Scraps" and "leaves" have the power to change political, royal, and military action. The wealth acquired in this manner threatens the dissolution of the dominant hierarchies, a problem Pope illustrates with the inappropriate blurring of public space designated by class and gender: "Statesman and Patriot ply alike the stocks, / Peeress and Butler share alike the Box, / And Judges job, and Bishops bite the town, / And mighty Dukes pack cards for half a crown" (141–44). As F. W. Bateson reminds us, the lines refer not just to the confusion of ranks (peeress and butler), but also to "the attendant confusion of the sexes. Normally . . . the women occupied the front-boxes in the London theatres and the men the side-boxes."[9]

The poem also illustrates how women exacerbate the dangers of paper credit. For example, in Balaam's decline caused by an excess of wealth, one of the final blows is his wife's gambling debts, an activity read as a type of speculative investment: "My Lady falls to play; so bad her chance, / He must repair it; takes a bribe from France; / The House impeach him;

Coningsby harangues; / The Court forsake him, and Sir Balaam hangs"
(395–98). Pope's attempts to contain and control paper credit with his
textual representation indicate his awareness of not just its insubstantiality, but its fundamental instability. Paper credit's value could rise and
fall with ease; it could enhance an individual's ability to gain wealth,
change position, or pose as someone else; indeed, there seemed to be no
limit to what paper credit could do. Like Dulness herself, it was
"Pregnant" (77) with myriad possibilities, a fecund image consonant with
fears of feminization.

Paper credit and the mechanisms of speculative investment shifted the
nature of property from a material, immovable, and stable form such as
land to fluid, immaterial, and multiple ones. The development of a system
of public credit, banking facilities, public and private lotteries, and joint-
stock companies that marked England's so-called "financial revolution"
all provided opportunities for financial speculation, diversified investments, and non-landed property.[10] With new financial institutions, the
types of negotiable paper available proliferated: lottery tickets, stocks, bills
of exchange, and letters of credit were among the numerous forms of
"credit"-able paper in circulation.[11] With the change in the nature of
value systems, property became increasingly unreal. The new financial
instruments of Exchange Alley were largely immaterial forms of property
that could be realized only imaginatively. When investors bought stock or
an annuity, they received nothing tangible for their purchase – usually only
a receipt for the stock or a numbered stock certificate or "bond."[12]
Consequently, there was no apparent relationship between sign and signified, between the paper receipt and the value it represented.

Critics of the new financial instruments often focused on their fundamental insubstantiality. In a 1720 pamphlet, *A Letter to a Conscientious Man*,
speculative investment is described as "a Business founded upon nothing
that is solid, rational, or honest, but meerly upon Artifice, Trick and
Catch."[13] In *Spectator* 191, Steele notes how "Caprice often acts in the Place
of Reason, and forms to itself some Groundless Imaginary Motive, where
real and substantial ones are wanting."[14] As Sandra Sherman suggests,
credit was "a mirage of signifiers lacking signifieds."[15] The investor had to
fantasize or create imaginatively a narrative that invested the purchase
with some meaning about the individual stock and the future performance
of the market.[16] Within this construction, unlike a mercantile economy
which is characterized by the accumulation and exchange of tangible
goods and products, finance capitalism is marked by invisible forces and
intangible (indeed imaginary) commodities.[17] Consequently, a speculator

could assess his accumulated wealth (with a value contingent on current market prices) only through discursive means. The rise and fall of stock, the whims of the marketplace, that affected the lives and fortunes of so many individuals did not "exist" or occur anywhere. It was not a "real" event; rather it was a phenomenon that could be known primarily through print sources like newspapers or stock sheets dedicated to the listing of various values. Even less reliably, value could be learned through the "word on the street," the rumors and opinions that influenced the price of shares. The workings of the new financial economy existed discursively, to be accessed on the page and recreated imaginatively in the mind of the investor.

While the term "paper credit" in early eighteenth-century England has been primarily associated with financial activities, I would suggest that it similarly informs, materially and symbolically, the volatile literary milieu of Grub Street. Like Exchange Alley, Grub Street and the literary market-place were driven by the proliferation and manipulation of symbolic instruments – writers jockeyed for position by continuing to produce texts that met changing demands from their reading and buying public. A writer's worth or "credit" depended on his or her production of literary commodities – a scurrilous pamphlet, a popular novel, or a piece of criti-cism. As with stock, a writer's "portfolio" of paper credit had a value that depended on the fluctuations of a marketplace influenced by fancy, desire, and the brief attention span of consumers. Just as an economic man relied on the buying and selling of stock and its capital appreciation, so too the professional writer of Grub Street depended on the buying and selling of texts, and their escalating value (or "capital appreciation") contingent on that text's reputation, notoriety, or popularity – in other words, the author's credit on paper. In an attempt to distinguish himself from the "hack" writers he disdained, Pope regarded his poetry as a type of property comparable to land that he similarly tended and cultivated. To a certain extent Pope succeeded in his attempts to materialize his literary property, although he, like all authors, had to confront the fundamental instability of language within a profession dependent on inherently immaterial signify-ing systems.[18]

The emerging prose forms of popular fiction (amatory fiction, the novel, secret histories), suffered a particularly keen insubstantiality similar to the new forms of property. Unlike history, which can purport to be "real," fiction by its very nature was seen as not real, a discourse of inten-tional deception designed, in part, to arouse fantasies and desires in the reader. Like the buying of stock, the reading of novels demanded of author and reader, or producer and consumer, the participation in or the creation of an imaginatively based narrative. Consequently, imagination and fantasy, unleashed emotions, and unregulated passions – all impulses distinctly gendered female – were seen as driving the engines of Exchange Alley and Grub Street. In these two different yet similar environments, individuals disenfranchised from the traditional avenues of power – women, non-aristocratic men, members of the middling and lower classes – gained new opportunities through paper credit.[19] As a result, both environments were potential sites for anxiety about the shifting constructions of gender and the centrality of "feminized" practices, and for the contestation and reconfiguration of socio-economic relations.

My book reads texts, activities, and symbolic practices at separate sites as mutually informing. Discrete financial and literary practices operate as connected parts of a relationally configured culture. Discursive texts of all types enable a culture to create, organize, and reproduce itself. They transform their reading subjects and in turn record the process of transformation. They simultaneously reflect and inform, resonate with and constitute both their socio-economic environment and the overarching culture in which they are contained. Fredric Jameson suggests cultural artifacts function as socially symbolic acts.[20] They create what Richard Johnson describes as "those social forms through which human beings produce and reproduce their material life ... become conscious, sustain themselves subjectively."[21] My study engages a variety of cultural documents – personal correspondence, novels, poetry, broadsheets, ephemera – through which individual subjects negotiate social change as well as their own relationships to different sources of power. The social, literary, and symbolic texts do a great deal of cultural "work" as they interpret and transform individual subjects, their construction of "reality," and their relationship with other subjects. By examining diverse discourses we can reconstruct (within limits) how they shaped eighteenth-century society, responded to cultural change, and emerged as sites of class struggle. A necessary and inextricable relationship exists between discursive forms and their constitutive possibilities, between contemporaneous social practices and material "reality" as that is variously understood.

The multiple activities in the literary and the financial spheres (Grub Street and Exchange Alley) would seem to be discrete and infrequently interacting. Yet these activities are never entirely separable, in part because of their reliance on similar discursive and imaginative possibilities, and in part because of the desires they simultaneously create and satisfy. The cultural practices of the emergent literary and financial marketplaces, like their textual manifestations, impinge upon dominant and residual elements of culture and mediate this moment of profound social change and the active (and often acrimonious) reconfiguration of the controlling hierarchies and symbolic relationships.[22]

Those controlling hierarchies and symbolic relationships were articulated through constructed categories such as class, literary hierarchy, and gender. Though, in fact, these categories were still deeply contested, a binary classification of culture developed in texts (like the *Dunciad*) that have traditionally been read by scholars as representative of the "Augustan" ideology. The resistant reaction by individuals such as Pope, Swift, and Bolingbroke to what they regarded as "the disorder and chaos brought to the traditional political and social world by money and financial innovation" has been termed "the politics of nostalgia" by Isaac Kramnick.[23] In his formulation, the more conservative political subjects retreated to elements of residual culture, to a highly idealized reconstruction of a patriarchal past, an aristocratic social and political order they perceived as threatened. That ideological position, which influenced subsequent constructions of the "Augustan" or the "neo-classical" age, produced an oppositional model of socio-economic relations, one valorizing the idealized components of the past and denigrating and resisting the practices of the present. Though Kramnick discusses the political activity of a specific social context, the attitude extended to other cultural activities and embraced what we might consider a "*poetics* of nostalgia," often read as the dominant cultural position. These eighteenth-century subjects created a fiction of the present that allowed them to organize the world into binary social, economic, and literary relations. Such binaries attempt to reinforce the status quo and to privilege a static (and thus controllable) vision of culture. A simplified model of this oppositional classification might include the following:

landed aristocrat	moneyed or "new" economic man
the country	the City, Exchange Alley
hierarchical society	social mixing/anti-hierarchical impulse
patronage, authors, history	Grub Street, hacks, novels
land, tangible commodities	paper credit
masculine	feminine
tradition, past	present, future

Of course, neither world ever existed as constructed. Scholars have appropriated an eighteenth-century cultural fiction as fact, often using the familiar oppositions as an *ad hoc* taxonomy (comfortable in our identification of "homo duncus"). We readily accede to the past's construction of itself because no other construction is available except other contemporary versions of the past. The construction of such a binary, which is inadequate, provides the only vocabulary we have to talk about these cultural relations. The terms, which construct a sort of phenomenology of culture, are provisional and yet necessary both for contemporary scholars and eighteenth-century subjects. Despite their obvious limitations (limitations inherent in any classificatory construction of social relations), these terms and concepts have infused discourse and continue to be a highly potent tool of cultural representation.

In fact, the artificial and tenuous cultural categories were not binary at all, or were binary only in so far as they can be conceived as part of a larger complicated series of cultural struggles along the allegedly stable lines of demarcation. Rather than being mutually exclusive, these relationships comprised a mutually informing dialectic; they illustrate sites of contestation and the processes of (re)producing culture. Eighteenth-century subjects like Pope lived within these contested structures prompting their vociferous adherence to a manageable (and identifiable) classificatory system. The act of scholarship often replicates the cultural relations it seeks to dissect. Current work that attempts to subvert this model inevitably carries the mark of such binary thinking. The critic attempting to locate Pope within consumer culture has to make sure he is not seen as a "hack" but rather as a purveyor of fine literary commodities. The recent attention to Eliza Haywood has proven her cultural significance but not without the obligatory references to her "scandalous" novels and allegedly disreputable past. Contemporary critical works, like eighteenth-century texts, draw upon these images and ideas in working through the cultural tensions, forcing us to distinguish between the constructed dialectic and the material practices that complicated those relationships. We need to be sentient of the interplay between the two. We must resist the effort to stabilize or tidy up our representation of the cultural landscape and instead reclassify it as a field in which dominant, emergent, and residual ideologies interacted, and in which different texts contributed to and recorded that process.

Read this way, a more complicated vision emerges of a culture wrestling to stabilize (and in the process create) the very categories destabilized because of the development of various social practices (both material and symbolic). Grub Street and Exchange Alley, and their various discursive manifestations, became a nexus of cultural indeterminacy and anxiety. Episodes that captured the popular imagination such as the South Sea

Bubble or the publication of *Pamela* or the *Dunciad* had the power to disrupt the already tenuous binary configuration of cultural relations.[24] Similarly, the activities, discourses, and concerns from apparently disparate domains such as the literary and financial profoundly penetrate and inform one another in both public and private documents. These texts complicate relationships often threatened to be obscured by a more monologic narrative of culture constructed by a dominant group.[25] Activities within the literary and financial spheres reconfigured, in fundamental ways, literary, social, and economic relations in early eighteenth-century culture.

The novel and speculative investment did not play identical roles in this process, and by linking them with the concept of "paper credit" I don't mean to stabilize a fundamentally dynamic relationship. The concepts central to my study do not remain stable during the course of the century or even during the period which my book explores. Indeed, the most volatile terms are, in some ways, the ones perhaps most fully recuperated. For example, with its increasing centrality in all economic relations the concept of paper credit is absorbed into the dominant Whig ideology. As A. O. Hirschman describes, the self-directed avaricious "passions" that motivate moneyed men are transfigured into outwardly directed and nationally beneficial "interests" to accommodate the actions of trade and investment.[26] The notion of paper credit in a literary sense is similarly moderated. The development of the novel, the introduction of women writers, the figure of the hack writer, among many other things, made the literary marketplace an expansive and unstable site of cultural activity in the early eighteenth century. Though the imaginative and material production of and demand for literary commodities grew throughout the century, access to the (real) material power of the print trade was limited. Genres such as the novel, initially regarded as "low" and popular, became increasingly codified and stabilized. The representations of women as readers and writers of the novel and as financial investors, along with the characterizations they simultaneously created and engendered, were modified and normalized as the emergent manifestations of cultural change were ultimately assimilated into the dominant ideology.

My first chapter discusses the verbal and visual representations of the South Sea Company stock crisis of 1720. The South Sea Bubble, as it is commonly known, was a moment of profound financial crisis that created an environment of socio-economic confusion and widespread cultural anxiety. The power of this incident arose both from the possibilities investment in the South Sea Company initially presented for a range of subjects, including women, and from the radical failure of those opportunities. The South Sea Bubble, as it was immediately represented and as it existed in cultural memory, was certainly a "popular" event, extensively discussed in public and private texts. Women's representations of their own financial actions in private correspondence and, in turn, the public representation of those actions sharply illustrate the tensions involving gender, class, and paper credit that characterize this period.

The cultural anxiety about gender and credit (and by extension about imaginative narratives) stimulated by the South Sea Bubble similarly informed the texts and professional strategies of Alexander Pope, Eliza Haywood, and Samuel Richardson. They all dealt with paper credit in multiple ways, whether addressing it discursively or encountering it materially. Each represented, negotiated, and, in various ways, profited from his or her participation in a marketplace dually influenced by the forces of a speculative literary and financial economy. As I suggested earlier and as my second chapter details, Pope's anxiety about the dunces and the infectious force of Dulness resided in the ways their activities were for him symptomatic of the broader "feminization" of culture. In representing the hack writers trying to sell their ever-increasing stockpiles of paper, Pope draws on the lingering suspicion about immaterial forms of literary and financial property, and his own ambivalence about the commercialization of literature and consumer culture. His sustained attack on Eliza Haywood specifically, and women writers generally, projects his apprehensions about the expanding place for women within the production and consumption of literary commodities. By gendering the dunces feminine, Pope also locates his poem within a pervasive cultural discourse expressing anxiety about the feminized economic man. But in doing so he raises problematic issues relating to his own ambiguous position. Pope, of course, was complicit in the very culture he criticized. Not only did he buy South Sea Company stock, but with literary projects like his translation of Homer he also profited handsomely from the same literary marketplace he attacks in the *Dunciad*. Contradictions dogged Pope's career. He simultaneously resisted and embraced those cultural forces he represents as feminized. Though he profited greatly and worked hard to control the physical appearance and the value of his text as a material commodity, he still expressed a lingering anxiety about the minimal materiality inherent in signifying systems. He knew he was living in a paper world.

The insubstantiality and the need to earn credit were particularly acute problems for a woman writer like Eliza Haywood, the subject of chapters 3 and 4. One of the most popular and prolific novelists of the early eighteenth century, Haywood published at least thirty-seven texts between 1719 and 1731. For Pope, she embodied his worst fears about the feminization of culture, as he demonstrates with his depiction of her in the *Dunciad*. Like Pope's, Haywood's publications and activities within the literary marketplace revealed an awareness of her dependence (as a writer and a woman) on a world of paper credit. She wrote primarily fiction (considered titillating and scandalous by her contemporaries like Pope) for popular consumption by a primarily female audience; she tried to appeal to her audience's passions, desires, and interest in an imaginative displacement of self. Like most authors (except Pope), she did not own the copyrights to her works, and lacked access to the real control within print culture; she could earn only various types of "credit" within the literary marketplace. She capitalized on the allure of her texts and the marketability of her constructed authorial persona – both intangible, imaginatively based commodities.

Her novels from the 1720s represented fictionally the forces she encountered materially. She explored in specific terms a woman's ability to negotiate sexual and financial economies. While her early career indicates her ability to accumulate primarily paper credit, in the 1740s she attempted to gain power within the material production of the print trade, to translate her credit into property. In 1741, she opened a bookseller's shop, a short-lived venture, and she continued to operate as a producer, distributor, and assembler of texts, perhaps trying to make her world less speculative within a culture still attempting to assimilate the forces of paper credit. In the later part of her career, Haywood created unauthorized spaces in which to react to the dominant practice.

By reading Haywood in the context of Pope and Richardson, I want to resist the tendency to place women writers in an exclusively female literary tradition or to add uncritically another woman to the canon. While numerous excellent studies of eighteenth-century women writers exist, they variously read these women discretely or as part of an alternative literary history.[27] Haywood's significance can better be understood by recontextualizing her within the professionalization of authorship and the development of Grub Street. Her personal and professional interactions with a range of authors, including Pope and Richardson, compel us to analyze her within that context. Yet, her extraordinary (and atypical) rate of literary production, the forty-year duration of her career, and her multiple roles within the print trade make her activities in the literary marketplace exceptional rather than representative. I devote two chapters to Haywood because she is one of the most significant woman writers of her time; because her experiences illustrate the situation for women more broadly within the literary marketplace; and because a clearer understanding of Haywood enriches (and enhances) our ability to comprehend the writers like Pope and Richardson with whom she had both material and symbolic interactions. Haywood wrote actively during the period of Pope and Richardson's greatest literary productivity; her longevity confounds a strictly chronological organization of my book since she is contemporaneous with both authors. I have made the Haywood sections the center of the book organizationally because, in many ways, she is the center of the study. The chapters on Haywood, while focused on her, simultaneously illuminate our understanding of her male contemporaries by placing them in a dialogical relationship that enables us more fully to understand their connections. Though Pope and Richardson have traditionally been read as the dominant voices of the period, situating them within a volatile literary marketplace, examining their discursive struggles with someone like Haywood, and recontextualizing their literary activities allows us to reassess their "dominance" and their place within eighteenth-century culture.

Additionally I focus primarily on Haywood's novels, rather than her periodicals or dramatic texts, because of what that genre meant for women as readers and writers at this time. Haywood's narratives offered women discursive representations that challenged the dominant construction of gender and depicted women acting in empowering and at times transgressive ways. They provided an imaginative displacement of self and a vehicle for women to conceive of the world and their relationships within it differently. The experience of reading the novel (as a genre) privileges privacy, self-identification, and a narrative investment that other genres (drama, poetry, newspapers) do not. The novel also potentially reaches a range of readers across a wide social spectrum, as indicated by the immense popularity of something like Haywood's *Love in Excess* (1719) or Richardson's *Pamela* (1740). As a genre, the novel potentially changes the way people see themselves as subjects acting in the world. There is a larger cultural inscription not of a type of discourse *per se* (although that was certainly part of it), but of the imaginative possibilities fiction – amatory and otherwise – offered the reader. The transformative power of the text created not only opportunities for self-fashioning on the part of the author – certainly all three of the authors in the study recognize and exploit the opportunities for transformation – but also for the reader. This discursive possibility enables sustained participation in the "narrative" speculative investment demands.

While Haywood's novels would seem to have little in common with those of Samuel Richardson, it appears increasingly apparent that, as first suggested by Margaret Doody, Richardson not only read (and indeed published) some of Haywood's work, but he appropriated her narrative techniques in service of his own more conservative social and literary agenda.[28] With the publication of *Pamela* in 1740, Richardson in a sense recuperated the novel from its "scandalous" and feminized origins. He strategically capitalized on the cultural credit Haywood accrued by appropriating her language, narrative devices, and fictional situations and reinvesting them in his own didactic novels that, in later literary history, came to represent the dominant form of "the novel" in the eighteenth century.

In addition to codifying the generic expectations of the novel, Richardson's texts (and, to a certain extent, career as a printer) illustrate how, by the 1740s, the notions of speculative investment, fictional duplicity, and paper credit so troubling twenty years earlier, are increasingly normalized (in part because of the naturalization of their narrative demands). Within his texts, which as epistolary novels are necessarily located in a paper world, he specifically explores the effects of the speculative economy on his fictional female subjects. For example, he makes Pamela a type of domestic stock-jobber. Though a romance, *Pamela* is filled with the language of credit and speculation as Pamela strategically constructs a persona (and social position) based on the production of letters and journals, on her "paper credit." Her value exists in and can only be known through her discursive construction of self. With *Pamela*, Richardson domesticated the more volatile notion of paper credit in a manner consistent with a broader shift in cultural attitude. A growing middling class (and an ascendant Whig government) tried to obscure its inevitable connection with more passionate and unstable aspects of trade, and control the concept of credit which increasingly became a necessary mechanism in all sorts of economic transactions.

Richardson's understanding of the significance of paper credit was undoubtedly heightened by his prominent position within the Stationers' Company, the guild for printers and booksellers, and that organization's inextricable ties to speculative investment. The Stationers' Company was unique among guilds because its funds depended on a joint-stock company, the English Stock, that had monopoly rights to print a variety of texts such as almanacs, primers, and Psalters. As a result the English Stock gave members specific and enduring economic inducements to support their company. The print trade was not just symbolically aligned with speculative investment for the reasons I have suggested above. Rather the specific financial interests of printers and booksellers were inextricably tied to a speculative financial venture, an aspect of the print trade and Richardson's career no one has yet explored.

The prominence of cultural studies, the emergence of the new economic criticism, and the increasingly sophisticated discussions of women writers have produced significant work in areas related to my project. Traditional scholarship in economic history and political philosophy such as that by J. G. A. Pocock, P. G. M. Dickson, and Howard Erskine-Hill laid the groundwork for subsequent discussions of a more literary or theoretical nature. Similarly, Isaac Kramnick's discussion of the "politics of nostalgia" offers one of the first examinations of "Augustan ideology" and the work of Bolingbroke in a socio-historical context. Colin Nicholson explores "capital satires" (but not the novel) in *Writing and the Rise of Finance*; his account discusses the Augustan resistance to speculative investment, yet he does not explore the issues of genre or gender.[29] In *Finance and Fictionality in the Early Eighteenth Century*, Sandra Sherman provocatively discusses the homology between literature and finance; but her study, limited only to Defoe, does not address women within both marketplaces or the consequences of the literature–finance relationship as the century progresses.[30] Jean-Christophe Agnew, Kurt Heinzelman, Walter Benn Michaels, Marc Shell, and, most recently James Thompson have variously dealt with intersections of economy, literature, and constructions of value.[31] Like Sherman's, their work, within different literary periods, underscores the inextricable link between the financial and the literary, and the symbolic and material marketplaces that inform cultural texts. Scholarship in the history of the novel (beginning, of course, with Ian Watt) has increasingly attempted to explore the formation of modern subjectivity and the ideological, philosophical, and epistemological conditions that contributed to the development of the novel as a genre. Nancy Armstrong's *Desire and Domestic Fiction*, J. Paul Hunter's *Before Novels*, Michael McKeon's *Origins of the Novel*, and John Richetti's *Popular Fiction before Richardson* each, in different ways, touches on the aspects of cultural context and attempts to describe the desires that are central to many of the social practices I am discussing.[32] More specifically, discussions of women as writers and readers of the novel have demonstrated the centrality of women in the emergence of that genre. The shift from recuperation of women writers to more complex analysis has provided a clearer understanding of the full field of discourse as demonstrated by the work of Janet

Todd, Ros Ballaster, and Cheryl Turner, among many others.[33] Other studies discuss women and various types of economies. Most recently, Catherine Gallagher in *Nobody's Story* looks at constructions of female authorship in the literary economy. Though she ignores Haywood, she offers some provocative claims about women in print culture. Women's role within the discourse of mercantile capitalism is the subject of Laura Brown's *Ends of Empire*, but she does not address speculative investment.[34]

My own project complements and differs from previous work because of my focus on the relationship between finance and the novel, and the cultural possibilities paper credit (in its multiple forms) offers to an early modern subject seeking a way to satisfy various desires. Paper credit invites and requires subjects to create and participate in innovative narratives that alter the way they are able to envisage their lives. The gendering of the activities in the financial and literary marketplace, which has not been discussed, arises, in part, from these narrative requirements and illuminates the construction of gender in the early eighteenth century. Additionally, an investigation of Haywood, increasingly recognized as a central figure in the development of the novel, provides specific examples of the manifestation of the cultural tensions in material and discursive texts, but also broadens our understanding of her work and the work of her male and female contemporaries. By linking the three authors – Pope, Haywood, and Richardson – I wish to discuss them in a way that enables us to view them and their cultural milieu differently. The nexus of Grub Street and Exchange Alley, the centrality of paper credit, and the relationship among three of the most important authors of the period, have not been discussed before. By reconfiguring the strategy for looking at this period, I hope to suggest how we can reconceive of the larger cultural configurations in early eighteenth-century England.

CHAPTER ONE

Women, credit, and the South Sea Bubble

Writing to Henrietta Howard, Countess of Suffolk, in June 1720, Elizabeth Molesworth, the wife of an army captain, describes her fascination with the financial opportunities available to those able to purchase stock in the South Sea Company. Like many individuals in London, Molesworth was titillated by the possibilities of the new financial world; indeed, she confesses to being "almost South Sea mad." "Good Lady Sutherland, mindful of her absent friends," secured a five-hundred pound subscription for Molesworth and her husband. By June, their stock had doubled in value. Molesworth's letters express her excitement about the financial gain and reveal the cycle of desire into which she is placed: "this has but given me a taste of fortune, which makes me more eager to pursue it."[1] Though indicative of her own personality (she calls herself "greedy"), her sentiments are symptomatic of a culture infatuated with the untold and heretofore unrealized potential for advancement through various stock schemes. The infectious nature of the pursuit ("a taste . . . makes me more eager") evinces the self-perpetuating process of investment and (paper) profit that drove such projects. The infinite expansion heralded by the South Sea Company was particularly enticing to those, like Elizabeth Molesworth, who, because of class or gender, previously lacked any opportunity for meaningful financial improvement or autonomy. There was the persistent sense that paper credit generally and the South Sea Company particularly afforded an unique and significant chance to change one's situation.

Certainly the South Sea Company's relationship with the British government was innovative in financial history.[2] In 1720, the government transferred part of the national debt (some £50 million) to the South Sea Company. The joint-stock company, which held the trading rights to the British South Seas, assumed the debt and offered individuals who held government annuities – such as long- and short-term annuities or lottery tickets – the opportunity to convert them to company stock.[3] No fixed

rate of exchange was determined, so the plan relied on the promise of
capital appreciation. Dickson describes it as "a confidence trick entirely
dependent on the rise in the market price of South Sea stock."[4] Individuals
persuaded to convert the amount owed on their government debt to an
equivalent amount of South Sea Company stock hoped for the steadily
increasing market value the company forecast. In addition to those
who held government annuities, the company also sold stock to those
individuals able to get their name on a company subscription list. The
conversion of the debt began in January 1720, when the stock stood at
£128. During a series of four subscriptions, the value rose dramatically
and by the June 25 date of Elizabeth Molesworth's letter, it stood at
£1,000. Investors like Molesworth who got in on the Third Money
Subscription saw the value of their stock double.

The rapid rise in the stock's value heightens Molesworth's enthusiasm,
yet that enthusiasm is tinged with frustration due to her inability to
purchase as much stock as she would like: "I cannot forbear repining that
it is not in my power to put myself in [Fortune's] way, that I might share
those bounties of which she is at present so profuse." Indeed, her father
had to provide the capital for the initial £500 subscription.[5] Her letter
casts into sharp relief the class tensions, envy, and dissatisfaction that
might previously have been suppressed or felt less acutely: "I find that
philosophic temper of mind which made me content under my circumstances, when there was not seeming probability of bettering them, forsakes
me on this occasion; and I cannot, without great regret, reflect that, for
want of a little money, I am forced to let slip an opportunity which is never
like to happen again."[6] Such pointed discontent in one's circumstance in
the face of potential improvement is particularly striking. The vehemence
of Molesworth's letters suggests how profoundly the South Sea episode
affected the cultural temperament by creating fissures within the increasingly strained class and gender hierarchies that informed eighteenth-
century society. The "opportunity which is never like to happen again"
(and presumably had not presented itself before) aroused in Molesworth,
and others, a simultaneous optimism and dissatisfaction fed by the introduction of previously unimagined possibilities and new cultural or personal
narratives of improvement. Molesworth's private sentiments capture the
tone of the public discourse which explored the desires, confusion, and
social disorder created by the unchecked investment activity, and intensified by the stock's eventual collapse. Though the value of South Sea
Company stock peaked in August at £1,100, within less than a month, due
to an overselling of the stock and the company's failure to actually trade in

anything, the price of the stock plummeted to £190 and remained below £200 for the rest of the year. Eager and hopeful speculators who bought or converted when the stock price was rising suddenly possessed nearly worthless pieces of paper.

The individual largely responsible for the decision to allow the company to assume the national debt was Chancellor of the Exchequer John Aislabie, who had to defend himself in 1721 before the House of Lords against charges that he accepted bribes and gave the company preferential treatment.[7] Professing his innocence, Aislabie insisted that he was "visibly carried on with a Spirit very different from [his own] ... suited to the Frenzy of the Times."[8] With the word "frenzy," a slightly gendered term, Aislabie attempts to place responsibility for his actions, like those of unfortunate investors, on a moment of temporary insanity and uncontrollable excitement. In language reminiscent of Molesworth's claim she was "South Sea mad," he pleads that the possibilities offered by the South Sea Company infected him with the enthusiasm for stocks and infinitely rising returns that gripped Exchange Alley and much of London. In pursuit of what dramatist William Rufus Chetwood terms "Imaginary Profit," titillated investors acted on their fascination with the mysterious possibilities of paper credit.[9] With his careful rhetoric, Aislabie tries to tap into the increasingly widespread attitude that speculative investment – financial ventures that depend on stocks, credit, and the fluctuations of the marketplace – was associated with hysteria, disorder, and unregulated passions, with the same "feminizing" forces that motivated the economic man.

The conjunction of these two discourses – Molesworth's private desires and Aislabie's public defense – reveals how profoundly the eight-month South Sea episode affected multiple segments of the population. The South Sea scheme altered the material practice and, in turn, the symbolic representation of men and women of all ranks who tried to capitalize on the new financial activities. The South Sea Company venture, like other economic schemes enabled by the financial revolution, introduced new ways for people to think about themselves and to act within the world; it resulted in a pervasive cultural crisis that destabilized and ultimately reconfigured the constructed hierarchies of class and gender.[10] As this chapter details, critics of the new financial activities focused on the perceived social disorder resulting from the volatile financial status and social mixing (in both a symbolic and material sense) enabled by paper credit. More significant, however, was the use of gender in the pattern of representation. This chapter explores how the intangible nature of speculative investment prompted representations of stock-jobbers and moneyed men preoccupied with paper credit as "feminized" creatures guided by the fickle female goddesses who symbolically control the new economic world. Such a pattern of representation was intensified by the consistent investment by middling and upper-class women who sought profitable outlets for their funds.

Between the 1690s and 1753 women held on average 20 percent of the stock holdings in annuities and major funds such as the East India or South Sea Company.[11] As Molesworth's letter indicates, women were increasingly present – physically and economically – in Exchange Alley and investment activities. The texts discussed in this chapter repeatedly locate women symbolically and materially at the center of the culture disruption, as they warn of speculative investment's feminizing influence on culture as a whole. As represented, women's participation in speculative investment obscures the binary categories of public and private, or financial and domestic, as women insert themselves into a public financial space. Their participation also potentially conflates the gendered distinction between business and pleasure. Female subjects are represented as newly discovering the "pleasure of business," speculative investment, and the imaginative financial economy. Yet they pursue the pleasure of business in a way that potentially compromises the "business of (providing) pleasure" within a sexual economy focused primarily on the desire of men. Women devote their energies to financial (rather than romantic or sexual) schemes, or they use the capital obtained through men within a sexual economy to fund their forays into a speculative financial economy.[12] As women enter the new financial arena, the pleasure of business and the business of pleasure become mutually enabling and mutually reinforcing activities that threaten male control of women. That loss of control reinforces the feminization already associated with a culture in which the new economic man appears increasingly central.

The discourse surrounding the South Sea Bubble uses gendered characterizations to express cultural anxiety about the development of paper credit, the increasing participation of women in speculative investment, and the perceived feminization of culture. Criticism of women's financial interests echoes contemporaneous criticism of their fascination with popular fiction; both depict women transfixed and aroused by imaginatively based pursuits that divert them from their appropriate activities. As the last section of this chapter suggests, and as subsequent chapters detail, the equally immaterial and potentially disruptive world of Grub Street, another market dependent on paper, was represented as similarly enabling women to pursue the pleasure of business and learn the business of (their own) pleasure by reading and writing fiction.

I

As discussed in the Introduction, the new "economic" or moneyed man emerged as a figure of concern in the discourse about social action, property, and economy in late seventeenth- and early eighteenth-century England. Devoted to speculative financial activities, the "economic" man created anxiety about the nature of his loyalties and motivations. Unlike the essentially paternal and stable figure of the landed citizen, the economic man symbolically gave free rein to his passions and became susceptible to the "frenzy" Aislabie describes; like Molesworth, he too could become "South Sea mad." Indulging his financial appetites, the new economic man departed from the neo-Harringtonian model of citizenship within the tradition of civic humanism. The highly nostalgic discourse of civic humanism constructed the idealized male citizen as an individual "rendered independent by his property and permitted an autonomous engagement in public affairs."[13] By owning land, the citizen avoided a compromised or self-interested relationship with government, and contributed to the moral economy and the political stability of the nation. By contrast, the economic man appears to abandon the land for a disordered and unstable milieu defined by paper credit, volatile signifiers, and increasingly immaterial forms of property. While, in fact, moneyed men frequently used their new wealth to purchase land, the perception of their detachment from "real" property persisted. Like his perceived abandonment of the land, the feminized economic man's preoccupation with his own fantasies, desires, and imagination caused him to circulate as a vision of an undesirable socio-economic future.

Describing the activities of Exchange Alley, Thomas Gordon draws on the power of this feminized figure when he claims stock-jobbing has turned Great Britain into a nation of "old women." In *A Dissertation on Old Women* (1720), he exhorts his "Brethren and Countrymen" to "either properly and patiently put on Petticoats; or resume our Manhood, and shake off this shameful Delusion, this filthy yoke, put upon our Necks by dull Rogues from Jonathan's; plodding dunces!"[14] His language locates "manhood" in the past as a residual cultural practice in contest with the emergent feminizing "delusion" of a world of speculative investment. To wear the yoke – and presumably the petticoat – of involvement in an intangible financial system is to reject the past and to involve oneself in an "upside-down world" populated by emasculated men and "plodding" economic dunces. The term "dunces," which Pope uses to describe the hack writers of Grub Street in the 1728 *Dunciad*, reveals disregard and contempt for participants in the new economic milieu. It also suggests the affinity between action in the literary and economic marketplace. In his discussion of the so-called literary dunces, J. Paul Hunter observes they "espoused the present and sought the values of the future."[15] The observation applies equally well to the participants in Exchange Alley. Stock-jobbers, like hack writers, pursued future profit and power based almost exclusively on the proliferation and manipulation of paper. While the stock-jobber resided in the present, his decisions and actions depended on his ability to anticipate future events in the financial market. Like a dunce creating a position in Grub Street dependent on the changing whims of the literary marketplace, a "dunce" of Exchange Alley had to produce and manipulate paper and symbolic instruments to maintain his credit in an unforeseeable, but potentially desirable, future.

In this environment, virtue became located in the past, and commerce, in Pocock's words, emerged as "the active form of culture itself."[16] The enduring characteristics inherent within the civic humanist construction of the classic citizen – duty, hospitality, loyalty, heroism – gave way to ephemeral values such as worth, opinion, and credit so important to the new economic man; as Steele observes, credit is to the Trader "what Honour ... Fame or Glory is to other sort of men."[17] The qualities desirable for a stock-jobber or a man of credit mirrored those coveted by a "fine lady" in the marriage market; both relied on reputation (credit or virginity), assets (net worth or dowry), and potential for future gain (regular dividends or children). A stock-jobber's success in the marketplace depended largely on public estimation of his value and credibility, for "credit is undone in whispers" just as a woman's reputation could be easily undone by gossip.[18] John Dennis, in *An Essay upon Public Spirit*, claims that the increased participation in financial speculation has destabilized the characterizations of both genders and "transformed our sexes": "We have Men that are more soft, more languid, and more passive than women; Men who, like women, are come to use Red and White ... On the other side we have Women, who ... in Revenge are Masculine in their Desires, and Masculine in their Practices."[19] Stock-jobbing put men in a submissive, culturally feminine position, because it forced them to depend on opinion, reputation, and the approval of others, and allowed them to privilege their expressions of passion, imagination, and desire.

The perceived threat of stock-jobbing increased with the fear that individuals like aristocrats and merchants, allegedly dedicated to national rather than self-serving interests, might also be lured by the seductive qualities of speculative investment – a business where one could seemingly increase one's wealth without any discernible work. The author of *Some Considerations on the late Mismanagement of the South-Sea Stocks* (1721) condemns a pattern of disregard for tradition and the values of honor, service, and hospitality. He constructs a nostalgic, indeed utopian, image of the past as he ponders what Britain's ancestors would think if they now saw

Their Descendants, instead of spending their Fortunes as they had done in the service of their Country, and instead of keeping up that antient Hospitality for which this Nation has been so famous; to see those, I say, who inherit their Honours and Estates, stock-jobbing their estates in that Infamous Place called Exchange-Alley, and debasing the Honour of their Birth, in begging the Favour of a Subscription (to their own undoing) of such who were hardly company for their Footmen.[20]

The ancient laws of hospitality which strategically reassert the power and status of the landed citizen have been forsaken symbolically and literally. The "descendants" not only leave their spacious and established family estates but potentially "job" them away in the crowded and newly sprung location, Exchange Alley, the site of social mixing and destabilized hierarchies. The geographic and ideological shift constricts and diminishes the male citizen by replacing the authority and identity of landed wealth with the anonymity of paper credit. The description reasserts the organizing principles he describes as endangered as he distinguishes between descendants and footmen, estates and Exchange Alley, nation and self. The loss of status is compounded by the descendants' subordinate relationship to social inferiors to whom they debase themselves by "begging" favors.

Driven by what one writer suggestively terms the "itch" of stock-jobbing, such men abandon their traditional position to pursue a quick profit and the pleasures of sanctified gaming that "depraves, and debauches the Morals and Manners of Mankind." This itch not only diverts landed citizens from their customary role, but also afflicts merchants who, theoretically, maintain the values of trade, responsibility, and industry. While merchants certainly relied on new financial instruments and forms of credit to facilitate their enterprises, they were typically represented as involved in tangible commodities which distinguish them from a stock-jobber. Yet even merchants succumb to the attraction of speculative investment which *An Examination and Explanation of the South Sea Company's Scheme* (1720) describes as turning them aside from pursuing their proper Business and Callings whereby they might maintain and enrich themselves and their families, as well as the Means of bringing Treasure into the Kingdom, and encouraging of the Manufactures of Great Britain, the Decay whereof is more owing to the Itch the People are fallen into of Stock-jobbing than to any other Cause whatsoever.[21]

A merchant's involvement in speculative schemes serves neither the kingdom's public nor the family's domestic good – it only satisfies the individual's "itch." The subsequent "decay" stems from the implicit shift from a world of material goods and property ("Treasures") to an invisible universe of paper credit, stock schemes, and unseen market forces. The language critical of stock-jobbing alters the terms of evaluative discourse; luxury goods, often regarded as the cause of a moral lapse in their own right, gain new acceptance in the face of intangible property.[22] The social and personal disorder created when speculators pursue passion, pleasure, and self-interest threatens the social fabric and, more important, the cultural construction of masculinity.

The economic man's subordination to potentially emasculating allegorical female figures of disorder – unstable "goddesses" like Credit, Fortune, and Luxury – further threatens his cultural performance of masculinity. These female images, upon which Pope draws with the figure of Dulness, continue a long misogynist tradition and retain what Michael McKeon describes as "that association with the volatility of exchange which they possess under older, patrilineal assumptions."[23] For example, in a 1706 representation by Defoe in *The Review*, Credit appears as a vacillating young woman unduly influenced by the forces around her; she simultaneously reacts to and shapes the surrounding commercial world.[24] Addison continues this image when, in *Spectator* 3, he describes Credit as "a beautiful Virgin, seated on a throne of Gold." An "infinitely timorous" young lady frequently "troubled with vapours," Credit has a tendency to "change colour, and start at every thing" she hears. "In the twinkling of an eye," Credit would "fall away from the most florid complexion, and the most healthful state of Body, and wither into a Skeleton. Her recoveries were often as sudden as her Decays, insomuch that she would revive in a Moment out of wasting Distemper, into a Habit of the highest Health and Vigour."[25] Her physical and emotional vacillation imitates the delicacy and sensibility cultivated by ladies of quality to increase their sexual charms and desirability (consonant with the images in Pope's Cave of Spleen). Her counterpart Opinion, who lacks Credit's financial influence, possesses a seductive quality and appears to offer endless sexual pleasures. Opinion is little more than the popular perception of a speculator or stock's worth, an imaginary construction. The figure's indistinct yet infinitely seductive persona can distract and arouse everyone, an image that underscores the role of opinion in a financial environment: "Her Voice was pleasing ... she seemed to have a tongue for every one; every one thought he heard of something that was valuable in himself, and expected a Paradise which she promised as the Reward of his Merit. Thus were we drawn to follow her, till she shou'd bring us where it was to be bestow'd."[26] Her ability to lead and seduce speculators accounts for their willingness to invest, for Aislabie's "frenzy."

These allegorical female figures assume a much more specific form during the South Sea crisis when James Milner illustrates the situation in *Three Letters, Relating to the South-Sea Company and the Bank* (1720).[27] Milner represents the two most important financial institutions in England as women: the Lady of the South Sea and the Lady of the Bank. Milner's letters depict the changing fortunes of the two companies following the government's transfer of its debt from the Bank of England to the South Sea Company, rapidly increasing the stock price of the latter as a result. The first letter, written March 1720, portrays the Lady of the Bank "in deep mourning" (5) after the decision favoring the South Sea Company; "the object was too melancholy to be entertaining, when I consider'd her former glories, and how often I had seen her wallowing in her Millions ... It gave me a melancholy Idea of the Vicissitude of human affairs" (6). The Lady of the South Sea, "now worth as many Millions as the other would be thousands in a little time" (5), sits "on her throne in a most magnificent manner." Like an imperious ruler, she is surrounded by her sycophants and those wishing admission, "all paying her the utmost Adoration" (22). And "[a]t her Feet were the poor Annuitants in mourning, petitioning to be admitted Sharers in the glorious Harvest" (5) – individuals holding government annuities who wished to convert them to stock. Potential suitors, "the poor annuitants," woo the Lady of the South Sea to persuade her to satisfy their financial desires and exchange their debts. Like a coquette rejecting importunate suitors, she resists their sexual and financial advances and initially "she spurned them from her with these words, No long Annuities!" The image refers specifically to the company's reluctance to honor exchange agreements with holders of long annuities which required a larger (and less advantageous) financial commitment. The scene is also part of a consistent pattern that portrays potential investors as suppliants, suitors before the unpredictable female figure of the South Sea Company.

Aislabie increases the sexuality of that image when he characterizes the South Sea Company as a prostitute seducing men in "a scheme more Voracious and destructive than a Lady that passes her Time in the Hundreds of Drury"; he specifically compares the company to a woman involved in the business of pleasure.[28] Similarly, *The Battle of the Bubbles* (1720) by a "Stander-by," represents the South Sea Company as the female figure "Oceana" who brings men to a state of frenzied arousal. Sexually insatiable, Oceana seduces, emasculates, and, in a sense, devours a succession of male lovers to satisfy her own desires: "She bewitch'd thousands to fall in Love with her, and to spend their whole fortunes upon her: And what is monstrous in her, is, that tho' she has reduc'd 'em all to skin and Bone, yet her Lust is not one bit abated; and She runs a whoring after new Lovers every Day."[29] In an attempt to satisfy her persistent lust, Oceana financially destroys the men she bewitches. She feeds her own pleasures by forcing men to divert the normal course of their business and "spend their whole fortunes upon her." She cannot escape the cycle of desire ("her lust is not one bit abated"), just as Elizabeth Molesworth remains unsatisfied after just a "taste of fortune." Both female subjects remain "eager" in their pursuit. The representation of Oceana anticipates later depictions of women who similarly make pleasure and business mutually reinforcing. This description, like the previous ones, embodies many associations of negative and stereotypically female qualities – avaricious sexuality, emotional instability, hysteria – that characterize financial activities dependent on speculative investment and paper credit. The range of female types being depicted – coquettes, prostitutes, monstrous women – make up a continuum of specifically feminine dangers that threaten to erode (or perhaps mutate) masculinity and diminish male control of financial structures.

The associations continue in the visual representations of Fortune and the Lady of the South Sea Company that appeared in prints circulating in London, typically of French or Dutch origin, depicting the South Sea Bubble and other speculative stock schemes on the Continent. A 1720 print titled *A Monument dedicated to Posterity* revises the iconic associations of Fortune to fit a world of speculative investment. Fortune, traditionally depicted with a cornucopia scattering coins, here showers her followers with contracts, stocks, and "bubbles" – she offers paper and air rather than gold to the men and women clamoring beneath her. The medieval image of the wheel of fortune is now a wagon wheel with the names of stock companies inscribed upon it as their fortunes regularly rise and fall. The text below the print describes how "books of Merchandise" are "crushed and turn beneath [the] Wheels of [the] Chariot, representing the destruction of Trade and Commerce." The tangible goods of trade are destroyed by the wagon wheel of Fortune. Folly drives that wagon and wears her distinctive attire, a fool's cap and jester's stick, as well as "her Ample hoop petticoat, which is also a folly of the time."[30] Just as Thomas Gordon used the petticoat as the emblem of men's (or "old women's") cultural impotence ("put on petticoats; or resume our manhood"), so too the visual representations underscore that quintessentially female garment's associations with folly, speculative investment, and feminization.

A contemporaneous print entitled *The South Sea Company, having risen to the top by Wind, now laments her loss with a rueful aspect* also highlights female sexuality in its depiction of the scheme. The South Sea Company is represented as a woman reclining in a state of dishabille, a pose reminiscent of eighteenth-century pornography. She would appear to be a woman of pleasure. She seems to be lamenting her devalued stock, expended resources, and absent investors – her "loss" seems financial. Nevertheless, her bare breast, unshod foot, and coy pose with her finger in her mouth also suggest she is a woman who is sexually spent (with all the economic force implicit in that image), and lamenting the loss of her lovers. Her failure in business is visually indistinguishable from the cessation of her sexual pleasure.

For the iconographic female figures associated with the financial revolution, pleasure and business exist simultaneously and are, in fact, mutually reinforcing, as these visual female images and the discursive descriptions indicate. Figures like Oceana, Fortuna, the Lady of the South Sea derive pleasure from their sexual and economic seduction of men desirous of their physical and financial charms. The mutually reinforcing imagery of pleasure and business, and the conflation of the two similarly dominates representations that focus on women's significant material involvement with the activities of the new financial world. The iconographic female figures pursue pleasure and business with the resultant subordination, indeed threatened emasculation, of their male followers. Women participating in the material world of Exchange Alley are represented as pursuing the same desires, possibly with the same potential consequences.

2

The representations discussed in the previous section draw, in part, on an existing cultural discourse about women, feminine characteristics, and speculative financial practices. The allegorical figures of fickle goddesses guiding the new economic world depend upon traditional iconographic

Figure 1 "A monument dedicated to posterity," 1720.

Figure 2 "The South Sea Company, having risen to the top by Wind, now laments her loss with rueful aspect," 1720.

and philosophic constructions of Credit and Fortune. They capture the emerging associations of speculative investment with "feminine" traits of passion, imagination, and fancy. The representations also exploit the role constructed for women in England's economic expansion and the mercantile capitalist ideology. The recurrent image of woman as "capricious consumer" underscores the culture's simultaneous dependence on and repudiation of female consumption of luxury goods.[31] During the period surrounding the South Sea Bubble, texts dealing with speculative investment depict women as consumers of *stocks*, and as eager participants in the world of Exchange Alley. They suggestively represent women of the middling and upper classes as enthusiastic speculators who use stock-jobbing to gain funds that supplement or substitute for pin money or other financial resources. The anxiety about women's participation in stock is expressed in terms similar to those that discuss women reading and writing fiction, a similar vehicle for a woman's imaginative (and often literal) displacement of self. Both forms of paper credit, fiction and stocks, offer women a new way to find pleasure. Because Exchange Alley and Grub Street were relatively new and unformed cultural spaces, women were able to penetrate and negotiate them in unanticipated ways.

The cultural anxiety about women's new financial interests, the perceived feminization of culture, and the diminished control over (feminized) men had a material basis in the pattern of women's investment activity. A striking pattern of women's consistent and continued investment exists. From the 1690s through the middle of the eighteenth century, women of diverse social ranks (primarily the middling and upper classes) were an important minority of all owners in stocks, holding, on average, 20 percent. For example, women held 16.6 percent of Bank stock in 1709, a percentage that rose steadily to 20.7 percent in 1724 and 25.4 percent in 1744.[32] Peter Earle stresses "the enormous importance of women, particularly widows, in the London investment markets."[33] Women often had a great deal of stock in their jointure, because, unlike land, stocks were not taxed and were a form of property a married woman could retain as personal estate. Stocks and government funds were often viewed as a good, passive investment. The opportunity for women's participation was enabled in part, suggests James Carswell, "because the law had never thought of it."[34] A married woman, normally considered a *feme covert* and unable to act on her own behalf financially, could be considered a *feme sole* with respect to her separate estate or personal property. The personal property, which would include pin money, was to be used for maintenance, and for the purchase of paraphernalia (jewelry, clothes, personal items); obviously it could also be used as a possible source of investment funds. Thus a married woman, spinster, or widow could legally use her own funds to buy stock. Although, as Susan Staves reminds us, "by the end of the eighteenth century, allowing married women such powers of alienation with respect to their separate estates was found to be intolerable,"[35] during the 1720s, women could legally act in Exchange Alley. Women could also buy lottery tickets or take out insurance policies, both forms of speculative investment.[36]

While women of all ranks held stock, aristocratic women owned vast shares in a variety of funds and viewed speculative investment as another, temporarily fashionable form of gaming. Henrietta Howard, initially a member of the court of the Prince of Wales, later mistress to King George II, and always a woman of fashion, invested in both the South Sea Company and the Mississippi land scheme devised by John Law that took the Paris market by storm in 1719. While Howard probably invested in part because of that activity's popularity, her always precarious financial situation also gave her pressing economic reasons to try to increase her wealth. Her correspondence during this period demonstrates her pre-occupation with various speculative schemes; the Earl of Islay, who acted as Howard's financial agent, wrote her from Paris with detailed updates. In September 1719 he expresses confidence in the investment and boasts that though "The subscription was full ... Mr. Law was so kind as to allow it me," enabling Howard to invest. Though he admits that Howard may think "the levity of this country has turned" his head, he claims, with the enthusiasm of an investor, that "every body has made estates that have been concerned in them [stocks] for four or five month."

When, by January, Howard's stock has dropped in value, Islay continues to rationalize the market's actions (which of course defy logical explana-tion) by suggesting that "the meaning of it is nothing else but people's sell-ing their actions in order to buy the new primes." He concedes he is "not insensible of distant dangers which may attend the funds here" but claims the objections come from those who don't have "any true notions of the principles of these matters."[37] Although Howard lost money in the Mississippi scheme, she invested in the South Sea Company and her abiding interest in stocks was apparently well known to her female cor-respondents. In addition to the exchange with Elizabeth Molesworth, Howard jokes to Mrs. Campbell, maid of honor in the court, that her new husband Colonel John Campbell "bows to no other altars than those erected in 'Change-Alley" while visiting London in her absence. As a result of her high level of involvement, after the fall in stock, the tone of

Howard's letters changes. She admits to Campbell that the loss in South Sea value has affected her countenance: "I have kept the same grave unmeaning face I used to wear (which, to compliment me, you may call philosophical); the fall of stocks has given me a large field to amplify upon, and a thousand good reasons for its so doing."[38] Financial performance determines Howard's social performance.

Other ladies of the Princess of Wales's court, "the daughters of Earl Ferrers, the Duchess of Rutland, [and] the Countess of Gainsborough," invested and "were only a few of those who with or without their husbands, dealt in stock," as Carswell details.[39] The largest single holding in the Bank of England was that of Sarah Churchill, the Duchess of Marlborough, at £166,855; Churchill also was adroit enough to sell her considerable South Sea stock in August when the price peaked, and reinvest her profit in bank and insurance funds.[40] Lady Mary Wortley Montagu speculated in South Sea Company stock on behalf of her French admirer Nicolas-François Remond, her sister's mother-in-law Lady Gower and, of course, herself; she used her connections to get her name placed on a number of subscription lists.[41] Acting on advice from Alexander Pope, however, she lost her money by holding on to her stock too long.

Women's involvement in Exchange Alley enabled them to act within a public financial arena and create a new cultural space. In fact, in the City chocolate houses designed for female speculators sprang up. Carswell suggests the "true centre of fashion" shifted to the City, where ladies "had rented a shop a few doors away from Blunt's office in Birchin Lane, and turned it into a club for tea-drinking and playing on the stock exchange."[42] Popular discourse surrounding the South Sea Bubble focuses on the unsettling effects of such activity. Milner, in describing his imaginary visit to the Lady of the South Sea, notes that, in addition to the "Jews, Stockjobbers, and Gamesters" paying their respects to the latest economic monarch, "Ladies were also there"; but "in respect to their sex," he refrains from making any reflections on such a scandalous activity (22). In Chetwood's *South Sea; or, the biters bit* (1720) the exemplary heroine Marinda demonstrates her "inclination for business" when she expresses her desire to "see the Bustle and Business of Change-Alley."[43] Thomas D'Urfey, in the "Prologue" to *The Two Queens of Brentford* (1720), describes how the price of stock has become a barometer for women's emotions:

> The Ladies too in Coach to Brokers run,
> The Fair, the Brown, the freckl'd, and the Dun;
> Fat Widows smile when dear Stock rises high;
> But if the vote comes that it falls – they cry.[44]

In the Preface to the comedy *Exchange Alley: or, the Stock-jobber turn'd Gentleman* (1720), the author complains that women's preoccupation with speculative investment distracts them from their "normal" pursuits: "if you wait upon a Lady of Quality, you'll find her hastening to her House of Intelligence in Exchange-Alley; and what is strange and wonderful, her every dress, Diamond shoe Buckles and Garters, neglected for the Stocks."[45] Just as men abandon their patriarchal duties to the land, women ignore their gender-defining activities to pursue economic interests. The very consumer goods that make the lady of quality a scapegoat in the representations of female luxury and its detrimental effects now become mementos of a desirable past when women could be lured by rather innocuous luxury goods rather than enjoying for themselves the intangible allure of speculative investment.

Women could use speculative investment to circumvent the financial restrictions placed on them by their husbands. Lady Pawn-Locket in Chetwood's comedy *The Stock-Jobbers or, The humours of Exchange-alley* (1720) describes the dividends from stock as "better than Pin Money" because, in part, available independent of her husband.[46] In *Exchange Alley*, Mrs. Cravemore pawns items often endowed with sentimental value – her "jewels, watch and tweezer case, and everything else" (21) – and commissions Cheat-all to buy her some stock. "To tell you the Truth," she insists, "I should not venture to commence Stock-Jobber, were it not occasioned by my Mercenary Spouse, who at this time allows me nothing for Pin-money – and alas! I want it, at least, every Day" (20). Mrs. Cravemore's "mercenary" husband, whose own greed does not allow him to provide his wife with the stipend she desires, might in another context be praised for his frugality and money-making ability; or perhaps he too is obsessed with stocks and his mercenary self-interest prevents him from sharing his discretionary income. When Mrs. Cravemore says she wants profits or pin-money "at least every Day," her desire (and her name) suggests both an economic and a sexual need. Her mercenary husband echoes the popular image of the preoccupied cit who is either unable or unwilling to satisfy his wife's sexual desires. Women pursue the pleasure of business because they are not getting sexual pleasure from men who are similarly preoccupied with financial pursuits. The representation of women's desire for personal spending money suggests male apprehensions that increased financial independence could jeopardize a husband's control over his wife in other areas as well. *Exchange Alley*'s author condemns such activities, advising that "when these extraordinary events are consider'd, and Women of the Town are become Dealers in the Stocks ... it is high time to pronounce Exchange Alley truly a Farce" (ii).

However, the concern persisted about the nature and degree of pleasure women derived from stock-jobbing. *The Stock-Jobbers* focuses on the financial, emotional, and material benefits of speculative financial activity. In a lengthy exchange, four women – wives of both merchants and aristocrats – discuss speculative investment in terms that suggest it surpasses pleasures usually provided and sanctioned by men:

LADY LOVE-PICKETT: I declare I do not see why these wretches should monopolize the Pleasure of Business to themselves; it is only to keep us in Ignorance of
all that's charming in Life: Like the Romish Priests, who refuse to let the Laity
know anything, for fear of usurping upon their Authority.

MRS. FIGG: I am sure my Neighbor, the Linen-draper's Wife, Mrs. Ghenting, had
the vapours for a Gold-Watch two whole years, as she herself told me; and so
she might still, poor soul, if her own Industry had not provided better for her.
Oh ! this stock-jobbing, 'tis better than a Turn in the Park in a Hackney
Coach.

LADY PAWN-LOCKET: Better than Pin Money.

LADY LOVE-PICKETT: I was going to say better than an Evening at Cards with
agreeable company.

MRS. SUBTLE: As for my Part, tho' I hardly ever saw the Inside of the City till
within these three weeks, I am grown a perfect trader. (23)

Stock-jobbing allows the women to transcend, however briefly, constraints on their activities and increase their knowledge, discretionary income, and power. Lady Love-Pickett's observation that men monopolize finance and guard their knowledge of Exchange Alley, "all that's charming in life," points to the careful control men try to maintain over the new financial instruments. She implies that women's ignorance is orchestrated by men, who "fear [women] usurping upon their Authority."

Despite the potential obstacles, these women have all realized some profit. Mrs. Subtle has gained an intimate knowledge of the City, a male domain of specifically financial activities. Though she calls herself a "perfect trader," presumably of stocks, her new knowledge of the "City" also suggests a familiarity with the urban vices and diversions a man like Pinchwife in *The Country Wife* fears his wife will discover. Just as Margery Pinchwife learns to operate sexually with her increasing knowledge of the City, perhaps Mrs. Subtle has learned to "trade" for herself in other ways as well. Mrs. Figg's story of her neighbor, Mrs. Ghenting, illustrates how stock-jobbing gives a woman a rare opportunity to use her "own Industry" to her financial benefit. Of course the "industry" involved is not physical labor *per se*, but rather the careful investment in stocks. Indeed, one of the criticisms leveled against stock-jobbers was the fact they didn't do any "real" work (a claim similarly made about domestic women). Mrs.

Ghenting's efforts in Exchange Alley transform her from a women beset with vapors to one able to acquire luxury goods by her own means. She becomes empowered financially and physically as she transcends the private sphere to secure public economic success. At the same time, Mrs. Ghenting abandons the rational, thrifty, mercantile world of her husband to pursue her own interests; she claims to retain the middle-class virtue of industry (now compromised) but she refigures it for her own purposes.

In these representations, while women of the middling classes use speculative investment to supplement their income and view it as an alternative to or another form of work, aristocratic women discuss speculative investment as entertainment, an opportunity to escalate their love of gaming to a new level of involvement and risk. Lady Love-Pickett no longer has to confine her gaming to only "an evening at cards with agreeable company," but can expand to the higher stakes and more public arena of stock-jobbing. John Dennis, in *An Essay upon Public Spirit*, explains how any type of gaming – from cards to stock-jobbing – robs women of their "natural" pleasure of being seen by men. Anticipating Pope's pronouncement that "love of pleasure" is one of women's two ruling passions (*Epistle to a Lady* l. 210), Dennis expresses his concern that gaming will overcome women's "natural" pleasure with and passion for men, and redirect it to self-sufficient (and self-interested) pursuits:

> The Women lock themselves up at Cards whole Days and Nights successively, and forget their natural Pleasure of being seen, and of being admir'd; and Avarice gets the better of their Pride, as Luxury in some of them had done before; and gets the better of their Pleasure likewise, gets the better of that Pleasure which is so natural to them, and makes them shew a stronger Passion than that which they have for Men. (18)

Women remove themselves from circulation within a sexual economy controlled by the variations in male affection and desire, to play an active role within a financial economy where they can benefit from the fluctuations in the price of stocks and other forms of negotiable paper. Dennis's passage addresses both the concern about female pleasure generally, and female pleasure specifically in speculative activities and gambling. There is a persistent fear that the pleasure women derive from stock-jobbing will supplant the satisfaction they derive from men; they will find a vehicle for self-pleasuring.

When Lady Love-Pickett terms financial interests "the Pleasure of Business," she suggests that the pleasure of business can serve as a substitute for sexual pursuits, or the business of pleasure. Stock-jobbing provides erotic and economic gratification. Indeed, the very language used to describe women's reaction to financial success is subtly coded with the language of sexuality. Women demand daily satisfaction from their investments ("alas! I want it, at least, every day"). They succumb to the "itch" for stock-jobbing. They demand the continued rise in the price of stock as a sexually desirous woman hopes for the continued (and repeated) "rise" of her lover ("Fat Widows smile when dear Stock rises high...but if ... it falls – they cry"). Mrs. Figg finds "this stock-jobbing better than a Turn in the Park in a Hackney-Coach," a vehicle often the site of illicit sexual encounters.

In other texts, stock-jobbing and sexual pursuits are represented not just as substitutes but as supplements to each other – the business of pleasure enables the pleasure of business. As one anonymous 1720 poem explains, "our greatest ladies" pawn their jewels, possibly a gift from a husband or male admirer, "for a sum to venture in the Alley." The process of capitalization and reinvestment is compared to the activities of prostitutes, who are represented as immediately investing their earnings in the stocks: "young harlots too from Drury Lane / Approach the 'Change in coaches / To fool away the gold they gain / by their impure debauches."[47] These women take the profits of their participation in a system of sexual exchange (the business of pleasure), in which male pleasure is privileged, and use them to achieve greater power in a system of economic exchange (the pleasure of business), where they can satisfy their own desires. Thus a circular pattern emerges: the business of pleasure, whether in prostitution, flirtation, or marriage, provides the capital needed to pursue the pleasure of business. Any subsequent profit (financial gain realized without work) can, in turn, enable women to attend to the business of their own pleasure.

The comedy *Exchange Alley* highlights the circularity of that sequence (which places women in another cycle of desire) when it satirizes the multiple insurance schemes, another form of speculative investment, offered for subscription. Bubble reads Cheat-all's list of insurance policies, which includes "An Insurance from Cuckholdom – Of Maidenheads – Noses Insured from Fire-Charter from the sole Property of the Cleanings of Necessary Houses – And for wiping Persons of both Sexes." The Fourth Subscriber, a woman of Drury Lane, approaches Cheat-all about insuring her "Maiden Treasures": "Sir, I live in the hundreds of Drury, and as I am often times Obliged to comply with some modish Liberties, I would willingly preserve my Maiden Treasure by Insurance – There's my Subscription" (15). Like an investor infatuated with the possibilities of the South Sea Company, she invests in a narrative (her insured virginity) that obviously has no basis in material reality. The use of "maiden treasures" as a marker of fraudulent speculative investment is particularly apt, for a woman's virginity resides in the same imaginative, intangible realm as paper credit. While a hymen is intrinsically material tissue, its value as a symbol of "maiden treasures" perhaps more powerfully resides in the imaginative realm fueled by a culture's emotional investment in a woman's "virtue." Its presence is marked by its absence, it circulates in a symbolic economy, and it exists primarily, if not exclusively, through a discursive construction (as Richardson's *Pamela* illustrates). The subscriber wants to "insure" her maidenhead to guarantee her continued, indeed perpetual, participation (as long as she retains a relatively youthful demeanor) within the commerce of sexual exchange. She wants the "regenerative hymen" Sherman ascribes to Defoe's Lady Credit. [48]

With her knowledge of the pleasure of business (in this case insurance) the woman of Drury Lane can continue to profit from the business of pleasure and potentially gains the ability to enter domesticated commerce as a still "virginal" bride. The exchange suggests how insurance or any form of paper credit could function as a disguise: a prostitute can maintain her virginity and obscure her professional background. Indeed, Cheat-all assures the subscriber her maidenhead will be as "safe, child, as that of a Lady of Quality at a Masquerade" – in other words, of course, not safe at all. Not only does the allusion draw upon the cultural anxiety about masquerades and disguise, it also anticipates the recognition that the anonymity of paper credit renders any marker of identity volatile and unstable.

In "An Excellent New Ballad upon the Masquerades" (1720), the anonymous poet extends this comparison further by explicitly equating a woman's "jobbing" for hearts at a masquerade with jobbing for stock in Exchange Alley, conflating sexual and financial economies. The masquerade "becomes a Rendezvous, / For Ladies that are Pretty" and ready to use any capital they have for financial gain. The text suggests that both kinds of "jobbing" involve women in a kind of prostitution – there is perhaps too fine a line between the business of pleasure and the pleasure of business: "At 'Change they job for money, / But Traffic here for Hearts: / The fairest Nymphs are willing / To Show you their Best Parts."[49] Locating the dual acts of "jobbing" at the masquerade heightens their already transgressive nature. More important, it intensifies the perceptions that women use stock-jobbing as a vehicle for pleasure. The masquerade represents a site of sexual, political, and existential freedom enabled by the anonymity of the mask. Terry Castle suggests that "one might describe the masked assembly as a kind of machine for feminine pleasure . . . [where] a woman was free to circulate . . . according to her own pleasure."[50] Certainly these texts reflect the perception that women achieve a similar opportunity through stock-jobbing and the anonymity of paper credit.

But the masquerade also represents a site of carnivalesque activity in which, as Castle observes, the "cardinal ideological distinctions under-lying eighteenth-century cultural life," including the fundamental markers of class and gender, were broached (6). A 1720 print, *The World of the Masquerade*, visually invokes the cultural space of the masquerade to repre-sent the anti-hierarchical, transgressive nature of Exchange Alley and the circulation of paper credit. Just as the lady of Drury Lane in Chetwood's farce gains a way to disguise herself as a maid through her adroit specula-tive investment, so too at the masquerade "Drury Punks for Maiden Ladies Pass, / And dress'd like Nymphs, decoy the Am'rous Ass."[51] In a sense, the activities and impulses of the masquerade become indistin-guishable from those of Exchange Alley. Indeed, Exchange Alley and the practice of speculative investment, like Grub Street and the commercial-ization of literature, arguably emerge as the primary site of carnivalesque cultural practice in eighteenth-century society.

3

This pattern of provocative imagery underscores the profound mark the South Sea Bubble crisis left on eighteenth-century society. But the fears and animosities stemmed from more than just anger about a society's ability to be financially duped. They were instead part of a larger cultural reaction to the frightening power of joint-stock companies, paper credit, and dematerialized property. The new objects of widespread cultural anxiety were "feminized" men led by their passions and emotions, empowered women diverted from their prescribed interests, and economies determined, in part, by the pursuit of pleasure. Significantly, the nature of this discourse was not limited to the criticism of Exchange Alley and the participants in speculative investment. It was also used to depict expanding production and consumption of literary commodities. The fears about new financial activities echo those expressed about the proliferation of primarily commercial writers, jobbing their own type of paper – writers who, at least in the *Dunciad*, are similarly represented as feminized. Just as much as a hawker of investment opportunities, the professional or hack writer of Grub Street depended on a text's reputa-tion, notoriety, or popularity for his or her livelihood – in other words, his or her credit on paper. Both booksellers and stock-jobbers attracted clients seeking participation in an imaginatively constructed "future," desiring "future" returns on their initial investment, either in the form of stock dividends or an enjoyable reading experience. Like a stock scheme, fiction was based on nothing "real" or tangible; indeed, it offered possibilities that may or may not have been realized. Speculators in fiction or in finance must make an emotional and economic investment. They must exercise the power of fantasy in pursuit of immediate gratification. They must use their imagination to envisage the outcome of the narrative implicitly being offered.

As a result, the emergence of popular fiction was another cultural development that threatened to conflate the business of pleasure and the pleasure of business. Readers of popular genres such as the novel, primarily women, engaged in an imaginative displacement of self through participation in a narrative they helped construct. Women reading fiction exercised their fantasies and imagination, and developed emotional attachments with texts that temporarily removed them from domestic concerns and restraints; in return, the text potentially provided a great deal of pleasure. Like women empowered, however briefly, by their forays into speculative investment, women reading (and writing) fiction were afforded the opportunity to transcend or surpass the pleasures potentially provided by men and gain knowledge not typically available to them. Women's transgressive behavior in a financial or literary milieu threatened to destabilize the gendered hierarchies represented as central to eighteenth-century culture. In the *Dunciad*, Pope, specifically describing Eliza Haywood, complains that "those shameless scriblers (for the most part of That sex, which ought least to be capable to such malice or impudence)" write novels that "reveal the faults and misfortunes of both sexes, to the ruin or disturbance, of publick fame or private happiness" (*TE* v, p.119). Pope argues that women are gaining from novels the knowledge and experience Chetwood, in *The Stock-jobbers*, suggests they are already getting in Exchange Alley. Indeed, as discussed in subsequent chapters, novels by Eliza Haywood offer specific strategies for women within the speculative world, illustrating how they can pursue both business and pleasure. When pursued by women, business and pleasure – in the form of reading and writing fiction, or investing speculatively – arouse similar resistance and anxiety, and stand as symptoms of an uneasy culture's simultaneous embrace of and resistance to the inevitable instabilities of social, literary, and gendered categories appearing on the eighteenth-century landscape.

CHAPTER TWO

Alexander Pope, gender, and the commerce of culture

The volatile literary environment of early eighteenth-century England manifested the same tensions that characterized the effects of the new economic order. The social fluidity, transgressive behavior, and speculative economic activity that marked Exchange Alley were, in a sense, replicated in the literary environment of Grub Street. Just as stock-jobbers and diverse investors, including women, competed for economic gains and enhanced (if fleeting) status, so too did a host of professional writers, speculators of another sort, compete for cultural or literary space and its potential profits both symbolic and material. Through the production, accumulation, and manipulation of various symbolic instruments – pamphlets, newspapers, novels, essays – professional writers could acquire (paper) credit from publishers and readers, and hope for the elevation (or perhaps inflation) of their literary stock. With what one critic has termed "the will to literary power," the professional or hack writers of Grub Street transformed the literary marketplace, and its attendant practices of reading, with their prolific output, innovative techniques, and multiple and often hybrid genres.[1] Their production of symbolic instruments was, like the economic man's various investments in stocks, subject to the whims of the marketplace (and often the publisher or bookseller), making the hack writer equally dependent on the goddesses of disorder, Fortuna and Credit, as well as the deity that completes the triumvirate, Dulness.

Textual representations of the commercialized world of Grub Street simultaneously recorded and created that site of literary production. A topographical location, Grub Street, like Exchange Alley, also existed as a discursive construction of cultural space that allowed an author like Alexander Pope to manage, contain, and thus control the professional writers he saw as literary mercenaries. Though a dynamic site of diverse activity, Grub Street was represented in a monolithic (and often antagonistic) vision by a self-prescribed literary elite such as Pope and his Augustan allies. The production of complex and varied texts and genres that characterized this literary milieu was erased under the damning rubric of "bad" writing. Alexander Pope's *Dunciad* was, of course, the most powerful (and, in part because of its existence in thirty-three separate editions and almost sixty impressions by 1751, the most persistent) representation of Grub Street and its denizens, the "dunces" – professional writers who sustained their often precarious existence through their rapid production of "paper credit."[2] In the *Dunciad*, Pope constructs a literary hierarchy that extends the binary of socio-economic relations (with which it was seen as inextricably linked) to socio-literary relations. Like his depiction of Exchange Alley, Pope's representation of the literary world is fundamentally oppositional: the frantic and mercenary hacks with their ephemeral devalued products stand in stark contrast to the privileged and "classical" gentleman-author who writes for a place in literary history.

Pope's ordering of eighteenth-century cultural production and the construction of a dominant hierarchy influenced the writing of literary history which, until recently, silently acceded to his model and maintained the "dunce" v. "poet," "hack" v. "anti-hack" mentality. In discussing the environment of literary production in the early eighteenth century, scholars have often cast Pope as the last outpost of high literary production in a marketplace increasingly shaped by successful businessmen like bookseller Edmund Curll. Pope and Curll metonymically function as opposing forces of high and low culture – "true literature" and "crass commercialism." Models of cultural relations threaten to perpetuate this binarism in an attempt to discuss the complex literary configurations. For example, Ronald Paulson, Pat Rogers, and, in a different context, Mikhail Bakhtin, have each theorized the practices of and relationship between disparate social formations and cultural categories as fundamentally oppositional. Paulson classifies eighteenth-century literary texts as "popular" and "polite."[3] Rogers labels Grub Street a literary "subculture," presumably in opposition to the dominant "culture" of Augustan literary production.[4] And Bakhtin, in his discussion of folk culture, identifies divergent cultural impulses as "classical" and "carnivalesque," categories which, though discussed dialectically by Bakhtin, are often reduced to a simple binary in critical shorthand.[5]

Certainly these models provide the scholar with a vocabulary with which to discuss these complicated cultural relations. Indeed, the literary production of Grub Street strikingly invokes the cultural dynamics of the carnivalesque: its irreverence, its suspension of hierarchical distinctions, its preoccupation with the body, and its invigorating energy all capture the carnivalesque impulse. As such, the products of Grub Street symbolically oppose the ordered, polite, and rational – "classical" – activity of high cultural production. Yet however illuminating these terms are (and I employ notions of the carnivalesque below), they must not be used in a way that risks replicating (in some form) the antagonistic and irreconcilable model Pope depicts in the *Dunciad*. The period is characterized not by boundaries but by transgressions, by the seepage of categories. The sites of cultural activity are mutually informing, indeed symbiotic. The dialogue rather than the opposition between constructed distinctions such as Paulson's popular and polite, Rogers's culture and subculture, or Bakhtin's classical and carnivalesque more accurately captures the cultural dynamic. As Peter Stallybrass and Allon White note in their discussion of the nature of symbolic hierarchies, high discourse with its "lofty style, exalted aim and sublime ends" is informed by "the debasements and degradations of low discourse." The two cannot be read apart but must be relationally configured.[6] In other words, the popular inevitably invades the polite, as Pope's *Dunciad* powerfully illustrates.

In part, the intersection or invasion of categories was inevitable because of all writers' dependence on paper credit. The *Dunciad* emphasizes the literary marketplace's connection with Exchange Alley and the influence of the "financial revolution" by using images of feminization consistent with the representations of speculative financial activity and the new economic man. The hack writer, as envisaged by Pope, emerges as a kind of new "literary" man (or woman). By worshiping Dulness and the marketplace, the Grub Street dunces subject literature to the economic laws of supply and demand. "They were manufacturing to order," writes Pat Rogers, " a product – literature – which in the past had largely been the preserve of the learned, the leisured, and the secure."[7] The commercial preoccupation altered the figure of the author and his text. Lady Mary Wortley Montagu complained that the profession of authorship had degenerated into a "trade." The mercenary attitude of authors, coupled with a lack of originality (exacerbated in part by the relentless need to produce), damaged the quality and status of "writing": "The Press is loaded by the servile Flock of Imitators . . . The Greatest Virtue, Justice, and the most distinguishing prerogative of Mankind, writeing, when duly executed does Honor to Human nature, but when degenerated into Trades are the most contemptible ways of getting Bread."[8]

Writers did not necessarily share her view. Indeed James Ralph, in *The Case of Authors by Profession or Trade* (1758), defiantly asserts that the "writer who serves himself and the Public together, has as good a Right to the Product in Money of his Abilities, as the Landholder to his Rent, or the

Money-Jobber to his Interest."[9] The function of writing as a trade and the construction of an author as a professional comparable to a "money-jobber" was increasingly accepted, if not celebrated, by those who operated in that capacity. In essence, then, the economic man and the professional writer were symbolically linked by their dependence on the imaginative forces that enabled their profession as well as the economic laws of the marketplace. There emerged a generation of modern subjects that could fashion a living out of the various manipulations of paper credit.

Though in the *Dunciad* Pope attacks paper credit in both its economic and literary manifestations, the poem is marked by a tension that underlies Pope's efforts to deny his associations with a world to which he is unavoidably and inextricably linked. The constructed hierarchy of the Augustan literary landscape quickly blurs in light of the phenomenal economic success Pope realized, his ongoing symbolic and material appropriation of Grub Street, and the confluence of commercial and literary activity. Popularity, frequency of publication, and profit were not only the concerns of authors writing to make a living wage, but of a self-styled artist like Pope.

Although Pope carefully controlled the production and distribution of his texts (holding copyrights, dictating format, etc.) in a way the typical writer in Grub Street could not, he did so in service of his consistent commercial preoccupations. David Foxon plausibly suggests that Pope's "quite distinct motive" for independence within the publishing industry was "to extract the maximum profit from his publications and to keep the copyright of his work under his own control."[10] Pope manipulated his early literary career to achieve the financial security that enabled him to write seemingly free of immediate material concerns. As Pope later wrote, "(thanks to Homer) since I live and thrive / Indebted to no Prince or Peer alive."[11] In fact, his translation of Homer – primarily a financial venture – was produced more rapidly (and made more lengthy) as a result of Pope's loss in the South Sea Bubble, an experience which fueled his suspicion of speculative investment and imaginary signifiers of paper credit. John Gay observed that Pope "has engag'd to translate the *Odyssey* in three year, I believe rather out of a prospect of Gain than inclination, for I am persuaded he bore his part in the loss of the South Sea."[12]

Sold by subscription, printed in quarto, and published in parts, Pope's translation of Homer, which David Foxon depicts as "revolutionary both commercially and aesthetically," provided him with a large profit at publisher Bernard Lintot's expense.[13] Selling the text by subscription, Pope capitalized on a profitable financial model introduced by speculative investment. Editions published by subscription, as W. A. Speck describes, "tended to be fairly expensive productions, confined to the more affluent members of society."[14] A subscriber usually paid part of the subscription immediately and then the rest upon receiving the book. The publisher and author have the money at the beginning of the project; their profit is guaranteed. The subscription process removed authors from the pressures and exigencies of the marketplace. Colin Nicholson, quoting Leslie Stephen, reminds us that "Pope's subscription technique meant that he 'received a kind of commission from the upper class' to produce his writing, and effected a break with past practice by replacing the individual patron with a 'kind of joint-stock body of collective patronage'."[15] Such advantageous financial arrangements incurred jealousy among less successful poets, and Pope's "collaborative" method of translating the *Odyssey* also made him vulnerable to charges of misrepresentation from his audience. He planned to get help from William Broome and Elijah Fenton on the translation of the *Odyssey* (since their Greek was better than his). Broome and Fenton, understandably, thought their work would be acknowledged. However, Pope recognized that the translation might be less attractive to subscribers if they knew Pope himself did not actually do all the translating. Capitalizing on the work of Fenton and Broome, Pope actually placed them in the position of the exploited hack writers he would satirize in the *Dunciad* (as indeed he satirized both men). The experience illustrates how Pope created his own type of literary factory to meet the demands of his public.

Foxon has also suggested Pope "swelled" his translation of the *Iliad* to ensure the profit he desired; he used larger type and formats and extended the margins and room for the annotations to each book. "What Madame Dacier [the French translator of Homer whom Pope attacked in the *Dunciad*] printed in three volumes duodecimo," notes Foxon, "Pope and Lintot swelled to six volumes in quarto or folio."[16] While Pope's efforts with Homer in part reflect his need to produce a text immediately considered a "classic," it also reveals his desire to extract the highest fee possible from his subscribers and his publisher. Such opportunities for increased textual production were ways an author like Pope could invest his paper credit in an attempt to construct a place for himself in literary history (all the while at great financial gain).

His well-documented desire to emulate a Virgilian career influenced his selection of genres, his self-fashioning of a socio-poetic persona, and even his decisions about the physical appearance of his works. Pope's motive in achieving independence within the book trade was not only the desire to improve his financial remuneration but the pressing need to control what Foxon describes as "the physical appearance and style of his works" which, I would argue, was central to his own sense of literary currency. After 1729, Pope eliminated the use of italics, capitalization, and catch-words from his own books in a return to a style visually allusive of the clean lines of a Latin text. This obsession with appearance makes the blue-bond format of the initial edition of the *Dunciad* all the more significant. Pope's pursuit of "classical status" also extended to what William Wimsatt has termed "the delineation and public projection of his own image." Pope's formal portraits – which only represented his head and shoulders – often evoked iconographic features associated with Greco-Roman portraiture: a Roman toga and a wreath of ivy leaves, a profile pose imitating a medallic representation, and use of the uroboros, the ancient symbol of eternity, all contributed to his efforts to transcend visually his temporal surroundings and to ignore his obvious physical differences.[17] Pope's skillful cultivation of his own poetic image – verbally and visually – indicates his desire to accumulate a surplus of paper credit in both an economic and a literary sense.

Poetry enabled Pope to increase his limited sense of personal power. He occupied a cultural position that might be read as "feminized," in contrast to the normative performance of masculinity dominant in a patriarchal culture. He was denied access to the public activities that authenticated masculine power. He lived a marginalized life constrained by circumstances largely beyond his control: his religion denied him the opportunity for a formal classical education, political involvement, or the possession of property within London; his physical infirmities limited his social and geographic mobility; and his elaborate process of "putting himself together" every morning made him dependent daily on personal servants. In *Lives of the English Poets*, Samuel Johnson describes how Pope "was not able to dress or undress himself, and neither went to bed nor rose without help."[18]

Pope recognized his inability to fulfill what his culture understood as the standards defining masculinity – an ideology he aggressively defended in his poetry. He also knew he was unable to engage in the libertine activities his early letters and poems imaginatively record. Physical disabilities and a life of constant pain undermined Pope's credibility as a rake, discouraged marriage, and, it is believed, prevented conventional sexual expression. He was acutely aware of being "that little Alexander the women laugh at."[19] Though he became infatuated with the Blount sisters and Lady Mary Wortley Montagu, Pope conducted these presumably unconsummated relationships primarily through language, substituting poetic for physical strength. He manipulated his poetic capital in his personal relationships, particularly those with women. As he told Teresa Blount, "were I a handsome fellow I should do you a vast deal of good: but as it is, all I am good for is to write a civil letter, or to make a fine speech" (*Corr.* I, pp. 349–50).

Pope's self-perceived feminization caused him to use his textual production to compensate for his fears of social and sexual inadequacy and to fulfill (if only discursively) his culture's construction of masculinity. He repeatedly suggests that writing good poetry is a vigorous, "manly" activity; literary authority contributes to sexual identity. In *An Essay on Criticism*, for example, in contrast to the "Patriarch-Wits" of the "Golden Age" (479), current writers "in the fat Age of Pleasure" "rhyme with all the Rage of Impotence" (609).[20] Writing marked by "Dulness with Obscenity" is as "Shameful sure as Impotence in Love" (532–33). Rival poets or critics who "cannot write" burn with "an Eunuch's spite" (30–31). The images of feminized dunces as symbolically emasculated illustrate Pope's representation of the writing of good poetry as powerful, authorizing, and "masculine." Poetry provided Pope with a form of creation in lieu of procreation – "no child of mine (but a Poem or two) is to live after me" (*Corr.* IV, p. 167) – and enabled him to offer women an immortality unavailable elsewhere. Language allowed Pope to reach unattainable women, to enact (verbally) physically impossible fantasies, and, most important, to create and control an ideal of a woman. He could immortalize and flatter or condemn and destroy his female subjects according to whether they fulfilled or threatened his constructed ideal of the gender. In essence, then, Pope was writing women in the image he desired: a discursive construction he could contain, control, and use as symbolic capital. Ann Rosalind Jones's characterization of writing from a male position has significant cultural resonance for a man living in an age defined by patriarchy, reason, and power. Jones suggests that to write "is to appropriate the world, to dominate it through verbal mastery. Symbolic discourse . . . is another means through which man objectifies the world, reduces it to his terms."[21] Pope's elaborate (and fictional) descriptions of erotic situations in his letters to Henry Cromwell, his manipulative attempts at seduction in his correspondence with Lady Mary Wortley Montagu, and, most obviously, his poetry reveal a man attempting to construct and control a world made more manageable on paper.[22]

At the same time, Pope was acutely aware that, as a poet, he relied on the cultural forces such as imagination and fancy he defined as feminized. As his description of the "Cave of Spleen" in *The Rape of the Lock* makes clear, Pope had an uneasy understanding that the sensibility creating female maladies was closely connected to the imaginative forces enabling literary production, "th' Hysteric or Poetic fit" (60): "On various Tempers act by various ways, / Make some take Physick, others scribble Plays" (*TE* II, p. 186, IV, pp. 60–61).[23] The fundamentally ambivalent (and perhaps androgynous) nature of the literary enterprise made Pope all the more vigilant in protecting – indeed cultivating – his own paper credit, and representing it as a rational, masculine pursuit. Of course, Pope also recognized that his carefully constructed socio-poetic persona, like his poetry, existed only through discursive representations that depended on a symbolic, rather than tangible, economy. Ronald Paulson observes that a writer or a poet "retains the stigma of paper objects as opposed to real objects."[24] That stigma aroused the same apprehension that Pope expressed about paper credit in a financial context, producing what Catherine Gallagher describes as Pope's "larger anxiety about the minimal materiality inherent in 'signifying systems'."[25] Pope attempted, as Richardson would later, to control interpretations of his "self." But he was assailed by circulating texts (both by him and about him) that complicated or compromised the illusion of him as a leisured, morally superior gentleman writing for primarily disinterested reasons. Although, as his interactions with Curll make clear, he could not always control his symbolic capital, literary worth, and the accompanying socio-literary persona, he never stopped trying. A mutually reinforcing relationship emerged between the symbolic and material economy. The more closely Pope could control the production, dissemination, and interpretation of his works, the more he profited from those texts in material and symbolic ways.

Any threat – real or imagined – to Pope's primary tool of power affected him on an intellectual, political, and sexual level. Consequently, the increasing success of female writers (which in itself manifested the feminization of culture) represented a force Pope feared personally and professionally. Critics of the *Dunciad* have traditionally emphasized its bleak prophecy of the triumph of fools; but, as the next section details, the poem can be read as Pope's reaction to women writing and the feminization that increasingly characterized literary activity. The epic's complex vision of culture delineates the inextricable connections between the financial and the literary, and reveals the profound ambivalence that informed Pope's attitude toward Grub Street.

The categories Pope established for himself were deeply contested within his own personal and professional existence. As discussed in the second section of this chapter, a series of pamphlets orchestrated by bookseller Edmund Curll following the 1728 publication of the *Dunciad* highlights those contradictions within Pope's career. These texts do not so much subvert the hierarchies constructed by Pope (although they retain a carnivalesque and decidedly transgressive impulse) as dissolve them in an attempt to represent Grub Street as an egalitarian site of literary production. Curll, in a sense, reconfigures the relationship between Pope and the marketplace and the other professional writers and booksellers. The responses to the 1728 *Dunciad* published by Curll (including responses by the women writers Pope attacked) underscore the precarious control Pope had over his literary texts, his cultural persona, and his discursive performance of masculinity. The exchange between the two men illustrates their competing negotiation of cultural authority, literary space, and Pope's construction of self. Curll's publications complicate and ultimately fragment the stable persona Pope carefully created and cultivated. Yet there is evidence Pope calculated the *Dunciad* as a vehicle for a protracted paper war (what Richard Savage called the "Dunce Wars") that would increase his literary stock and his economic gain. The *Dunciad* initially appears to be Pope's exclusionary gesture to silence the feminized and female opposition he believed was eroding culture as well as encroaching on his stature as an artist. But he attempts to silence the very voices he wants to engage in a profitable dialogue. The *Dunciad*'s radical ambivalence complicates our understanding of Pope as it reveals his attempts simultaneously to deny and profit from his growing portfolio of paper credit.

I

Pope dramatizes the cause of the culture's deterioration as specifically female – Dulness the woman. The rise of the female novel, the proliferation of Grub Street publications by and for women, and Pope's personal sense of diminished ability, make Dulness more than an abstract manifestation of duncian energy or yet another female monster in Augustan satire.[26] Dulness symbolizes Pope's escalating fear of a pervasive "feminization" that threatens to permeate nearly every aspect of English culture. The term "feminization" derives from the exclusionary practice Andreas Huyssen (in a different context) identifies as "the persistent gendering as feminine of that which is devalued."[27] Pope constructed the feminine image of Dulness to be read as a composite of all the evils of femininity placed in a position of cultural centrality. Drawing on the essentialist eighteenth-century assumptions about women, their sexuality, and their writing, Pope creates a powerful, emasculating, and dangerous woman to embody the worst aspects of the feminized economic and literary world.

With her uncontrollable fecundity, her feminine inconstancy, and her absolute power over the dunces, Dulness, Magna Mater to commercial writers, transgresses established boundaries and creates a powerful social incoherence that portends systemic disorder. By identifying Dulness with Magna Mater, Pope foregrounds his personal fears with images from classical sources as well as Renaissance and eighteenth-century mythographic works. Pope makes "Dulness larger and more terrible than she may at first appear," a composite figure that gained chaotic power from the associations with other female deities of disorder. Pope exploits what Faulkner and Blair term the "confused" historical and mythological accounts of Dulness to reinforce the idea of chaos which she embodies in the *Dunciad*.[28]

Magna Mater is most closely associated with the goddess Cybele, who led her eunuch priests or "Galli" in activities associated with incest, misdirected sexual energy, and castration. The Galli, who anticipate the intellectual eunuchs or dunces, worshiped Cybele and practiced rituals characterized by "frenetic dancing, wailing and the noise of clashing cymbals and tympanum."[29] The cult's disordered, "feminized," and literally emasculating activities share with the dunces a symbolic regression. Like Dulness, Cybele's maternal power debilitates rather than strengthens. Cybele and goddesses like her were characterized as "cruel, capricious, lustful; they were powerful." Simone de Beauvoir describes her as a fearsome mother: "[Goddesses like] Cybele were as much the source of death as of life, in giving birth to men they made men their slaves."[30] Dulness requires similar male subordination. She increases aggressive demands until she ultimately subsumes and emasculates her male followers. Pope's representation of Dulness exploits the supposed male fear of the mother and the reluctance to acknowledge her male followers' previous containment within and dependence upon a woman – "the chaos whence all have come and whither all must one day return."[31] In each consecutive book of the *Dunciad*, Dulness essentially leads her dunces back to the womb as she encourages their increasingly degenerate behavior: from "the Chaos dark and deep" (A.i.53) to "*Night* Primaeval and ... *Chaos* old" (B.iv.630) where "CHAOS! is restor'd; / Light dies before they uncreating word" (B.iv.653–54).[32] The regression bordering on stasis removes men from the sphere of masculine activity to the female realm of passivity.

Dulness's chaotic power arises largely from her uncontrollable ability to reproduce, and her physical prolificacy makes subversive an activity culturally constructed as normative for a woman. In the eighteenth century, children typically anchored a woman further within a private sphere like the home and a patriarchal institution like marriage; in the domestic arena, children became another means of subjugation. As Susan Stanford Friedman observes, "women's oppression begins with the control of the body, the fruits of labor."[33] However, Dulness controls her own body in order to oppress her dunces. She refuses defining circumscription and, with her very public maternity, is empowered by her transgressions of established male boundaries. Her activities confound male restraints or categorization; she resists the patriarchal construction of woman. As a result, Dulness creates social incoherence and assumes the power residing in what Mary Douglas terms the "inarticulate areas, margins, confused lines, and beyond the external boundaries."[34] Her undefined position disregards traditional hierarchies – social, sexual, literary – and fuels what Pat Rogers describes as the Augustan anxiety "not that things would fall apart, but that everything would somehow merge."[35] Dulness embodies the carnivalesque impulse of Grub Street. Bakhtin, speaking of the carnivalesque generally, writes: "the leading themes of these images of bodily life are fertility, growth and a brimming-over abundance. Manifestations of this life refer not to the isolated biological individual ... but to the collective ancestral body of all the people."[36] In an upside-down world, the "collective body" manifests itself in Dulness and the rapidly growing population of dunces.

Dulness's procreative abilities symbolically give her the power of physical and cultural reproduction and illustrate the ease with which texts are conceived and materially reproduced in the Grub Street environment. During this period, women's procreation "was perceived through an androcentric lens as a mindless, unconscious, uncontrolled act of the body," writes Friedman.[37] This characterization extends to Pope's understanding of hack writing. As what Irvin Ehrenpreis labels an "unwed or parthenogenetic mother," Dulness's ability to reproduce autonomously provides her with a vehicle for action, articulation, and control; with her double-birthing ability, she spawns dunces, genres, and texts that she can mold in her image.[38] Instead of marking her domestic conformity, this maternity is ultimately an aggressive action that provides her with the opportunity to rule, shape, or construct. For Pope that action took the all too material form of literary production such as Eliza Haywood's and the sheer un-controlled quantity of texts emanating from the popular press. As a result, Dulness's image hyperbolically embodies the patriarchally derived characterization of what Susan Gubar terms a "presumptuous, castrating or even monstrous" female author.[39]

Dulness's progeny and their literary creations assume similarly mon-strous forms which delight the goddess, who insists that culture "prepare / For new Abortions, all ye pregnant Fair !" (A.III.311–12) and applauds the literary miscegenation: "How Tragedy and Comedy embrace; / How Farce and Epic get a jumbled race" (A.I.67–68). The misshapen offspring illustrate the culturally constructed abnormality of female literary pro-duction as well as the eighteenth-century belief that a mother's emotional or intellectual state could influence the condition of her fetus. Paul-Gabriel Boucé explains how eighteenth-century male physicians attrib-uted stillborn or malformed babies to the "more or less monstrous marks" a mother's imagination could leave on the fetus.[40] In *De Morbis Cutaneis* (1723), Daniel Turner (1667–1741) states that without a doubt "Powerful emotional events during a woman's pregnancy gave rise to malformation of the offspring."[41] This belief encouraged male fear of a woman's repro-ductive ability and essentially pronounced it medically unsound for women to stimulate their imaginations – exactly the aim of reading and writing fiction. Ironically, as Roy Porter observes, assigning such powers to the female imagination makes the future of the race dependent on "what chanced to be racing through the mind of the weaker vessel, whose ration-ality was doubted at the best of times."[42] David Hume in "On Essay Writing" echoes this fear of a woman's excessively emotional or imagina-tive reaction specifically to a novel: "Most of them seem more delighted with the Warmth than with the justness of the Passion ... As the Fair Sex have a great share of the tender and the amorous Disposition, it perverts their judgement on this occasion, and makes them easily affected."[43] The novel appeals to a woman's "tender and amorous" and thus feminine dis-position; yet it takes the natural and feminine and perverts it by making it, in a sense, too feminine.

Dulness's exaggerated femininity is another source of Pope's anxiety. Feminine characteristics (as culturally constructed) are qualities designed to diminish and trivialize a woman's abilities, power, and interests, or keep her narrowly focused on her virtue, physical appearance, or reputation. The feminine virtues, when displayed in a controlled environment, make women the object of male desire. Pope gently satirizes Belinda's female whim, foibles, and designs to power which never really extend beyond the card table or the drawing room. Yet when Dulness displays feminine characteristics, she promises destruction, a "world turned upside down." When these feminine traits exceed their boundaries and define an individual in power, they become a profoundly destabilizing force. On a more personal level, Pope's reaction perhaps suggests how his own insecurities with women (indeed his ideal vision of woman is as a "softer man" [*Epistle to a Lady*, 202]) translate female attributes into dangerous cultural weapons.

Dulness shares the feminine inconstancy Belinda displays in *The Rape of the Lock*; like Fortune and Luxury, they are fickle and require diversions. When Belinda awakes, the sight of love letters immediately removes the ominous warning Ariel made in her dream; she can go from fear to pleasure instantaneously. Dulness's "love letters," or the scribblings of the dunces, provide her with the ever-changing stimuli she needs to remain content. Like Dulness, the capricious Belinda cannot remain constant in her mind (II.9–10) or in "the moving Toyshop" of her heart (I.100), and she always seeks new conquests. Though Pope obliquely condemns her inconstancy, he implicitly acknowledges its function in protecting a woman's other commodity – her virginity. As Ariel explains, a single woman surrounded by suitors needs such fickleness to guard "the Purity of the melting Maids" (I.71). Such inconstancy provides a woman with only the power of refusal and inaction, a passivity central to the male construction of female sexuality.

Despite this passivity, Belinda does possess the power to drain an object of meaning and replace it with a significance more appropriate to her diminutive world; indeed, Belinda feminizes and trivializes the world around her. However, her transformative powers are limited to objects within her rather narrow purview. The Bible on her dressing table assumes the value of a love letter while the sparkling cross on her white breast loses its religious aura, becoming an erotic tool to lure men – sacred icons become secular commodities for public consumption. As his critics noted, Pope performed the same gesture with his translation of Homer by attempting to market an epic as a popular text: he transformed a classic text into a popular and profitable commodity.[44] Similarly, Dulness drains the strength from forceful, masculine disciplines and reduces them to a product for the marketplace or an instrument for her own use: "There, stript, fair *Rhet'ric* languish'd on the ground; / His blunted Arms by *Sophistry* are born" (B.IV.24–25). With her beauty and charm, Belinda, like Dulness, controls the temperament of those around her; when she smiles "all the World was gay" (II.52) but when she frowns, "The pitying Audience melt in Tears ... For who can move when fair

Belinda fails?" (v.i, 4). Pope attributes this tendency, which becomes dangerous with Dulness, to a woman's power and to the malleable characters of effeminate men. Yet he praises this same quality in Martha Blount, who is "blest with Temper, whose unclouded ray / Can make to morrow chearful as to day" (*Epistle to a Lady*, 257–58); when used by a docile woman in a self-sacrificing manner, this temperamental influence is sanctioned and even praised.

The dunces, whether Belinda's Baron or Dulness's Theobald or Cibber, share a fundamental dullness with Pope's poetic women that ranges from a fascination with superficial and trivial concerns to a laborious preoccupation with minutiae: they are feminized in thought and deed. Again, Pope condemns women for practices and preoccupations that embody the male construction of gender and the sanctioned activities for women. *The Rape of the Lock* abounds with examples of triviality stemming primarily from Belinda's vanity, as she lives by Dulness's motto – "Learn but to trifle" (B.iv.457). However, Belinda's vanity is born of a concern with physical appearance, reputation, and image, all social constructions that trivialize her value. Belinda's hyperbolic reaction to her ravaged curl confuses virtue and vanity, and she disregards Clarissa's warning about mortality. Her culture's obsession with the immediacy of youth, beauty, and marriage denies her the ability to think about the consequences of age and the passage of time. She cannot think of herself in any but superficial terms.

Encouraged by Dulness, the "indolent" dunces, like Belinda, are preoccupied with the trivial and concentrate primarily on "trifles" of every kind, finding proper employment "in the study of *Butterflies, Shells, Birdnests, Moss*, &c. but with particular caution, not to proceed beyond *Trifles*, to any useful or extensive views of Nature, or of the Author of Nature" (*TE* v, p. 338). These feminized activities divert the dunces, causing them to neglect their real duties to govern, another traditionally male activity from which Pope himself was barred. The dunces' fascination with trifles also precludes the possibility of substantive, "real" work, and channels their energy into illusory pursuits. A hack and an economic man have only increasing amounts of paper to show for their labor. The dunces rely primarily on superficial appearance and are easily tricked by the phantom poet, as a woman might be duped by a false lover, or an investor swindled by a dishonest stock-jobber. While superficiality causes the inconsistency and gullibility Pope condemns in the dunces, women, and stock-jobbers, it also serves as the measure of a woman's value in a patriarchal culture where a woman's face is her fortune. In Dulness, such superficiality makes it easy for the goddess equally to value disparate things. She lacks a discriminating eye:

> (Diff'rent our parties, but with equal grace
> The Goddess smiles on Whig and Tory race,
> 'Tis the same rope at sev'ral ends they twist,
> To Dulness, Ridpath is as dear as Mist.)
>   (A.III.283–86)

This indiscriminate attention conveys a woman's complaisance, her willingness to be agreeable, meek or accommodating: "How soft is Silia! fearful to offend, / The Frail one's advocate, the Weak one's friend" (*Epistle to a Lady*, 29–30). Dulness also delights in the inconstant "motley Images her fancy strike" (A.I.63), and when she sees "a Mob of Metaphors advance" she is "Pleas'd with the Madness of the mazy dance" (A.I.65–66). Like a numbed public or an overly eager stock-jobber, she desires the sensation of immediate gratification without regard to order or meaning: "random Thoughts now meaning chance to find, / Now leave all memory of sense behind" (A.I.229–30).

The duncos, like women, for "Women and Fools are always in Extreme" (*Imitations of Horace* I.ii.27–28), also concentrate on minutiae to the exclusion of real meaning. Dulness sanctions the endless discussion of one issue to the point of inanity, work that destroys meaning. Her sterile self-absorption makes her observations meaningful only within her self-enclosed system of exchange: "explain a thing till all men doubt it, / And write about it, Goddess, and about it" (A.I.169–70). She shuns sharp rational thoughts in favor of continued trivializing: "revive the Wits! / But murder first, and mince them all to bits" (B.IV.119–20). She uses the tools of real scholarship to destroy rather than enhance meaning. She advocates "The critic Eye, that microscope of Wit," that sees only "hairs and pores" (B.IV.233–34) and never comprehends the whole.[45]

Dulness's actions are completely consistent with the role prescribed for women in eighteenth-century culture, where they are praised for excelling at detailed handwork like needlepoint, a diminutive art form like china painting, or the management of a household, activities that literally and symbolically reduce their field of vision. The mention of "hairs and pores" resembles the preoccupation with imperfection produced by the unattainably high standards created for perfect female beauty; a woman attempting to achieve that ideal focuses a critical eye only on her slight flaws and ignores her overall appearance. Ironically, when he criticizes the feminine characteristics shared by women and dunces, Pope implicates the patriarchal structure he supports, for he criticizes precisely the qualities women are encouraged to cultivate to meet male standards for beauty, chastity, or housekeeping. Here, as with his attack on Dulness's maternity, Pope decries the actions engendered by the social structure he casts as endangered.

A similar ambiguity characterizes Pope's most damning accusation about women – their desire to achieve increasing amounts of power and thus satisfy their "Love of Pleasure, and the Love of Sway"; "They seek the second not to lose the first" (*Epistle to a Lady*, 210, 214). The terms "pleasure" and "sway" do not immediately suggest a type of dangerous ambition; they instead connote limited and, to a certain extent, self-determined ambitions achievable by women. Yet Pope, by making them the shibboleth of Dulness, recontextualizes and thus reconstructs their meaning in a manner that endows the terms with sinister implications. Such a move confirms Pope's personal fear of the encroaching power of women and his broader apprehension that women writers who offer the public sensually pleasing texts will gain a point of entry to increase their power – their love of sway.

Sway suggests a type of subtle persuasion or influence, the kind of disguised force women, denied access to the public tools of power, have often used to achieve any sort of personal power. Sway allows one to redirect or divert an individual, his actions, or feelings; it causes him "to swerve from a course of action" or "from a path or line of conduct."[46] Rochester similarly uses the idea of "sway" in "A Satyr of Charles ii": "His scepter and his prick are of a length; / And she may sway the one who plays with th' other."[47] In Dulness sway becomes an insidious, coercive power that characterizes her dangerously effective strategy for control. As she feminizes culture, Dulness diverts it from its "proper" course, redirecting male genres, energies, and impulses. With "Arbitrary Sway" (B.iii.182) Dulness can rule like a tyrant and potentially satisfy her love of pleasure. The fact that she also controls "the young, the old, who feel her inward sway" (B.iv.73) indicates the pervasiveness of her power.

Moreover, Dulness metaphorically embodies the physical and mental movement characteristic of sway. Her "gentle sway" (A.iii.304), though describing her seductive power, is also suggestive of the way Dulness lulls her dunces into a passive state; she moves like a woman rocking a child, creating the illusion of movement while remaining stationary:

> What Dulness dropt among her sons imprest
> Like motion, from one circle to the rest;
> So from the mid-most the nutation spreads
> Round, and more round, o'er all the sea of heads.
>
> (A.ii.375–78)

The nodding dunces watch Dulness sway back and forth, hypnotized by the repetitive movement – an image appropriate in light of the dunces' delight in trite ideas, Dulness's repeated practical jokes, and her fondness for unimaginative, formulaic works. Dulness also exploits the sensual aspects of sway, luring her dunces, "Who gently drawn, and struggling less and less, / Roll in her Vortex, and her pow'r confess" (B.iv.83–84). Like a ship swaying on the sea of whim, pleasure, and fancy, she cannot personally, mentally, or intellectually remain stable. Her constantly shifting, indecisive mind becomes a fitting emblem for the increasingly sensationalistic work consumed by a public easily swayed from one feminized attraction to another.

Dulness's ability to "sway" the public increases her pleasurable power and enables her to humiliate, embarrass, and dupe the dunces. Their infantile activities, most strikingly in Book ii, originate with the commands of the woman at the center of the poem. The dunces' activity emblematically represents the world of Grub Street writers, the demise of education, art, and politics, and the imminent collapse Pope predicts for men, the patriarchy, and culture as a whole. The dunces perform "the exercises for the Poets, of tickling, vociferating, diving" (*TE* v, p. 295). The booksellers pursue the false poet Dulness constructs (B.ii.31–156), illustrating how the economic demands on booksellers have debased the book trade. Spurred on by Dulness, the dunces act like fickle women as they attempt to meet the needs of a feminized reading public. Rather than fighting heroically with swords or fists, the dunces tickle patrons with quills, a purely sensual "dext'rous task" (A.ii.191) that promotes a "pleasing pain" (A.ii.203) as "quick sensations skip from vein to vein" (A.ii.204). The masturbatory imagery implicit in the lines is appropriate for the activities of a hack writer who squanders vital energy (sperm or poetic ability) purely for self-gratification (orgasm or money from patron). The dunces' activities also parody or simulate the heroic activities of an idealized aristocrat; but, like their economic counterparts, the hacks actually operate in a world of intangible property, imagination, and deferred meaning. For example, in the noise contest the dunces, resembling a chattering group of women, create "one loud din" (A.ii.227) which provides immediate gratification but lacks any force or permanence: a cacophony void of coherence and signification, designed only "To move, to raise, to ravish ev'ry heart" (A.ii.215).

Similarly Opera, "a Harlot form soft sliding by" (B.iv.45), embodies the trivial and inconstant female and manifests Pope's vision of a feminized genre. With her "mincing step, small voice, and languid eye" (B.iv.46), Opera parodies the demeanor of a flirtatious woman:

In patch-work flutt'ring, and her head aside
By singing Peers up-held on either hand,
She tripp'd and laugh'd, too pretty much to stand...
Then thus in quaint Recitativo spoke.

(B.IV.48–51)

Her art form consists of little more than trills and "Chromatic tortures" (B.IV.55). With his footnote, Pope amplifies the "irregularity" of the music, which he terms "a variation and embellishment" : "They say it was invented about the time of *Alexander,* and that the *Spartans* forbade the use of it, as languid and effeminate" (*TE* v, p. 347). Equally troubling to Pope was the incomprehensibility of the Italian opera: the series of scenes from different librettos eliminated plot; the difference in language prohibited understanding; and the cast members' portrayal of characters of the opposite sex blurred the boundaries of gender. To Pope's mind, the success of opera depended purely on the superficial allure of spectacle: "The Attitude given to this Phantom represents the nature and genius of the *Italian* Opera; its affected airs, its effeminate sounds, and the practice of patching up these Operas with favourite songs, incoherently put together" (*TE* v, p. 345).

Pope's description of the Phantom of Opera indicates the ambiguous, corrupt sexuality opera also engenders in the material world; the castrati willingly mutilate themselves, sacrificing their virility in pursuit of profit or performance. As Robert Ness notes, these "unnatural monsters" (another product of the imagination) become for Pope "an obscene symbol ... of the kind of 'amphibiousness' that heralds chaos": "The basic distinction, that of sexual difference, was blurred in the castrati. In their epicene appeal, they usurped the position of 'legitimate' humans."[48] Like the Galli, the worshipers of Magna Mater, the castrati emasculate themselves to demonstrate their devotion to a feminized aesthetic. By transgressing established gender boundaries they contribute to a larger cultural confusion. Like the dunces, they happily live within a world of ambiguous sexuality, subverted power relations, and social incoherence.

In the *Dunciad,* this immorality and ambiguous sexuality characterize almost everyone Pope finds personally or professionally threatening – Dulness, the dunces, and female writers of Grub Street like Elizabeth Thomas and Eliza Haywood. Pope not only "made the theme of sexual licentiousness implicit simply through his choice of the Magna Mater as the prototype of Dulness," as Faulkner and Blair argue. He also suggests an abnormal sexuality by emphasizing Dulness's incestuous relationships with Theobald and later Cibber, "unchaste priests whose 'chastity' is lost to Dulness herself" (239). When she first spots Theobald, "She ey'd the Bard" and "pin'd" (A.1.109–10) and by the end of Book 1 she is "rapt" (A.1.255) in his presence. An equally smitten Theobald declares Dulness "First in my care, and nearest at my heart" (A.1.144). All her children are drawn to her "by a wonderful attraction" (*TE* v, p. 337). In the womb-like temple, a submerged Theobald, once son and now royal companion, slumbers with his head in Dulness's lap, a position suggesting an incestuous relationship: "in her Temple's last recess inclos'd, / On Dulness lap th' Anointed head repos'd" (A.III.1–2). Pope also highlights suggestions of the dunces' impotence and Dulness's unnatural and aggressive sexuality; Dulness "mounts the Throne" and instructs her son to recline "Soft on her lap" (B.IV.17, 20). The "Great Tamer" (A.1.143) enervates her soft king and the dunces who resemble dutiful women with their increasingly trivial and submissive behavior, underscoring the similarity between the corrupt and the effeminate within Pope's representation.

Pope fully exploits that connection in his attacks on Grub Street regulars Elizabeth Thomas and Eliza Haywood.[49] Like the dunces, these women symbolically exist within "a new world, to Nature's laws unknown" (A.III.237), where hack writing triumphs over "art," where women writers successfully compete with men for fame and profit, and where the dominant masculine culture must combat the powerful force of feminization. Thomas and Haywood were women who threatened Pope professionally, offended him personally, or, in some ways, controlled him textually.

Elizabeth Thomas (1675–1731), allegedly the mistress of Henry Cromwell, sold Edmund Curll the letters that Pope had written to Cromwell.[50] Curll promptly published them on August 12, 1726, as *Mr. Pope's Familiar Letters ... written to Henry Cromwell.*[51] These letters, which subsequently appeared in *The Female Dunciad*, reveal Pope's affected rakish attitudes and deal explicitly with his self-contained sexual fantasies. They undermine the socio-poetic persona Pope constructed. Thomas's actions, done primarily for profit, exemplify the nature of her literary activities. She achieved only limited success with her own writing, and she tried to transcend her literary obscurity through her associations with prominent authors of the time. She corresponded with Dryden, who gave her the name Corinna, she was the confidante if not mistress of Pope's friend Henry Cromwell, and, as a result of that relationship, she might actually have met Pope on at least one occasion. T. R. Steiner insists that Pope not only knew Thomas, but had actually spent "time in private company" with her and praised her knowledge and conversational skills. In fact, Steiner believes Pope "purposely obscured" his early London relationships with individuals like Thomas to facilitate his satire.[52] However, Thomas's impecuniousness and unscrupulousness prompted her to exploit those friendships by capitalizing on the information gained in the relationships; for example, she published an almost fictional account of Dryden's funeral shortly after she sold Pope's letters. And her sale of the letters, in light of the possible personal association between Pope and Thomas, may have been as personally hurtful as it was professionally embarrassing to Pope.

Ironically, another source of Thomas's published notoriety was the report of her unusual physical condition to the College of Physicians in 1730. In April 1711 Thomas accidentally swallowed a large chicken bone which created an obstruction that for years created a pronounced distention caused by the retention of bodily fluids: "her stomach, and belly, and head swelled to a monstrous degree," an uncomfortable situation relieved only by her use of purgatives and the expulsion of those fluids.[53] On one occasion, purgative medicines could not help her and "she was given over as incurable when nature unexpectedly helped itself, and in twelve hours' time by stool and vomit, she voided about five gallons of dirty looking water, which greatly relieved her for some days" (95). This account of Thomas's medical history was not only given to the College of Physicians, but appeared verbatim in the appendix to her published love letters, *Pylades and Corinna* (1731–32) and in Theophilus Cibber's *Lives of the Poets of Great Britain and Ireland* (1753). Apparently Thomas's bodily discharges were as well known as her poetry.

Pope's representation of Thomas draws directly on her medical history. During the booksellers' race of Book 11, Thomas urinates in the middle of the street and produces the lake into which Curll slides and falls:

> Full in the middle way there stood a lake,
> Which Curl's Corinna chanc'd that morn to make,
> (Such was her wont, at early dawn to drop
> Her evening cates before his neighbour's shop,) ..
> (A.11.65–68)

The inappropriate public urination signifies the lack of propriety and conformity demonstrated by Thomas's sale of Pope's personal letters; the private should not be publicly exposed. A woman of dulness, Corinna cannot recognize the proper boundaries – literary, patriarchal, or social. Curll, like the other dunces, delights in the discharge: "From the effluvia strong / Imbibes new life and scours and stinks along" (A.11.97–98). Although Pope claims in a footnote that he had "no thought of reflecting on her in this passage" (*TE* v, p. 106), Pope's likely personal familiarity with her affliction (and cure) suggests that, with this passage, he may have attempted to embarrass her as personally and publicly as she had him. Pope's scatological emphasis on the abnormality of Thomas's body reduces her to a physically defined individual and ignores her literary activities. He does to her precisely what he accused and hated his critics for doing to him.

Pope similarly reduces Haywood's distinguishing characteristics to the physical, and ignores or demeans her considerable publishing achievements. Eliza Haywood, as discussed more fully in the next two chapters, was arguably the most important producer of popular fiction before Richardson. Jerry Beasley notes that, during the 1720s, she was more closely identified with the novel "than any other native fiction writer ... Her efforts probably did more than those of any other single author to stimulate the production of native novels."[54] Maynard Mack contends that Pope's attack on Haywood was primarily an attempt to exact revenge for Martha Blount, who "had been sneered at as a common whore in a scandalous novel by Eliza Haywood as recently as 1725."[55] However, it seems just as likely that such an incident only crystallized Pope's growing antipathy to Haywood's Grub Street affiliations. During her career in Grub Street, Haywood associated with the larger network of writers – or dunces – whom Pope combated and she contributed to the paper wars following the *Dunciad*. Aaron Hill (1685–1750) wrote the epilogues to Haywood's first play *The Fair Captive* (1721).[56] William Rufus Chetwood (d. 1766), a competitor in the urinating contest, published many of her early novels, including the *roman-à-clef* in which she slights Martha Blount. And Edmund Curll (1675–1747) enlisted Haywood's contribution for a critical response to the *Dunciad* entitled *The Female Dunciad* (1729).

Her extremely popular novels, which tell of beleaguered heroines, disastrous romances, and corrupting world experience, embodied Pope's worst fears about feminized cultural standards. Haywood's unconventional personal life and frank discussions of sexuality gave Pope the opportunity to exploit the traditional patriarchal association between modesty and sexual morality in his attacks. Writing was often represented as an aggressively immodest act for a woman in the eighteenth century. As Patricia Crawford suggests, "silence, in all its forms, was an essential component of modesty ... in writing for publication, women risked their reputation."[57] Haywood's reputation suffered even further at Pope's hands. By focusing on the immorality that allegedly characterized her life and her fiction, Pope strategically ignores, indeed trivializes, Haywood's success as an independent female author by making his attack personal as well as professional. For example, using a Virgilian allusion (cf. *Aeneid* 5.285), Pope describes Haywood as having "Two babes of love close clinging to her waist" (B.II.158). Similarly, his reference to her "majestic size" with "cow-like udders and with ox-like eyes" (A.II.155–56) casts her fecundity, like Dulness's, as abnormal and almost animalistic – an image appropriate to his belief in her equally unnatural literary creativity.

His excoriating footnote mentions her "profligate licenciousness" and "most scandalous books," and describes her as one of

those shameless scriblers (for the most part of That sex, which ought least to be capable to such malice or impudence) who in libellous Memoirs and Novels, reveal the faults and misfortunes of both sexes, to the ruin or disturbance, of publick fame or private happiness. Our good Poet (by the whole cast of his work being obliged not to take off the Irony) where he cou'd not show his Indignation, hath shewn his Contempt as much as possible. (*TE* v, p. 119)

Though in part personal vendetta, Pope's footnote reveals a more general antagonism toward female writers which stems largely from his fear of their (seemingly aggressive) powers of articulation. Women's novels reveal information that could lead to "the ruin or disturbance" of public fame and private happiness, suggesting they maliciously provide gossip or knowledge that disrupts the status quo. Women writers and readers remove women from the domestic sphere by the power of fiction and its seeming unreality, a disruption in its own right; they also create and empower a community of women intellectually freed from male control.

Pope makes Haywood the first prize in the urinating contest, with a China Jordan or chamber pot for the second-place finisher. Here Pope parodies the section in Book 23 of the *Iliad* where the first prize for the third game is a tripod, while the second prize is a female captive (23.819). In his footnote to the *Iliad*, Pope comments on Madame Dacier's resentment of this passage, where the ancients "set (it seems) thrice the Value upon a Tripod as upon a beautiful female Slave" (*TE* VIII, p. 522). Pope ironically recounts Dacier's concern that "the Value of Women is not rais'd even in our Days," a situation he attributes to "a want of Taste in both Ancients and Moderns." He goes on to remind the reader "that these Tripods were of no use, but made entirely for Show, and consequently the most satyrical Critick could only say, the Woman and Tripod ought to have born an equal Value" (*TE* VIII, p. 522). In this passage, Pope simultaneously reveals the injustice of the plight of women while condoning the inequity. By making Haywood the first prize in the *Dunciad*, Pope indicates that she (much to his dismay) is not just for "show" but is an all too active member of the publishing community. With the Homeric allusion, Pope also increases the insult toward Haywood by suggesting that in the devalued, inverted, and distinctly un-heroic world of the *Dunciad*, a woman like Haywood *should* be the first prize for a urinating contest; a tripod would be too valuable.

By making Haywood the prize, Pope symbolically assigns her a more appropriate female activity – namely a silent, passive receptacle and object completely under male domination. He silences her by removing her from the primarily male world of competition, and he degrades her by characterizing her as libidinous. While the tripod is more highly valued in the *Iliad*, Pope notes that "Mrs. H. here is treated with distinction and acknowledg'd to be the more valuable of the two" (*TE* v, p. 120) – here in the empire of Dulness. Yet Pope's concession more powerfully reveals his contempt and disdain. Both prizes are powerless vessels to be filled by the various excretions of men, for just as the runner-up is encouraged to "Replenish [the China Jordan], not ingloriously, at home" (A.ii.158), so too will the winner of Haywood "fill" "the pleas'd dame soft-smiling" (A.ii.180). In the *Dunciad*, Pope controls Haywood and by textual means temporarily returns her to the submissive position "appropriate" for women, eliminating the threat she poses to him economically, professionally, and personally. Haywood's commercial success not only produced economic competition, but to a certain extent demystified the creative process, arguably another form of symbolic emasculation for a man like Pope. In response, Pope's poetic expression of contempt and indignation, "as vile a picture as possible" (*TE* v, p. 119), reasserts his power and exacts his revenge by placing Haywood in a poetic situation under his control; but, as I have suggested, this pose also displays Pope's constructed role as a solitary voice defending his literary space against the encroaching forces of feminized culture.

Consequently, Pope's complex vision cannot be adequately characterized by the term "misogyny," for his antipathy extends beyond women to all Grub Street writers, the new breed of economic men, and the insatiable and seemingly unstoppable middling classes. The politics of Pope's vision, while incorporating contemporaneous references, go far beyond them to redefine the issues of the *Dunciad* and Pope's other representations of culture. Despite its contemptuous tone, the *Dunciad* is not a poem written from a self-perceived position of strength, but a poem revealing a symbolically emasculated man's personal and professional anxiety about the increasing power of creating and mercenary male and female writers.

2

Pope's professional stature did not prevent him from attempting to manipulate the mechanisms of print culture to stimulate interest in his own publications. In fact, his relationship with Grub Street was marked by a simultaneous repulsion and attraction that manifested itself within the trajectory of his poetic career and in the works themselves. Pope initially engaged in verbal sparring with individuals he would label dunces. Early in his career he competed with his literary rivals, producing inflammatory pamphlets in a series of well-known episodes. In 1713, John Dennis wrote *Remarks on Cato*, where he condemned Addison's *Cato*, to which Pope had contributed the prologue. In defense of Addison, and himself, Pope published *The Narrative of Dr. Robert Norris, concerning the strange and deplorable frenzy of Dr. John Dennis* (July 1713), which portrays Dennis as a ridiculous and raving lunatic. This exchange determined the tone of their acrimonious relationship, although Pope significantly revised the history of their published feud when he declared in *Epistle to Arbuthnot*: "Yet then did Dennis rave in furious fret, / I never answer'd, I was not in debt" (*TE* IV, 107, pp. 153–54). The language of credit which informs the response subtly indicates that for Pope the symbolic and material economies of the literary marketplace were mutually informing. In 1716, after Edmund Curll published *The Court Poems*, a pirated series of mildly scandalous texts attributed to Pope, Gay, and Lady Mary Wortley Montagu, Pope secretly administered an emetic to Curll under the guise of a "peace-making 'Glass of Sack'."[58] As he wrote John Caryll, "I contrived to save a fellow a beating by giving him a vomit" (*Corr.* I, p. 339). Pope then wrote a graphic history of the event, *A Full and True Account of a Horrid and Barbarous Revenge by Poison, on the body of Mr. Edm. Curll*, followed by *A Further Account of the most Deplorable Condition of Mr. Edmund Curll, since his being poisoned*. The title of each pamphlet resembles that of a criminal biography and the texts emphasize the scatological consequences of Curll's "deplorable condition." The nature of the physical and then verbal humiliations also anticipates Pope's strategy of finding forms of retribution that did not demand physical strength. These early encounters demonstrate Pope's calculated ability to respond to a perceived injustice with a public, published, and potentially profitable literary response.

With a long-term view of his career, however, Pope recognized the value of investing in a position in literary history rather than "selling short" and settling for the more fleeting satisfaction of a pamphlet. Instead he used his rising literary stock to construct a transcendent position in the form of a socio-poetic persona that preserved his place as an august author seemingly separate from the unsavory fray of Grub Street. He sought to create and preserve his classical reputation from the disordering forces of the carnivalesque.

Although Pope professed an aversion to the milieu of the dunces, the *Dunciad* vividly illustrates his intimate knowledge of, if not fascination with, its subversive energy. As Stallybrass and White observe, "the mitigating fact of Pope's superior poetic ability [and I would add superior control over the production of his texts] could not save him from being immersed in the very process of grotesque debasement which he scorned in others" (117). The *Dunciad* draws on Pope's understanding of the situation of a commercial author and yokes the classical and the carnivalesque as an epic poem about the denizens of Grub Street. Pope uses the impulses of the arena of literary commerce to increase his poetic power – he controls the images within his own text while benefiting from their cultural resonance. He plans for the poem to demonstrate his mastery in a discursive struggle for literary authority.

Yet, his involvement with Grub Street exceeds verbal appropriation. During the period surrounding the publication of the *Dunciad*, Pope exploits the emerging vehicles of consumer culture to increase his own marketability. The poem's self-revealing hybridity suggests the contradictions inherent in Pope's career and marks the uneasy relationship between what Mark Rose, in another context, describes as "the traditional world of the author as a gentleman and scholar and the emergent world of the author as a professional."[59] The *Dunciad* plunged Pope into a protracted relationship with his alleged nemesis Edmund Curll. Pope's manipulation of Curll suggests that he benefited from the proliferation of pamphlets. Though Pope professed a lack of concern with financial rewards, claiming "I can be content with a bare saving game" (*Corr.* 1, p. 236), his exacting control of the production and sale of his works after 1727 indicates otherwise. He stood to gain a great deal from the succession of pamphlets that kept the *Dunciad* topical and justified his subsequent publications. They allowed him to cultivate the position of the besieged and morally superior author that enhanced his cultural currency. He could also represent himself as compelled to issue subsequent editions of the poem to correct or respond to the words of his literary enemies.[60] The extended exchange enabled Pope to refine his poem while gaining additional material for his work.

The paper war inaugurated by the *Dunciad* indicates that Pope's relationship with Curll, though born of animosity, was fundamentally symbiotic. Each man invigorated the other's career. As competing businessmen and rivals for control of Pope's poetic image, the men's professional relationship manifests the homosocial desire Eve Sedgwick identifies as central to the male power relations present in a patriarchal society. Sedgwick describes male homosocial relations, conducted through the exchange of an erotic object, a woman, as a way to maintain and transmit power. "The bond that links the two rivals is as intense and potent as the bond that links either of the rivals to his beloved . . . the bonds of 'rivalry' and 'love,' differently as they are experienced, are equally powerful and in many senses equivalent."[61] The rivalry between Pope and Curll analogously defined their commercial and textual relationship. While competing for cultural space, literary authority, and multiple forms of paper credit, their rivalry also focused quite specifically on mastery and control over Pope's poetic construction of self.

Just as superiority within a romantic triangle validated the masculinity and cultural potency of the victor, control over Pope's texts and socio-poetic persona was integral to his sense of authenticity within eighteenth-century society. The affinities with a homosocial relationship increase in light of Pope's erotic, compensatory use of his poetry, the connection he drew between literary authority and masculine sexuality, and his perceived inability to engage in a conventional sexual rivalry. Certainly Pope demonstrated an intense emotional commitment to the object of his rivalry with Curll – not a woman, but his discursive construction of self and the accompanying body of work.

However, in a sequence of pamphlets responding to the *Dunciad*, Curll constructs an equally potent persona for Pope in order to compete with the poet in the commercial and cultural space of Grub Street. Curll transcodes Pope and his work with the imagery of the carnivalesque and situates him within the print trade's market economy. His technique reveals Pope's reliance on paper credit, his affinities with the feminized world of hack writers, and his dependence on a potentially counterfeit persona. Curll's transgressive gesture highlights the desire for financial and symbolic currency that drove both men.

Using three basic strategies, Curll's publications destabilize Pope's position within an implicit literary hierarchy as they locate his texts as utterances within a larger cultural discourse. First Curll demonstrates the intertextuality between the work of Pope and his Grub Street con-temporaries, denying either dominance. Curll's pamphlets correctly intimate that the *Dunciad* could not exist without Pope's construction of Grub Street as its foil; understanding the poem requires a knowledge of that commercial literary environment.[62] Second, Curll expropriates and radically alters the context of Pope's texts, public and private. His youthful letters to Henry Cromwell, the allegedly scandalous sections of his poetry, and his responses to Grub Street attacks, coupled with Curll's commentary, contradict Pope's socio-poetic persona. Finally, Curll focuses on Pope's physical body, which the poet strove to obscure. He circulates verbal and visual images of Pope's body and makes it another contested construction within their exchange. Curll metaphorically (re)presents Pope's physical body in a manner that invokes Bakhtin's concept of "grotesque realism" with its emphasis on "degradation, that is the lowering of all that is high, spiritual, ideal, abstract": and thus "a transfer to the material level, to the sphere of earth and body."[63] It renders the body as incomplete, with orifices emphasized and "its lower regions given priority over its upper regions."[64] The carnivalesque figure starkly opposes the classical image of the complete finished man which Pope tried to construct poetically and failed to achieve personally. Though we now read these attacks on Pope's physical disabilities as cruel, Curll's preoccupation with the body indicates his recognition of Pope's compensatory strategy, which privileges the power of the cerebral and denies his own physical limitations. "Reconstructing" Pope in those terms, Curll casts him as the symbolic manifestation of these contradictory forces of high and low, classical and carnivalesque, the lofty mind and the base body. Pope becomes a hybrid, a physical embodiment that violates the same cultural categories he casts as central.

Curll's *Compleat Key to the Dunciad*, published on May 28, 1728, constructs the illusion of textual and critical interdependence between Curll and Pope, an intimacy that allows Curll to "co-author" the *Dunciad*. The epigram on the first page of the key connects the men and casts them as literary equals: "How easily Two Wits agree, / One finds the Poem; One the Key."[65] Though the "key" actually depends upon the *Dunciad*, Curll inverts the power relationship and makes readers of the *Dunciad* depend on the key to get the fullest meaning of the poem. Revealing the names Pope omitted and assuming the role of translator, Curll heightens the poem's satiric sting and pre-empts Pope's voice (and arguably prompts the subsequent apparatus Pope provides with the *Dunciad Variorum*). Curll continues this ploy in the *Curliad* when he expresses gratitude that "Mr. Pope has corrected two small faults in my key" (12); in return, Curll lists the faults he has detected in Pope's work. Pope's later textual references to Curll demonstrate how the bookseller has penetrated his text, causing him to react, rethink, or revise his words.

During the following year Curll exploits the marketability of Pope's name and the constructed intertextuality between the two men. Within his pamphlets, Curll strategically advertises other anti-Pope materials that had been "lately published," and he tries to lure readers into his shop, "where may be had, *The Progress of Dulness. The Popiad.* And *A Key to the Dunciad.*"[66] Curll also furnishes scholarly footnotes that refer the reader to the growing Curll library of Pope material: "See *Pope's* Familiar Letters to *Henry Cromwell*, Esq.; Page 28. Vol. 1"[67] or "See the Remarks on Mr. Pope's Temple of Fame subjoined to the Progress of Dulness."[68] Essentially, Curll offers what Terry Eagleton, discussing Samuel Richardson's addenda to *Clarissa*, terms a "kit" for reading. A "great unwieldy container," writes Eagleton, the kit is "crammed with spare parts and agreeable extras, for which the manufacturer never ceases to churn out new streamlined improvements, ingenious additions and revised instruction sheets ... One text ceaselessly spawns another."[69] Curll and Pope both act as manufacturers, "spawning" successive editions of their respective works. By making frequent reference to an extensive array of Pope-related publications, Curll invites the reader to construct his own collection. Taking Curll's invitation to heart, Pope himself assembled a Grub Street "kit" with perfect copies of the pamphlets bound in three volumes for his library at Twickenham.[70] Samuel Johnson recounts Jonathan Richardson's visit to Pope, when he discovered the poet reading the bound pamphlets. Looking up, he reportedly exclaimed: "these things are my diversion ... such things are sport to me."[71] The painter observed Pope's "features writhen in anguish" (188), revealing the conflict he experienced between reading the texts as pieces in a larger game – a sport or diversion – and seeing them as stains on his literary reputation.

As Curll exposes Pope's material connections with Grub Street, he also expropriates Pope's texts and "reconstructs" his body to highlight the carnivalesque aspects of the poet's life and work. Curll heavily exploits Pope's letters to Henry Cromwell. Written between approximately 1706 and 1712 in what James Winn terms Pope's "rake period," the letters recount Pope's various experiences with women and include the infamous Rondeau and the parody of the First Psalm. While these youthful letters didn't necessarily damage his literary reputation, they did deflate his moral reputation because they demolished his image as a morally superior man, which in many ways was the linchpin of Pope's socio-poetic persona. As Pope remarked to Aaron Hill in a moment of uncharacteristic (and perhaps feigned) humility, "I vow to God, I never thought any great matters of my poetical capacity ... But, I do know certainly, my moral Life is superior to that of most of the wits of these days" (*Corr.* III, p. 166).[72] In the Cromwell letters, however, Curll discovered "a vicious Scene" as "painted by the profligate and profane Pen of Alexander Pope of Twickenham, Esq." (vii).

In *The Female Dunciad*, published August 8, 1728, Curll supplements these letters with commentary by a "female critic" who describes them as "sufficient testimonies of Mr. Pope's Immorality, Profaness and Obscenity."[73] Her comments, which create another type of dialogue between Pope and the Grub Street critic, highlight the portions of the letters that express interests more appropriate to a hack than to the "morally superior" master of Twickenham. One of the more damning letters is that of December 21, 1711, in which Pope discusses his desire for the Blount sisters, "two such ladies, that in good faith 'tis all I'm able to do, to keep myself in my skin" (9). Affecting a libertine attitude, Pope wishfully comments:

Let me but have the Reputation of these [ladies] in my keeping, as for my own, let the Devil, or Dennis, take it for ever! How gladly wou'd I give all I am worth, that is to say, my Pastorals, for one of their Maiden heads, and my Essay, for the other? I wou'd lay out all my Poetry in Love, an Original for a Lady, and a translation for a Waiting Maid! (10)

The letter makes explicit Pope's use of poetry – "all I am worth" – as a supplement to (and substitute for) the masculine desirability that would give him sexual currency with women. Pope's poetic endeavors potentially compensate for his limited sexual prowess. Read in economic terms, the exchange posed in the letter – pastoral for maidenhead – reveals Pope's recognition that a shrewd investment of his high cultural status and his poetic material (his capital or paper credit) could potentially yield interest in the form of physical (i.e. sexual) satisfaction. Pope wants to use the business of poetry as a means to gain the pleasure of sexual intimacy (if only imaginatively realized). Though, by revealing his sexual fantasies, the letter obscures the moral superiority Pope declared for himself, it also reinforces the hierarchies important to him. Pope does not conflate the high and the low but rather attempts to play one against the other. He aims to exchange the products of the mind for the pleasures of the body, while preserving a central literary and social hierarchy (an original for a lady, but just a translation for a waiting maid). Though intentionally amusing, the letter reveals the discrepancy between Pope's verbal fantasies and physical realities, and his discomfort with the complicated situation he had created for himself with his use of poetry and language as a compensatory tool.

Seemingly aware of Pope's compensatory strategy, Curll heightens the incongruity of his sentiments by publishing the Cromwell letters with a novel by Eliza Haywood, *The History of Clarina*. Given the realities of eighteenth-century literary production, Haywood possibly did not write the text specifically for *The Female Dunciad*. Nonetheless, the juxtaposition of the two texts constructs the illusion of a dialogue between Haywood and Pope, an interaction underscored by the epistolary form of the novel. The fictional text effectively complements Curll's portrait of Pope and comments specifically on the role of the satirist in its opening paragraphs. Dedicating the novel to an unnamed male satirist, Haywood praises the "sweetness" of his "disposition, and that Tenderness with which [he] consider[s] the Errors of [his] Fellow Creatures" (17–18) in his "endeavour for a Reformation of Manners" (17). She remarks that should she find, "in the Course of your Papers, all the little Inadvertencies of my own Life recorded, I am sensible it will be done in such a Manner as I cannot but approve" (18). Though Haywood makes no specific references to Pope's scurrilous representation of her in the *Dunciad* (a text which certainly alludes to the "inadvertencies" in her life), the comment resonates with the potent images of the poem.

The novel depicts the "deformities of vice" in a way that might be read as metaphorically descriptive of Pope's relationship with literary women like Haywood. The lovely and wealthy Clarina, too closely influenced by her maid Aglaura, is entranced by a letter from Merovius (actually Aglaura's son) which describes his attempted suicide motivated by his unrequited love for her. With Aglaura's help, Merovius persuades Clarina to marry him secretly; after spending all her money he then abandons her, now pregnant. Alone, estranged from her family, and "destitute of all the Necessaries of Life" (38), Clarina subsequently lived "the Life of a kept Mistress" (40), her reputation ruined. Merovius's metamorphosis from devoted suitor to vindictive spouse parallels the alternative representation of Pope in *The Female Dunciad*, and the final metamorphosis described in a poem of the same name at the end of the text. "The New Metamorphosis. Being a Familiar Letter from a Gentleman in Town to a Lady ... Occasion'd by the Dunciad," asks why "a Poet renown'd for Politeness, and Fire, / Has stain'd all his Laurels in Puddles and Mire"; "What Merit so bright, can encourage a Poet / To attack all the World, with his Jingle and Low-Wit!" (43). Just as the *Dunciad* has ruined the reputation of various authors, male and female, so too, the poem suggests, has the text – and the metamorphosis it marks – ruined Pope's reputation: "Could not the great Wit, the prime Bard of the Nation, / Be content to enjoy such a vast Reputation." Rather than "admiring" his poems, readers are now "forc[ed] ... to dread them."

Like Clarina, Haywood has had her reputation destroyed by a faithless man, and her text highlights Pope's (new) reputation for viciously representing women.

The text replicates the multiple discourses that comprise literary culture. It also implies that Pope's letters would be of sufficient interest to the readers of the female novelist, a titillation Pope would certainly resist. The maneuver attempts to ally Pope with the feminizing forces he despises. *The Female Dunciad* juxtaposes Pope and Haywood, letters and commentary, Twickenham and Grub Street, to show how their intersection more accurately represents Pope's hybridity. Curll later assures his customers: "As to Mr. Pope's Letters, every impartial Reader" will find Pope's "Judgement both of Men and Books, is exactly conformable to present Sentiments of the Author of the *Dunciad*" (*Curliad*, 23).

In addition to the Cromwell letters, Curll captures by textual means any responses his work elicits from Pope – such as his denial of *A Popp upon Pope*. The pamphlet, often attributed to Lady Mary Wortley Montagu, appeared on June 1, 1728. It recounts the alleged beating of Pope "by two evil disposed persons out of spite and revenge for a harmless lampoon [the *Dunciad*] which the said poet had writ."[74] Though the piece begins with a pious admonishment against brutalizing Papists, it quickly concentrates on graphically describing Pope's beating. Hoisted over the back of one man, "poor master Pope" is beaten with a rod by another who "did, with great violence and an unmerciful Hand, strike Mr. Pope so hard upon his naked Posteriors, that he voided large Quantities of Blood, which being yellow . . . had a great Proportion of Gall mized with it, which occasioned the said color." The description diminishes Pope to the level of a schoolboy beaten for a minor infraction, "the harmless lampoon." As Kristina Straub reminds us, "the spectacle of the schoolboy's bent knees or his bared ass before the corrective birch constitutes a semiotic terrain upon which are continually being inscribed masculinities defined in power relation to each other" (69). While the identity of the two assailants remains unknown, Pope's masculinity, through Curll's discursive rendering of the event, is left not only subordinate but contested. Left "weltring in his own blood," with the lower half of his body naked, Pope is reduced to a base physical level. The physical displaces the cerebral, leaving Pope disordered, raving "for Pen, Ink and Paper," no doubt in an attempt to regain textual control over a physical situation. The humiliation is heightened when Miss Blount arrives to carry Pope home in her apron. The verbal image of Pope being whipped by two men upon his "naked posteriors" capitalizes on the sexual ambiguity implicit in Pope's marginalized body and his

Catholicism, and the description subtly underscores the homoerotic implications of the scenario.

The pamphlet did not go unnoticed by Pope, who took out an advertisement in the June 14 *Daily Post* to denounce the piece. "Perhaps," suggests Maynard Mack, "he feared that, however fictional in this instance, the idea might catch on; more likely he found its patronizing tone toward Martha as well as himself too humiliating to go unchallenged."[75] In his denial, Pope declares, "Whereas there has been a scandalous Paper cried about the Streets under the title of A Popp upon Pope, insinuating that I was whipped in Ham-walks on Thursday last. This is to give Notice that I did not stir out of my House at Twickenham all that day." Ironically, that brief notice only provided Curll with more material, for he reprinted it next to "A Popp upon Pope" in his longer pamphlet, *The Popiad*.[76] The propinquity of these pieces traps Pope within another Curll publication – literally binding him and his words to Grub Street and again creating the illusion of dialogue between the two men. Pope's brief statement might actually have interested readers in *A Popp upon Pope* and looks insignificant if not arrogant next to the far more titillating and explicit essay.

Pamphlets like *The Popiad* depict Pope – verbally and visually – with grotesque realism contrary to the classical images of the "finished, complete man" that he strove to construct poetically.[77] Indeed, the paper wars attempt to deny Pope any physical dignity or credibility. For example, the well-known frontispiece to *Pope Alexander's Supremacy* (1729) had a composite of Pope's head atop a monkey's body. In response to Pope's portrait of Appius in *An Essay on Criticism*, John Dennis had written of Pope: "As there is no Creature in Nature so venomous, there is nothing so stupid and so impotent as a hunch-backed toad." Curll's last anti-Pope pamphlet of 1728, *Codrus: or The Dunciad Dissected*, takes Dennis's comment to a hyperbolic extreme with Elizabeth Thomas's fable "Father Pope and his Son, or the Toad and the Ox." "Father Pope" rewrites Pope's biography as an animal story allusive of the broadsheet theme of the "World Upside Down."[78] The fable describes Pope as a toad "deformed in shape, of Pigmy stature: / A Proud, Conceited peevish Creature" (12), who achieves great poetic success. The text inextricably links the toad's grotesque physicality with its poetic ability, depicting the poetry as a type of bodily discharge, an overflow of bad humors. Pope's satires are "stinking venom" (18) and "nauseous slaver" (18), and, in the case of the *Dunciad*:

> Take away the filthy Part,
> Of *T–d*, and Spew, and Mud and Fart:
> (Words which no Gentleman could use,

And e'en a Nightman would refuse.)
There nought remain'd, save to the elf
A Disemboguement of himself.

The toad's animosity and competitiveness ultimately cause him to explode, revealing he has neither "Limb, nor Bone, nor flesh, nor Skin," and is nothing but a "splatch of squalid gore" (21). This consistent yoking of physical and poetic echoes Pope's representations in the *Dunciad*, where he depicts the texts of women writers as grotesque or abnormal physicality: Corinna's (Elizabeth Thomas's) public urination; Eliza Haywood's distended, udder-like breasts and her "two babes of love"; and Dulness's amorphous body and uncontrollable fecundity which spawns countless dunces and "dull" texts. While Thomas's representation is designed to satirize Pope, it actually highlights perhaps the most serious and complicated issue for him personally and professionally. Pope's poetry simultaneously springs from and denies his physical condition, what he calls in *Epistle to Arbuthnot*, "this long disease my life." He compensates for his physical limitations and social and religious marginality through the forceful use of language that allows him to touch, influence, or affect a range of people, particularly women. Yet that marginality and distance, in part, enables Pope's distinctive poetic voice. Curll seemingly recognizes Pope's strategy and attempts to deflate his persona not only through a symbolic inversion within a literary hierarchy, but also with his further feminization. The images of grotesque physicality underscore Pope's compromised sexuality, an ambivalence Curll exploits by making Pope's body the locus of attack. Emphasizing the connection between the body and the mind, Curll conflates the dichotomy seen as central to eighteenth-century rational masculinity and represents the poet's body as a (if not *the*) source of the poetic.

In the summer of 1735, Curll went one step further; he made "Pope's Head" his shop sign in Rose Street, Covent Garden, and used a line engraving of the same image as the frontispiece in his books. Curll describes his intention "to hang him in effigy for a sign to all spectators of his falsehood and my own veracity."[79] The gesture captures the essence of the men's relationship. Curll's appropriation of Pope's physical image materially manifests the symbolic medium of their exchange. They were competing for control over Pope's persona, literary commodities, and the economic rewards of both; they each sought control not just over Pope's "body" of work, but over the representation of the body itself. By using Pope's image to mark the site of commercial activity, Curll literally merges the tenuous oppositions that characterize this period: the literary and the commercial, the classic and the carnivalesque. Curll's shop sign, like the *Dunciad* itself, is a testimony to what Stallybrass and White term a "hybridization" of culture. A hybridization "produces new combinations and strange instabilities in a given semiotic system. It therefore generates the possibility of shifting the very terms of the system itself by erasing and interrogating the relationships which constitute it" (58). To have "Pope" in a sense advertise for Curll certainly shifts the terms of their relationship. Yet, the iconic use of Pope as the marker of the commerce of culture symbolically enacts the reciprocal activity that enables the literary production of both men.

Curll's attacks on Pope stemmed from his own experience of manipulating the power of language, print culture, and paper credit to elevate his financial if not social situation. Curll notes that he and Pope began in similar social positions, "Mr. Pope is the son of a trader, and so is Mr. Curll, – par nobile," and have reached similar heights in their respective fields: "Mr. Pope is no more a gentleman than Mr. Curll, nor more eminent as a Poet than he as Bookseller."[80] *The Curliad, A Hypercritic upon the Dunciad Variorum* (1729) presents the men's relationship as one of competition, reciprocity, and dialogue within a shared discursive space. The Steele epigram on the title page, "Soon will that Die which adds thy name to mine; / Let me then Live join'd to a Work of Thine," accurately articulates the symbiotic nature of the relationship.[81] Curll describes their verbal jostling as mutually beneficial, a sort of literary (and financial) *quid pro quo*: "Whatever mention Mr. Pope thinks fit to honour Me withal, in any of his Labours, I shall always take it in good part ... If I have done Him any service, he is, in our Shop-stile – heartily welcome" (19). The reference to his print shop's reply to a customer – "heartily welcome" – casts Pope as a consumer and their relationship as commerce. Curll claims that he has "generously" printed Pope's material, albeit pirated, for twelve years, and that he "shall continue his Fame" (21) by printing editions in years to come. Just as the *Dunciad*, arguably Pope's most powerful poem, gained much of its force from Pope's appropriation of Grub Street, Curll similarly prospered by connecting himself to Pope. He observes that "A fitter Couple, sure, were never hatch'd; / Some marri'd are, indeed, but we are match'd."[82]

The men's relationship continued after the 1728 *Dunciad* as they manipulated each other, prompting attacks, responses, and mutual notoriety. A well-known example of Pope's cunning occurred in 1735. Using an anonymous middleman, Pope tricked Curll into buying a "collection" of his letters that contained his correspondence with members of the House of Lords. Curll advertised the impending publication of the letters and was, of course, promptly arrested. Pope later used the self-generated publicity to sell his own authorized edition of the letters. Pope could be said to have "won" that round since the appearance of Curll's five-volume edition provided Pope with the needed excuse to publish an authorized version of his own correspondence.[83] Yet it remains equally potent that Pope needed the "unauthorized" version of his correspondence to justify his own self-congratulatory gesture of publication, another strategic move to enhance his poetic persona.

Curll's representation of the two men's relationship within his edition of the letters provides an important postscript to the "dunce wars" and the men's respective effects on print culture. In *Volume Four of Mr. Pope's Literary Correspondence*, "An Essay on the Character of Mr. Curll," allegedly written by "A. Pope," claims Curll "carried his Trade many Lengths beyond what it ever before had arrived at, and that he was the Envy and Admiration of all his Profession."[84] To this passage Curll notes: "if he has carried the Art of Bookselling beyond all his Contemporaries, has not Mr. Pope done the same by the Art of Poetry" (149). The statement characterizes the men as successful innovators who redefined their professions. In doing so, it elides the distinction between the art of bookselling (commerce) and the art of poetry (literature). As James Ralph's previously mentioned comment suggests, booksellers, poets, publishers, and writers are, like stock-jobbers, all tradesmen in an expanding commercial space.

Curll's publication of Pope's letters and the accompanying commentary support the traditional image of Curll as the opportunistic bookseller whose marketing skills and unscrupulousness made him a parasite who profited from his consumption and reproduction of "real" literature. That the "unspeakable Curll," as biographer Ralph Straus calls him, manipulated or bribed the aristocracy and the clergy to lend their names and thus credibility to his publications is beyond question. He also exploited hack writers by publishing their works to his financial gain while limiting their profits. He antagonized "gentlemen-authors" by pirating editions of their texts, composing keys to their popular works, or printing scandalous pamphlets attacking them personally or professionally. But this behavior, motivated primarily by a desire for fame and economic gain, allowed Curll to compete in and, in a sense, reshape the literary marketplace.

In many ways Curll's actions replicated those of Pope, a man similarly interested in fame, status, and financial profit. Pope and Curll, each in his own way and for his own reasons, attempt to cast Grub Street and the more sweeping emergence of the print trade as a cultural site marked by oppositions, antagonism, and mutually exclusive categories. The more interesting and potent areas of that milieu exist in the margins, the seepage, the transgressions that ultimately define and empower the literary production of both men. Though Curll attempts to subvert the persona Pope has so carefully constructed, he complicates rather than diminishes it. He places it more fully and accurately within the context and interactions of the commerce of culture (a gesture comparable to that of modern literary scholars). While Pope's literary texts remain dominant, his socio-poetic persona and the modern subject lurking within grows ever more complex and unattainable. Just as the tendency to read cultural relations with a hack/anti-hack mentality has dominated eighteenth-century literary history, a similarly binary reading of Pope as a subject emerges. A strain of scholarship sympathetic to Pope exists, as exemplified by someone like Maynard Mack: scholars who read Pope much in the way he presents himself in *Epistle to Arbuthnot* – as a besieged, morally superior poet writing for altruistic and often generous purposes. Others, like Pope's contemporary John Dennis or any number of modern scholars, read him as embittered, spiteful, and malicious – a poet whose work is fueled by personal vendetta as much as a desire to produce "objective" social commentary. Obviously neither "Pope" can accommodate the actual historical practice, motivation, and "intention" behind the poet (to which we will never have access). Did Pope resist those cultural forces he saw as threatening to his vision of literary and economic culture? Yes, as evidenced by his construction of those as corrupt, devalued, and feminized actions. Was he complicit in those cultural innovations, profiting from the apparatus of literary production and, in various ways, from the structures of the new financial order? Of course. And his marked and sustained involvement in the literary and financial sphere arguably fueled the compensatory antagonism with which he represented the dunces in both.

Pope, despite his association with the social and literary elite, suffered from his own marginality. His religion, his political beliefs, his physical condition, and of course his pen forced him into an uneasy situation where he, in a sense, had continually to earn his position, a position that could be terminated at any time (as demonstrated by his relationship with Lady Mary Wortley Montagu). Similarly, his relationship with colleagues like Swift was marked by a broader marginality, for they battled the political and economic forces above them while resisting the competing energy of Grub Street below. Pope straddled the world of the elite and the popular, claiming the former as the rightful domain of the Virgilian model of his career, yet simultaneously exploiting the energy and opportunity of the latter.

Ultimately we need to reconfigure the hierarchies and cultural relations that define literary production at this time. The questions an examination of Pope raises anticipate the interpretation of Eliza Haywood's position within the commercial culture of professional authorship. Symbolically aligned with a literary entrepreneur like Curll, Haywood and her texts are often read as popular rather than culturally or generically significant. But I would suggest her literary ambition, though not fully realized, was no less palpable than Pope's, her authorial persona no less complicated a construction, and her presence in the literary marketplace no less essential to understanding fully the dynamics of eighteenth-century culture.

CHAPTER THREE

Eliza Haywood and the culture
of professional authorship

In the *Dunciad*, Pope figures Eliza Haywood as the nexus of his anxieties concerning the feminization of culture, the increasing prominence of immaterial signifying systems, and the emergence of symbolic economies. She manifests what Pope perceives as a threat to the existing social and literary order. Like his depiction of the dunces, Pope's representation of Haywood has largely determined her place in literary history until her recent emergence as the subject of feminist reconsiderations of the novel. Pope's "Haywood" retained a certain currency in scholarly discourse due in part to an inability to locate her fiction within the master narrative of the "rise of the novel," to correct perpetuated biographical inaccuracies, and to ensure the availability of her texts in modern editions. These factors, among others, contributed to the critical perception of her as "just" another Grub Street author.

Though she functions metonymically for Pope and subsequent scholars as the referent for "woman's bad writing" (in great abundance), the power of the image bespeaks Haywood's obvious presence in the marketplace and her significance within eighteenth-century literary production. Although Pope renders her silent and passive, his portrait (unwittingly) validates her position and her work's powerful appeal. As Barbara Babcock reminds us, what is socially peripheral is often symbolically central, as Pope's treatment of Haywood demonstrates.[1] By recontextualizing her image and appropriating her name, Pope capitalizes on the recognized currency she has established and exploits her authorial persona for his own gain. Attempting to present her as the literary void against which other more respectable (and typically male) writers are measured, Pope actually reveals her centrality within the cultural landscape, her associations with a vital and commercially recognized literary product, and her considerable amount of "paper credit."[2]

By Haywood's paper credit, I refer to her credibility as a certain kind of author owing to the considerable popularity and consistent sale of her books. She depended on her ability to produce, manipulate, and circulate symbolic instruments – literary commodities that demonstrate her credit on paper. She relied on an imaginative narrative, a fundamentally intangible product, to establish and maintain her authorial position and cultural currency. Enabled by the mechanisms of print capitalism, Haywood tirelessly produced innovative and popular texts for a growing reading public and, in the process, destabilized the constructed hierarchies that previously would have limited her success. She had to acquire paper credit in multiple economies simultaneously. As a professional writer in a competitive market, she had to produce salable commodities at a consistently rapid pace to sustain her relationship with booksellers. As an author of fictional texts for women, she had to engage and increase her community of readers with her narratives depicting women circulating within patriarchal society. And as a woman writing she always, at some level, had to negotiate the cultural resistance to her discourse and the public appropriation of her life and works within a gendered literary economy.

This chapter explores how Haywood accumulated the "paper credit" that allowed her to circulate within and ultimately transform the symbolic and material economies of print culture in early eighteenth-century London. The chapter first discusses how she operated within the commercial literary marketplace and gained the ability to sell her texts on the basis of the reading experience with which she came to be associated. Examining the characteristic components of her fiction provides insight into her popularity and, more important, helps explain why her books were consistently treated as transgressive. Her commercial involvement, innovative texts, and departure from the existing literary hierarchy symbolically aligned Haywood with the feminized economic man, an alliance underscored by her representation of the ideology of the sexual economy. As the next two sections illustrate, Haywood discursively and imaginatively engaged the issues she encountered materially. Two novels from the middle of that decade, *The City Jilt* (1726) and *The Mercenary Lover* (1726), demonstrate how Haywood represents her fictional female subjects' attempts to deal with the economic forces that characterize her own existence. She constructs new models for women to follow in the dual (and often simultaneous) economies of finance and romance. Her texts depict negotiations of sexual and financial capital, offer alternative constructions of female sexuality, and redefine the boundaries of women's experiences in both the symbolic and the material world. Consequently, Haywood becomes an important figure with which to explore the activities of a

woman writer within the nascent literary marketplace and to assess how
the economies of professional authorship and speculative finance reflect
and inform the representation of women in her fiction.

I

During the period of Eliza Haywood's greatest productivity (1719–28), the
literary marketplace and the profession of authorship expanded tremendously with the increasing participation of a range of writers, including
women. The nearly exponential rise in the number of books published
and sold in the first three decades of the eighteenth century signaled the
emergence of a new consumer culture defined, in part, by the commercialization of literature. As Paul Langford observes, "the sheer volume of
printed matter produced in the period is striking testimony to the extent of
the reading market."[3] Haywood benefited from this expansion. Though
she claimed to lament that "the poets, at least the would-be ones, debase by
a thousand servile practices, the Noblest Art into a Trade,"[4] she demonstrated an ability to operate effectively in a competitive environment
where production and profit were the primary motivations; as she
acknowledged in the preface to *The Injured Husband*, "The press is set to
work only to gratify a mercenary end."[5]

Haywood wrote copiously and variously, and established her presence
within the cultural discourse. Motivated by what one critic terms "the
unremitting need to produce," Haywood's production of texts was
unmatched between 1719 and 1728.[6] She was "unassailably dominant in
quantitative terms" and her prolificacy no doubt contributed to Pope's
characterization of Dulness as mindlessly reproducing.[7] Simply put,
during the period of the 1720s she published far more texts than any other
woman author. In his 1749 *A General History of the Stage*, William Rufus
Chetwood observed that "[a]s the Pen is her chief Means of Subsistence,
the World may find many Books of her Writing, tho' none have met with
more Success than her Novels more particularly her *Love in Excess*" (the
book he, of course, published).[8] Similarly, David Erskine Baker in *Biographia
Dramatica* (1764) described her as "perhaps the most voluminous female
writer this kingdom ever produced."[9] Her first novel, *Love in Excess*, went
through six editions in London and one edition in Dublin.[10] She produced
at least twenty titles between 1719 and the 1724/25 four-volume collection
entitled *Secret Histories, Novels and Poems* which would appear in two subsequent editions in 1732 and 1742. Between 1725 and 1730 she published
thirty-three more works. Though the marketplace was growing steadily,

there were still commercial risks involved in publishing women's fiction, regarded as a more speculative and competitive venture. Haywood attracted an audience consistent enough to publish (and presumably sell) her work at the rate of roughly one novel every three months.

Of course Haywood's popularity did not translate into extensive financial remuneration. "Authors," writes James Raven, "were the very last participants to benefit from the eighteenth-century book bonanza."[11] Haywood, like most writers of the time, did not hold her own copyrights and received only the initial payment for the text; as Terry Belanger observes, "it is likely that very few writers before the end of the eighteenth century could earn a good living exclusively from the writing of such works."[12] Nevertheless, her publication patterns demonstrate how even those on the margins of literary respectability and material control still possess a measure of cultural authority.

From the beginning of her career, Haywood positioned herself to improve her opportunities for success, as indicated by a letter she wrote to a potential patron shortly after the publication of *Love in Excess*. Describing a new translation for which she sought financial support, Haywood reveals her understanding of print culture and her subtle efforts to establish herself as a producer of consistently viable commodities.[13] "The Stage not answering my Expectations," Haywood writes, "has made me turn my Genius another Way":

I have Printed some Little things which have mett a Better Reception than they Deserved, or I Expected: and have now Ventur'd on a Translation to be done by Subscription, the Proposalls whereof I take the Liberty to send You: I have been so much us'd to Receive favours from You that I can make No Doubt of yr forgiveness for this freedom, great as it is, and that You will also become one of those Persons, whose Names are a Countenance to my undertaking.[14]

Exploiting the pose of modesty (claiming the three volumes of the best-selling novel "mett a Better Reception than they Deserved"), Haywood hopes professional literary authorship might satisfy her "expectations" left unanswered by the stage. She also tries to capitalize on her newly won fame by selling a translation by subscription. She may have thought the momentum from her first novel's great success would enable her to establish new connections with patron-subscribers who could contribute a certain status to her literary endeavors, or display what she termed a "Countenance to the undertaking."

Published by Chetwood, Haywood's translation of *Letters from a Lady of Quality to a Chevalier* (1721) was her only text sold by subscription during the nearly forty years of her career.[15] The list of subscribers includes Lady

Howard (to whom she would later dedicate *The Injured Husband*), Aaron Hill, and the Dowager Lady Herbert.[16] The relatively expensive edition was certainly of a higher quality than most of Haywood's subsequent publications. This proposal sought three shillings ("each book in quires, or 5 shillings bound in calf gilt back"), while typically her texts appeared as inexpensive duodecimo volumes. Like Pope, she wanted to benefit from the financial opportunities available in an increasingly commercialized literary marketplace. (Indeed she later claimed that her "ambition" was to be "as universally read as possible.")[17] Unlike Pope, Haywood did not amass a large sum of money. Nor, despite the relative popularity of the subscription (309 subscribers), did she embark on this type of venture again. Books sold by subscription were often prestige productions, translations, "lofty" genres such as history, and collections of periodical essays or works by a single author. The nature of that enterprise was not consistent with Haywood's abilities or interests. I would suggest her lack of involvement also stemmed in part from the way she positioned herself as a writer within the trade.

Haywood thrived in the open market and her rapid rate of composition suited the immediacy and topicality of her texts. She occupied a precarious professional position that relied on her ability to accommodate public taste, to create and respond to the desires of consumers, and to compete actively within print culture. She was closely associated with a recognizable commodity because of her distinct authorial persona and the cultural assumptions about women writers. Quickly, Haywood's name alone served to characterize a type of fictional discourse (in terms of status, genre, and narrative experience) and it possessed a clearly defined value. The volume of her production, the nature of her fiction, and her careful self-promotion enhanced her increasingly valuable reputation.

Haywood's ability to manipulate the marketplace may have stemmed, in part, from her theatrical experience and her associations with other professional authors. Her tenure with the Theatre Royal Company at the Smock Alley Theatre from 1714 to 1717 exposed her to the vicissitudes of an audience and perhaps to the limitations of her own talent. When Haywood returned to England, she used the connections she had made while in Ireland and received help from William Rufus Chetwood (assistant to Smock Alley manager John Ashbury), who published *Love in Excess*.[18] Chetwood, who became prompter at Drury Lane, dedicated *Love in Excess* to actress Anne Oldfield, using his own associations to forge a new venture and subtly place Haywood in a pre-established literary and theatrical network including the literary circle surrounding Aaron Hill.[19]

This entrée, coupled with the prodigious number of books she wrote, made Haywood desirable to numerous publishers.

The events in her personal life also resulted in a certain notoriety that contributed to her commercial success. After the publication of *Love in Excess* (1719), which marked Haywood as a writer of titillating stories of passion, she no longer lived with her still unidentified husband, under circumstances that remain unclear.[20] She later refers to herself as a "widow," and in a letter from 1728 comments on the untimely death of her spouse. This ambiguous status, coupled with her relationships with Richard Savage and William Hatchett, resisted categorization. She resided in a perpetually liminal position that provided the opportunity for critics to exploit the stereotypical connection between sexual promiscuity and a woman's alleged verbal immodesty in the form of published fiction.[21] As Paula McDowell notes, "venturing into printing has always meant granting one's public the right to make one's private life a public commodity," a situation particularly treacherous for British women writers.[22] A popular perception of Haywood as a libidinous, scandalous, immodest woman actively circulated. While she couldn't control what hostile critics wrote about her, Haywood subtly manipulated those negative associations to her own advantage in the marketing of her texts. She attempted to subvert the efforts of her critics by complementing her paper credit with a constructed personal history that functioned as another textual commodity. This pose provided her fiction with more authority (or perhaps authenticity), and increased its sensational qualities. A contradiction marks Haywood's ascent in the world of print culture. Her calculated authorial persona depends on the culturally inscribed assumptions about sexuality, textuality, and femininity exploited by her detractors. Yet the popularity of her texts, the independence with which she apparently lived, and the model of female subjectivity her fiction provides all challenge the then-prevalent cultural construction of woman.

Haywood capitalized on her undefinable position. Cultivating the voice of experience, she subtly used her sexuality to frame her texts and increase their appeal. For example, in the preface to *A Spy on the Conjurer; or . . . Memoirs of the Famous Mr. Duncan Campbell* (1725), Haywood dedicates the book to "My Lord —," and provocatively recounts the time they conceived of the book. She offers the text "according to the Promise I made you that agreeable Evening we passed together last summer at Bellsize." Haywood also hopes her story will "entertain [his] Fancy, at times when Business leaves a vacancy" just as she herself "entertained" him the previous summer.[23] Through her text, she will provide a pleasurable alternative to business. The topics Haywood lists in the table of contents continue this slyly sexual tone. She includes letters to Duncan Campbell from "a Lady, willing to be persuaded, the best action she could do, was to cuckold her Husband," "From a Servant-Maid under Temptations from her Master," and "From a Lady complaining of Mr. Campbell's discovering the Intrigues of wives to their Husbands." The descriptions of each of these letters could (and often did) also act as a summary of the plot of a Haywood story. Such a table of contents naturalizes the situations Haywood offers fictionally and suggests that such extreme experiences happen to women in the discursive and material world.

When she describes the difficulty a woman writer confronts, Haywood employs the language of gendered discourse, as though her relationship with the reading public were controlled by the same forces that inform male–female relationships. "It would be impossible to recount the numerous Difficulties a Woman has to struggle through in her Approach to Fame," she writes in the preface to *The Memoirs of the Baron de Bosse* (1725).

If her Writings are considerable enough to make any Figure in the World, Envy pursues her with unweary'd Diligence; and if, on the contrary, she only writes what is forgot, as soon as read, Contempt is all the Reward, her wish to please, excites; and the cold Breath of Scorn chills the little Genius she has, and which, perhaps, cherished by Encouragement, might, in Time, grow to a Praise-worthy Height.[24]

A woman writer and her text must negotiate the same obstacles and disadvantages in a literary marketplace as a woman confronts in a social or sexual "marketplace" where women compete for male approval. Were she "cherished" by encouragement or some other support, she might perhaps succeed; yet her "wish to please" may "excite" envy, contempt, or scorn. Laura Runge observes, "the gendered packaging of the early fictions employed the language of heterosexual romance, thus reproducing and naturalizing a paradigm of female subordination and male control."[25]

Haywood was under the (primarily) male control of booksellers who recognized her ability to "please" her audience and emphasized the cumulative weight of her literary production. The title pages to her novels or advertisements for her texts incorporated references to the growing collection of Haywood novels: "Written by the Author of *The Mercenary Lover*, and *The Memoirs of the Said Island*," or "By the Author of *The Masqueraders, or Fatal Curiosity*." Haywood's publishers understood the value of her name, placing it on the title page, and her genre, "novel," another word prominently displayed, often in the largest typeface. The end sheet facing the title page of *The Rash Resolve* (1724) lists seven

Haywood texts also available, lest the reader had missed one. All of these texts (accurately or not) claim to be at least a second edition, increasing the volume and thus appeal of Haywood's work. These titles become a kind of literary spreadsheet, a marker of previous performance. This technique not only targeted Haywood's established audience, by alerting the reader to the nature of the commodified reading experience, it also advertised other books for sale.

Her narratives benefited from what Catherine Gallagher calls "the powerful novelty of fictionality" that intrigued eighteenth-century readers.[26] She entered the marketplace at a time when there was a desire for a variety of texts and a sustained interest in narratives, particularly those for and by women. The London world of readers sought the pleasure, the stimulation, and the fanciful possibilities offered by fiction. The imaginative re-creation of self, the conventions of reader identification, and the habit of reading all worked together to create a climate conducive to the popularity of Haywood and writers like her. J. Paul Hunter suggests that the new readers in the market were those "most likely to wish to change their circumstances, to be dissatisfied with their lots, to have ambition above the station they were born into."[27] They possessed an "increased taste for commerce within a larger world (whether of trade or ideas)" (77). They sought a mechanism (literary or financial) that enabled them to envisage their life (and their future) differently. They were a reading public quite simply with desires.

Haywood satisfied some facet of those desires by writing fiction that emotionally engaged readers in a discourse with relevance to their lives. Her texts interrogate existing cultural norms, encourage alternative (and potentially empowering) models of behavior for women, and validate desire as a motivating force (while simultaneously condoning appropriate ways of channeling that energy). Writing with the familiarity of a woman talking to a younger companion, Haywood creates a narrative intimacy that elicits a commitment, an emotional and economic investment, from her readers. In exchange, she provides information about specific social, sexual, and economic dilemmas of women in a manner she hopes will be instructive: "If the examples I have sate down to write, may correct that Error in but one among the Number who shall read it, I shall think my time well employed."[28] This strategic pose ostensibly adheres to the conventional didacticism that will increasingly characterize the novel. Haywood frames her texts with apparent conformity while simultaneously challenging the underlying precepts of such conventionality. More pointedly, she emphasizes the relevance of her work, which she intentionally distinguishes from the romance. Haywood withholds the idealistic if not utopian resolution such texts provide.[29] She revises or extends the notion of a "happy" resolution to include a woman's ability to exact a specifically economic revenge, to establish a relationship with another woman that could be called a romantic friendship, or to retire from society altogether.

Haywood also emphasizes the more general applicability of her fictional situations and the need to represent accurately the emotional and physical experiences of her characters. She claims to present not only "the Gallant, the Tender and the Comick" but "above all ... the Facts [that] shall either be directly true, or have so great a resemblance to Truth, as not to be distinguished from it."[30] She attempts to draw characters "as they really are ... no poetical Descriptions, no Flight of Imagination ... if I have not made them speak just as they did, I have at least made them speak as Persons in their Circumstances would naturally do."[31] Her texts often deal with what she termed "those of a middle state" : "Nature confines not her Blessings to the Great alone, and where a fine Genius has the Improvements of a liberal Education, it will undoubtedly be the same in one Rank as in another."[32] Consequently her female subjects are frequently the daughters of bankers, merchants, or aldermen: individuals of the middling classes consistently located in the socio-economic and often geographical milieu of the City of London. Haywood assimilates and reinscribes the needs of her reading community, and provides the detailed topicality her audience demands. She locates herself centrally in the social network and speaks as a seeming equal to a wider social group; she develops the "ordinary, neutral middling speaker position" that Stallybrass and White describe as emerging at this time.[33] This calculated subject position also allows Haywood to advise her readers on specific relevant issues.

Haywood's narrative voice highlights her connection with her audience and facilitates her ability to instruct. Writing largely without the luxury of revision, Haywood capitalizes on the enforced immediacy of her own literary production and stylistically cultivates that directness. She defines her work in relation to the opportunities and obstacles she faces because of her gender: "As I am a woman, and consequently depriv'd of those Advantages of Education which the other sex enjoy, I cannot so far flatter my Desires, as to imagine it in my Power to soar to any subject higher than that which Nature is not negligent to teach us."[34] Haywood positions herself and her work against a primarily male literary tradition. For example, in the preface to *The Fair Captive* (1721), she claims that her play lacks the "embellishments of poetry, which the little improvements my Sex receives from education, allowed me not the Power to adorn it with."[35] While partially an effort to avoid the harsh commentary of critics, Haywood's observation emphasizes the gendered difference always present in her professional pursuits. Haywood says she has "nothing to value myself on, but a tolerable share of Discernment," which limits her subject matter to the world she observes around her: women's experiences in social, sexual, or affective relationships.

Through the romantic yearnings of her female characters she explores the effects of love and sexual desire. In Haywood's fictional universe, love is an overwhelming emotion that threatens to become "the whole business of our lives . . . Love is what we can neither resist, expel nor even alleviate, if we should ever so vigourously attempt it."[36] While mutual love between two people "which Fancy inclines and Reason guides" will result in "a Partner for Life," passion or false love demonstrate "how little Reason has to do in the Affairs" of the heart.[37] Sexual desire "hurries people on to an immediate gratification . . . tho' never so prejudicial to themselves or the person they pretend to love."[38] Haywood's description of women's desires enables her to extend and revise the boundaries of represented female sexuality, traditionally theorized within masculine parameters. Active, desiring, and desirable female subjects, Haywood's characters resist their culturally constructed gender roles. In *The City Widow* (1729), the libidinous Bacchalia attempts to seduce Sylander aggressively: "She hung about his neck, press'd his lips with such a fervency, as if her very soul issued with her breath, then kiss'd his eyes, and suck'd his cheeks, which blush'd at her extravagant fondness."[39] Haywood's characters are concerned with the visceral and the fleshly. Love, hatred, and desire are not abstract philosophical constructs but physically felt sensations.

While some of her texts reinscribe familiar cultural narratives and affirm certain types of gendered relationships, she more profoundly interrogates the existing sexual economy and reconceives of sexuality in terms that position her subjects not simply as women within a larger male system of heterosexual exchange and homosocial relationships.[40] Instead she provides alternative sexual and economic practices for women that typically envisaged potentially empowering behavior. This changed behavior not only reconfigures socio-sexual relations but possibly economic ones as well, as women challenge male control of financial resources. Haywood represents her fictional subjects dealing with the economic forces that characterize her own market existence. But she does more than demonstrate that romantic heterosexual relationships are fundamentally ones of obligation, debt, and credit. She places her characters in financial situations specifically defined by speculative investment. As discussed in chapter 1, popular representations depict women investing speculatively in stocks and inappropriately diverting their sexual energy. Haywood creates female subjects who derive pleasure and satisfy their desires from such financial activities. They learn the pleasure of business. At the same time, Haywood as an author makes a business out of providing pleasure to her readers. As Ros Ballaster notes, "Haywood herself makes a profit" (194) from the adventures of her female characters.

Haywood's commercial success, the transgressive nature of her discursive practice (as understood within dominant culture) and gender symbolically link her – and by extension her reading public – to the feminized economic man discussed in the previous chapters. The figure of the overly emotional, imaginatively stimulated, and inherently unstable stock-jobber or man of (paper) credit was a repository of cultural anxieties concerning the new commercial, financial, and literary milieu. The perception existed that the increasingly intangible constructions of property, the unleashing of the passions, and the encroaching power of consumer society all threatened to erode the social, literary, and gendered hierarchies seen as central to the stability of eighteenth-century society. As Pope suggests with his representation of Haywood in the *Dunciad*, the perceived expansion of moneyed men's cultural power, like the success of the commercial or woman writer, depended on the privileging of characteristics culturally constructed as feminine: emotion, desire, fancy, imagination. The economic man and the commercial writer were symbolically linked by their dependence on the imaginative forces that enabled their profession as well as the economic laws of supply and demand. Most broadly speaking, a professional writer (male or female) and a stock-jobber depended on the inherently unreliable forces of the consumer mentality that defined their existence – opinion, the whim of the marketplace, passions, and appetites. They sought to arouse in their reader or investor a desire, an emotional commitment, that would prompt (an occasionally impulsive) action. An author and a stock-jobber both need to persuade a potential client (reader or investor) to participate in an imaginatively constructed narrative. The stock-jobber described a financial future marked by rising prices, financial gains, and, consequently, the opportunity to improve one's socio-economic position. He offered the possibility of a better existence which in turn could satisfy the investor's emotional, financial, and acquisitive desires. He also hoped the individual would continue to invest.

Similarly, a writer of fiction advertised a future reading experience with a fictional text designed to provide an escape (however abbreviated) from the reader's present situation, to offer models for future behavior (or fodder for subsequent fantasies), and to introduce the imaginative possibilities of conceiving of one's life differently. While the author could only offer the intangible reward of satisfaction, s/he could motivate the reader to act – to purchase another text. The affinity between a female writer like Haywood and the stock-jobber was highlighted by the culture's gendered representation of both the financial and literary activities. Just as the new economic man defied the implicit hierarchies that inform social interaction, so too a writer like Haywood ignored literary tradition in her pursuit of popularity and a living wage. The convergence of Haywood's popularity and the increasing fascination with speculative investment (as demonstrated by the frenzy surrounding the South Sea Bubble) revealed a cultural desire for participation in narratives that reflect on the present and the future: the same desire that fueled the broadly based impulse for commercial and consumer goods.

Haywood's texts metaphorically and structurally replicate the process of deferral, continuation, and imaginative participation that characterizes speculative investment. In her fiction, as Michael McKeon accurately describes, "love is sheer inconstancy, like commodity exchange an endless circuit in which the movement toward completion and consumption, a perpetual imagining of an end which must never come, becomes an end in itself."[41] The "love" relationship within Haywood's fiction, the perpetual imagining of an end which must never come, mirrors the implicit understanding on which speculative investment depends: the continued deferral of complete repayment until a date which will, of course, never arrive.

Haywood also required an emotional investment from her readers on both the symbolic and material level. Her authorial expectations duplicate in microcosm the structural paradigm that defined her market existence. At multiple points she withdraws from the narrative and forces her reader to supply the details, the ideas, or the consequences of the situation at hand. Usually these gaps occur at moments of emotional intensity that surpass "the ability of her pen": "It wou'd be as needless as impossible to set forth, as it deserves, the distracted State in which this Night was past, both by Clitander and Althea, to be told what has happen'd between them, will better enable the Reader's Imagination to conceive their present Wretchedness than any Thing I am able to say."[42] Such coercive participation in the text, while perhaps a symptom of Haywood's limitations as an author, forces readers to invest in the story and to expend emotional and imaginative currency. It serves further to arouse and summon the readers' powers of their own fantasies. Though this technique is not unique to Haywood, it is symptomatic of the changing expectations for narratives specific to this cultural moment. Haywood relies on investment, credulity, a willingness to commit, and, of course, desire. The alternative models of female behavior Haywood offers reside in a world of increasingly feminine and specifically economic power, often acquired through the use of intangible rather than substantive things. Like women empowered, however briefly, by their forays into speculative investment, women reading (and writing) fiction were afforded the opportunity to transcend or surpass the pleasures potentially provided by men and gain knowledge not typically available to them elsewhere.

2

Two of Haywood's texts from 1726, *The City Jilt* and *The Mercenary Lover*, illustrate her ability to address simultaneously the construction of sexuality within male–female relationships and the financial and symbolic economies that shape and inform women's lives. One reason for Haywood's success was her ability to engage a relevant discourse about gender and sexuality; she also provides strategies for women to produce and manipulate their own paper credit. Her model for personal and financial action was particularly powerful in a post-South Sea Bubble culture marked by opportunities and disappointments. *The City Jilt: or, The Alderman Turn'd Beau; a Secret History* (1726), representative of Haywood's fiction from this period, explores the relationship between the sexual and the financial economies and illustrates the types of currency available within those systems of investment and exchange.[43] In presenting the tale of the abandoned Glicera, Haywood offers various ways that women can use the multiple kinds of "capital" available to them. Specifically, she demonstrates how a woman can combine the opportunities provided by speculative investment with the exchange value of her own sexuality to increase her power and improve her situation. In representing strategies for women to profit from men, she also alerts women to the dangers of men primarily interested in financial gain.

Avarice is the primary passion the text explores, as Cowley's title page quotation suggests:

> Virtue now, nor noble Blood,
> Nor Wit by Love is understood;
> Gold alone does Passion move:
> Gold monopolizes Love.

That preoccupation corresponds with the novel's specific location within the City of London – the financial world of merchants, money men, and stock-jobbers. Glicera, "one of the most lovely and accomplished Women of the Age" (67), is the daughter of an eminent tradesman "reputed one of the richest Citizens of his Time" (69). His wealth attracts numerous admirers for Glicera, one of whom, Melladore, wins her heart. Significantly, Haywood withholds a description of their romantic courtship, suggesting its illusory (and largely irrelevant) nature. "Nothing happening between them but what is common to Persons in the Circumstances they were," writes Haywood, "I shall pass over in silence the Days of their Courtship" (67). She deflates the idealism and optimism courtship demands. She doesn't want to distract her reader from the larger project of inscribing the cultural codes of male–female relationships with new possibilities.

On the eve of the wedding Glicera's father dies and his penury is revealed: "[he] left behind him little more than would serve to defray the Expences of his Funeral, and pay the Debts he had contracted" (69). Never doubting the sincerity of Melladore, Glicera details her financial situation to him.[44] In language typical of the sex–money axis, he insists that "her adorable Person was of itself a Treasure infinitely beyond his Merit" (70).[45] However, in actuality, "the real Love he had was to the Wealth of which he expected she would be possess'd; but that being lost, his Passion also vanish'd, and left behind it only that part of Desire which tends to Enjoyment; – the nobler Inclinations all were fled, and brutal Appetite alone remained" (70). He retains only a desire doubly directed toward sex and money. He succeeds in seducing Glicera, whom he abandons once she becomes pregnant. Instead of honoring his obligation to Glicera, Melladore marries Helena, allegedly worth 5,000 crowns, "Charms which in his avaritious Eyes far exceeded those *Glicera* was possessed of" (78). His changed emotions and his refusal to marry Glicera illustrate the motivation of the seducer and resemble the psychology of the investor in stocks (or even more broadly the consumer mentality). Both are sustained by hope and the arousal and then perpetual (and indefinite) deferral of desire. Once sated, desire no longer exists. "The very word *Desire* implies an Impossibility of continuing after the Enjoyment of that which first caused its being," claims Melladore. "Those Longings, those Impatiences so pleasing to your Sex, cannot but be lost in Possession, for who can wish for what he has already? "(76). Indeed, commercial and finance capitalism are driven by the perpetual substitution of one desire for another, the imagining of "an end which must never occur" to which McKeon refers.

Melladore's treatment of Glicera profoundly changes her approach to the world and the sphere in which she operates. She laments: "Ah! what a dreadful Revolution has thy Ingratitude caused within my Breast" (75), a change that alters her mental attitude and increases her awareness of the profitable ways she can exact revenge. For Glicera, the revolution is political in the fundamental sense of the word. She intends to shift the power relations between the sexes as she uses the coded behavior of her gender to exact specific financial rewards and subvert cultural conventions for her own gain. Such empowerment becomes increasingly "revolutionary" in light of Glicera's specifically financial means of revenge. She achieves a new calm and acquires an "implacable . . . hatred in her Nature, not only to *Melladore*, but to that whole undoing Sex . . . despising therefore the whole Sex, she resolved to behave to them in a manner which might advance both her Interest and Revenge" (78–79). If men like Melladore act out of interest and desire, she will be guided by interest and revenge. Initially revenge supplants any sexual desire Glicera may have and her "interest" is inextricably linked to her ability to arouse and sustain (but never satisfy) sexual desire in men. She resembles the previously discussed allegorical female figures of Credit and Opinion as represented in the *Spectator*. Opinion encourages and promises the satisfaction of sexual desire: "her voice was pleasing . . . she seemed to have a tongue for every-one . . . [everyone] expected a Paradise."[46] But ultimately Opinion provides nothing for her promises. Similarly, Glicera promises many but satisfies none. Glicera "gave Encouragement to the Hope of as many as sollicited her" to increase the number of suitors and raise their expectations. Male anticipation intensifies her power and her suitors' frustrations when they are denied: "nothing is capable of giving more Vexation to Lovers than a Disappointment when he thinks himself secure from the Fears of it" (79). She arouses men's desires and then repeatedly defers gratification while earning interest – real financial gain – for her efforts: "having as large a Share of Sense as Beauty, [she] knew so well how to manage the Conquests she gain'd, that not one whose *Heart* confess'd the Triumph of her Eyes, but made a Sacrifice also of his *Purse*." She operates with the belief that "nothing discovers the Passion of a Lover so much as parting freely with his Money" (83).

While Glicera attracts a number of different men, she specifically cultivates a relationship with the "immensely rich" Alderman Grubguard, a man whose "age and Dotage [made] her believe she should be able to profit herself more by him than any other of her Enamorato's" (79). His physical appearance runs counter to his passion. He is so old that his "wither'd Face, and shaking Limbs," "palsied Tongue, and toothless Gums" hardly suggest "that in those shrivell'd Veins there was Warmth sufficient to maintain *Life*, much less to propagate *Desire*" (79). This asexual, slightly feminized demeanor is heightened when Glicera, as a practical joke, persuades him to dress the part of the Beau, complete with embroidered coat, lace, and powdered wig.[47] The transformation indicates her control over Grubguard, and her ability to place men in a submissive (and, in Grubguard's case, feminized) position. The language used to describe the terms of their relationship – "profit," "portion," "paid" – underscores the financial basis of the interaction. Glicera receives "Rings, Toys for her Watch, Plate of all kinds, and Jewels" with the promise of a future settlement (80). Because she never intends to consummate the relationship, the combination of Grubguard's financial expenditures and continued sexual frustration temporarily provide a satisfying form of revenge.

Yet Glicera is not the only woman in the text who uses money to exact revenge. After Melladore's marriage, his wife, Helena, is accused of being an illegitimate child and thus an illegal heir – an accusation she and her mother deny. Initially, Melladore believes his wife and his mother-in-law, and he finances their defense himself. He spends his ready money, cashes in his stock, and even borrows money because he believes the case is a good investment. He anticipates a monetary reward for "the Damages he should recover of his Adversaries" and he believes "all would be returned to him with ample Interest" (86). Thus, when the accusation turns out to be correct, Melladore is ruined by the court costs and legal fees. "He had now not only married a Wife without a Fortune, but also a Woman basely born" (86). Additionally, Helena "had no bounds to her Desires, but sought the immediate Gratification of them, let it cost what it would" (87). Her concerns and pleasures are purely financial and commercial. In fact the letter she receives from her lover, Villagnan ("a kind of a Merchant, one at least who by retailing some petty Commodities between *England* and *Holland*, assumed to himself that Name" [88]), is more of a financial report than a billet doux as he highlights Melladore's economic inadequacy: "his ready Money is not only gone, but he is about to mortgage those Acres which were designed your Jointure ... save what you can out of that general Ruin in which you else will certainly and shortly be involv'd" (87). Like Melladore, Helena's passion relies on financial property rather than emotional attachments.

Villagnan invites Helena to go with him to Holland (a destination that allies him with the speculative investors located in that country) but when

Melladore discovers the plan, he locks Helena up in the house until Villagnan's boat has sailed, preventing her elopement.[48] He thinks he has disappointed her sexual and financial desires – her pleasure and her interest. However, when released, she exacts her revenge by obtaining "on the Credit of her Husband, not only all manner of Apparel, Jewels, Plate, rich Furniture, but also several large Sums of Money" (90). She gains the consumer goods she desires at no cost to herself, since legally Melladore is responsible for payment. Because of his public expenditures and debts, Melladore's creditors demand repayment simultaneously, a common pattern at this time. "The least hint of unreliability," observes John Brewer, "could produce a debtor's collapse as his creditors unceremoniously competed with one another to ensure the security of their assets" (204). Melladore resorts to mortgaging his estate to Grubguard. As a result, the two women's financial revenge (unwittingly) works in concert, for the debt Helena incurs is what ultimately enables Glicera to gain financial control over Melladore and reclaim the property that would have been hers.

When Glicera learns of Melladore's situation, her longing for his mortgage and thus financial control over him is greater than any sexual desire she previously experienced and the language underscores that intensity:

to be assur'd that he was also ruin'd in his own Fortune, inevitably undone, fill'd her with a Satisfaction so exquisite, that for a moment she thought it impossible it could be exceeded; but soon it gave way to an impatient Desire, which gave her an adequate Share of Disquiet. – She long'd to be the Mistress of that Writing which gave the Person who had it in possession the Power of all that *Melladore* was now worth in the World. (91)

Haywood uses language that completely reverses the gendered roles of the sexual experience. Melladore is "ruined," "undone," terms in previous Haywood texts that code a woman's loss of virginity or sexual violation. He has also been stripped of his socio-economic markers of male power. Glicera, by contrast, has a climactic experience which she thinks cannot be surpassed. Her satisfaction is exceeded only by her desire, which when satisfied by possession of the mortgage will presumably bring another wave of "exquisite satisfaction." Having decided never to circulate again sexually, Glicera supplants sexual experience with financial transactions (and ambitions).

The exchange of sexual for financial favors also determines the basis of her relationship with Grubguard (though not in the way he anticipates). She is ostensibly willing to consummate their relationship in exchange for Melladore's mortgage. Using her female companion Laphelia as her negotiator, Glicera offers "possession of her Charms" for "possession of the Writing" (96). Grubguard, ever the economic man, is eager to make an immediate exchange, but Laphelia chides him for his approach: "you talk as if you were in *Change Alley*, where they chaffer one *Transfer* for another. – Is such a Woman as *Glicera* to be had by way of Bargain?" (96). The language places the transaction in Exchange Alley; his reaction is like an overly eager stock-jobber anxious to traffic his financial wares for sexual ones. He plans to "lose" the mortgage at Picquet as, in previous weeks, he has lost so much to Glicera that he removed "all need of lamenting her want of Money" (84). The use of gaming to gain the mortgage further underscores the speculative nature of Glicera's whole endeavor.

Though Glicera feigns ignorance about the exchange, she reveals an astute knowledge of the legality of property transactions when she obtains the mortgage. She requests a lawyer be summoned to the house immediately, since "before you can act as *Mortgagee*, there must be a Label annexed to the Writing, testifying that these Deeds are assign'd to you for a valuable Consideration receiv'd" (98–99). She also refuses to rely only on the face value of the mortgage: "I will have a Lawyer then to do it immediately . . . for I love not a Shadow without a Substance" (99). Glicera is especially aware of the hazards of "a shadow without a substance" since that is precisely what she has offered Grubguard all along – the promise but not the delivery of sexual goods (also an image consistent with speculative investment generally, where individuals act because of the promise rather than the materialization of financial returns). Indeed, she summarily dismisses Grubguard and berates his inappropriate desires when he attempts to collect his payment.

Holding the mortgage on Melladore allows her to determine the direction of his life. Melladore, in an attempt to placate Glicera, admits he made a mistake by abandoning her, and laments that he, "like the foolish Indians . . . barter'd *Gold* for *Glass*, exchanged the *best* for one of the vilest that ever disgrac'd the name of Woman" (101). But the terms of his alleged remorse reveal that he has not altered his perception of male–female relationships. For Melladore, they still reside in the world of finance and trade. He is not sorry for any emotional pain, social alienation, or dishonor he may have caused Glicera. He only regrets that he made a bad deal. Financial control, by either Glicera or Melladore, means power in the most basic sense and at the end of the text Glicera has all the power. Glicera provides Melladore with the money to buy a commission in the army and allows him to repay the mortgage with his military wages. This plan enables her to get him out of the country and to collect his money. An ineffectual soldier, he dies in his first battle, providing Glicera with the satisfaction of both his death and the financial holdings she would have received if they had married as originally planned. Upon Melladore's death, she moves into his former house and retires completely from both business and pleasure; she has earned enough to support herself in comfort and withdraws from both sexual and financial circulation. Her desire for interest and revenge has been sated and she lives the rest of her life in retirement, a narrative resolution Haywood provides in many of her fictional texts.

Glicera's actions provide an alternative model of behavior that eschews circulating as a commodity in an economy of male heterosexual desire. Instead Glicera exploits male desires to finance her own speculative invest- ments. Her ability to capitalize on the male desire for pleasure finances her pursuit of business. The detail with which Haywood discusses mortgages, investments, and various types of capital elevates the text above a figura- tive discussion of those activities. She provides specific advice that can be used in actual personal interactions. The text represents a series of hier- archical relationships that are disrupted by a woman's ability and desire to control her own finances, a woman who understands the function of credit. This kind of innovative representation of female sexuality and sub- jectivity significantly departs from cultural expectations and enhances Haywood's credibility with her growing number of readers (increasing her own "paper credit"), while also signaling the transformative and de- stabilizing implications of her fictional discourse.

3

The City Jilt provides women with a specific model for economic revenge and a contemporaneous text, *The Mercenary Lover* (1726), initially appears to follow a similar formula as it explicitly illustrates the dangers women face from avaricious men. Though the female characters in this text do not successfully negotiate those dangers, their experiences provide an instructive example of behavior to avoid. Two sisters, Miranda and Althea, have been left co-heiresses "of a very plentiful estate" (9). Clitander, the "mercenary lover," is a man "of no higher Rank than a Trader" (10), who woos and wins Miranda for her fortune rather than her person. When Miranda marries Clitander, "Money was the only Darling of his mercenary Wishes, and the Estate of which *Miranda* was Co-heiress, was the sole Inducement to his addressing and marying her" (12). He made himself "the solid Business of her most serious Inclinations" (10). Once married, Clitander seduces Miranda's sister, Althea, who becomes pregnant. He attempts to obtain all of Althea's estate through a legal deception, and then he poisons her. Though his crime is discovered by his wife, he is not legally punished because of insufficient evidence and his own persuasive powers. His wife Miranda subsequently keeps his letters to Althea to inoculate herself against his contagious charm that might prompt a reconciliation. On one level, Haywood provides an example of the mercenary and unscrupulous male lovers women should avoid, and demonstrates the importance of controlling absolutely one's sexual and material property. She illustrates what McKeon, describing her fiction, terms "the analogous pathologies of exchange value and sexual libertinage."[49] As a sexual and financial predator, Clitander's desires are mutually informing and mutually enabling, and he serves as a clear warning to women.

However, Haywood's discursive and ideological agenda addresses more than the complicated issues related to the financial situation of women in the sexual marketplace. *The Mercenary Lover* also represents metaphorically Haywood's own situation as an author confronting the financial and cultural exigencies of the *literary* marketplace. Clitander operates as Haywood's surrogate within the text, and functions in a manner analogous to her own discursive, social, and economic practices. Throughout the novel he manipulates specifically textual devices to achieve his goals; he "authors" the situations into which he positions Althea and Miranda. Clitander capitalizes on the credulity, desire, and fantasies of his "readers." He creates and controls their romantic situations. He relies on the imaginative, emotional, and sexual powers of discursive texts to shape, arouse, and ultimately seduce these women. Most important he, like Haywood, performs these actions primarily for economic gain. With the character of Clitander, Haywood demonstrates and to a certain extent justifies the power of the text (romantic and otherwise) to inform, reflect, and influence various types of readers. Indeed, Haywood rather than Clitander is truly the "mercenary lover."

Haywood also uses Clitander to broach the ideological concerns expressed within her novels. By mediating her voice, she deflects her own narrative authority while still performing the cultural critique central to much of her work. She expresses her resistance to existing assumptions about gender, marriage, and power relations through Clitander's interrogation of hegemonic cultural constructions that have been inscribed as "natural." He voices such opinions, and even murders Althea, but is never punished or silenced for these transgressive actions; indeed, his wife remains susceptible to his persuasive powers and must reread his letters to Althea, the texts that document his past actions. The continuity of his discourse provides it with a validity that causes Haywood's readers to assimilate his words. Clitander's dual role within the text – simultaneously a predatory male and the voice of Haywood's feminine cultural critique – offers the reader two distinct though inextricably linked ideological messages and blurs the boundaries of gendered behavior.

This dynamic complicates the effect of Haywood's novel. On the one hand, she illustrates the dangers women face from too great a credulity, an overactive imagination, and a susceptibility to the powers of persuasion. However, she simultaneously demonstrates how judiciously capitalizing on those same forces can empower one's life, as it has her own. She wants to de-gender the social tools Clitander uses and provide a model for action equally applicable to both sexes. Though a man, Clitander's sex is repeatedly neutralized. Despite his aggressively male sexuality, he is often relegated to a culturally feminized position. His financial and social status are conferred by his wife. He acts in the private rather than public sphere to gain his power. While his wife Miranda is often called away by "the Affairs" and business of her family, Clitander "scarce ever stirr'd from Home" (18). He demonstrates a vast familiarity with romances and other feminine texts; he displays a knowledge of the discourse of feminine superstition though he is equally conversant with legal conventions. These contradictory facets connote Clitander's complex role in the text. His very name, Clitander, seems to couple clitoris, the marker of female sexuality, with an approximation of the root of "man", *ander* or *andro*.[50] The multivalence of his name bespeaks the androgynous models Haywood offers as she destabilizes the established system.

The experiences of Miranda and Althea illustrate the dual economies of romance and finance in which most women must operate. As co-heiresses, the women have a clearly marked economic value which makes them attractive to suitors. However, the sexual value of the two sisters and their ability to circulate in a competitive marriage market differs sharply. Unlike Miranda, Althea lacks vivacity and a facility with social inter-action. She

was extreamly cautious who she entertain'd; and as she seem'd little ambitious of creating Admiration, was also not very inclinable to pay it: Hope, being the chief Food of Love (especially in an Age where few Men, like the Heros of Antiquity, can patiently submit to a seven Years Service, before they receiv'd the Reward of a Kiss of the Hand) she afforded so little of that, that she had but few of those who declar'd themselves her Lovers. (10)

Hope, like Desire, must be encouraged and sustained, but she is stingy; she won't "pay" or can't "afford" the mutual flattery that comprises the code of courtship.

The inherent modesty and sexual reticence that limit Althea's desirability in the marriage market increase her attractiveness to her brother-in-law Clitander. Not content with only Miranda's estate, though he possessed the "Moiety of it which was her Proportion," Clitander directs his energies toward gaining Althea's money as well "and put Invention on a continual Rack for some Contrivance to bring the long'd-for Aim about" (12). He imagines Althea will never marry, or at least not without his approval, in part because of her growing affection for him: "the Aversion she ever had for Marriage, she had now another Motive added, to induce her to continue in a single Life, which was, that she wou'd rather that Part of the Estate she was possest of shou'd at her Death descend to him and his Heirs, than any other Person in the World" (13). Clitander considers arranging for Althea to marry a dupe of his choosing, or murdering her outright. He fears the uncertainty and unreliability of feminine emotion that might prompt Althea to marry and escape his control. Nevertheless, he depends upon the volatility of those emotions for his own plans when he ultimately decides to seduce her himself. With her seduction, he hopes to be able to satisfy both his sexual and his financial desires, a "double pleasure":

Tho' Avarice was his prevailing Vice, and the love of Money had so entire a Possession of his Soul, that no other Charms had Power to inspire him with a real Passion, yet he was not without those Desires which are too frequently mistaken for the Influence of the god of tender sighs . . . With strong and vehement Desires he burn'd to enjoy her. (16)

He strives for "absolute Possession" of her estate and her body (17).

Althea's inexperience makes her particularly susceptible to his plans. He secretly and subtly touches her as "he began to appear more open, [and] wou'd often take her Hand and kiss it with Raptures"; "he sometimes took her in his Arms" (19). His physical persistence arouses her sexual desires which are further stimulated by the effects of the immodest texts Clitander persuades Althea to read. "[H]e desir'd she should peruse" texts that would "insensibly melt down the Soul, and make it fit for amorous Impressions"; she read "the Works of *Ovid*, the late celebrated *Rochester*, and many other of more modern Date, and of this Kind it was that he furnished the Study of his intended Victim, to the two worst Passions of deprav'd Humanity" (17). With Ovid and Rochester, Haywood codes the sexual licentiousness which Althea encounters. Though the novel is not specifically mentioned, the texts "of a more modern Date" could suggest romance or amatory fiction. Clitander's plot validates the power of the text to inspire, influence, and persuade. The fundamentally intangible power of discourse, of paper credit, will arouse and motivate Althea and enable Clitander to achieve his very tangible "double pleasure."

In addition to controlling Althea's reading material, Clitander uses his own "invention" to author the sequence of events; he depends on keeping Althea's "Mind in Play" (46), stimulating her emotions, imagination, and passions. He believes there is "no Difficulty which his Genius, Resolution, and the Fertility of his Invention cou'd not surmount" (31).[51] Immediately after the consummation of their relationship, the "barbarous Author of it, now began to exert his utmost Wit and Eloquence to dry her Tears" (24). In a letter, he asks her to use her mind to "bring back in Idea our past Endearments! remember to what a vast Excess of unrestrain'd Delight we have been transported; and while the extatick Image is in View, judge of the Fervour of *Clitander's* Flame" (47). Clitander urges Althea to read the text of their sexual history.

In one sense, the imaginative possibilities Althea discovers after beginning her sexual relationship with Clitander allow her to enjoy a new "Freedom of her Thoughts, [she] felt a kind of Pleasure, in giving way to Pain"(26): "the Idea of *Clitander*, his Charms, his Fondness, and imagin'd Honour and Sweetness of Disposition, took their Turn to triumph over the faint Remains of Modesty and Virtue; and the Felicity of being belov'd by a Man, whom she consider'd as the Wonder of his Sex, seem'd to her sufficient Reparation for that she had resign'd in the rewarding it" (26–27). This relationship is located only in her imaginative manifestations, stimulated by the various "texts" Clitander offered; she loves the "idea" and "image" of the man. Althea lacks the interpretative skills to distinguish appearance from reality. His power to "new-form [her] Mind" and "tune every jarring Thought" (48) impairs her ability to perceive him accurately. For example, when he poisons her at a celebratory ball for her sister Miranda, Althea cannot discriminate between the anxious look of a murderer and that of a man in love: "the Success of his Designs made his Eyes sparkle with a Delight, which the deceived *Althea* observing, imagin'd was owing to his Love and Tenderness" (51). Though her experience and exposure to various texts increases, Althea's interpretative skills do not improve commensurably.

When Clitander learns Althea is pregnant, he creates elaborate scenarios based on superstition and crude prognostication to persuade her she will die in childbirth. "[H]e was continually filling her Ears with

Stories of Women who had died in Child-birth, wou'd sometimes, in a well counterfeited Terrour tell her, he had heard a Weasel squeak, at others, that a Raven had perch'd upon the House, pretend some ominous Dream: In fine, scarce a Day pass'd over without his bringing her an account of some fabulous Prediction" (28). Haywood marks the inappropriateness of this type of "authoring" by revealing the false basis for Clitander's accounts – "counterfeited," "pretend," "fabulous." Haywood's work tries to replace superstition and old wives' tales with models for action, advice, and clear thought. Fear erodes the type of self-actualization that she ultimately details and encourages in her work. While admonishing women to control their own textual choices, she obviously depends on the authenticity, desirability, and persuasiveness of a text. She carefully discriminates between positive and negative models of textual authority. Haywood endorses tacitly a woman's unmediated access to discourse and relies professionally on the motivational and constitutive authority of a printed text, yet she cautions against relinquishing control over the selection of and access to legal, economic, or social narratives.

Clitander attempts to control the legal and economic discourse central to his goals. Having convinced Althea she may die in childbirth, Clitander persuades her to establish a will, with him as the executor, to provide for their unborn child: "you shall bequeath your Lands, your Money, Jewels, and whatsoever valuable Goods you have to a fictitious Person – we may easily invent a Name; – and . . . I must be left *Trustee*, or if you please his *Guardian*, and your *Executor*" (30). The alleged document relies on stock narrative devices – a fictitious person, the invention of a name. Instead of a will, however, Clitander draws up a Deed of Gift which bestows the entire estate on him. He depends on his ability to control Althea's access to and interpretation of the text. Though he needs her to sign the document without learning its true function, "Chance, more than Suspicion, made her desire to read it first" (32); Clitander, unwilling to be revealed as "the Villain he was in Reality" (33), insists on reading it to her. He "began not to read, but to speak such Words as were suitable to the Instrument for which she had given Orders, what he utter'd being altogether different from the real Contents" (34). As he "reads" the document, Althea, "perceiving that his Tongue consulted his own Invention more than the Parchment," recognizes the discrepancy between the printed and the spoken text. More than simply a gap between sign and signified, his duplicity reveals not only the inherent unreliability of language, but also the unreliability and duplicity of the overarching signifier of his and all Haywood texts: man. (Indeed, perhaps Clitander's functional androgyny is another aspect of that unreliability, the multivalence of gender.) The discrepancy between language and meaning, or action (particularly sexual action) and signification is profound. This gesture, and Althea's moment of recognition within the text, allows Haywood to instruct her readers to exploit this discrepancy (much as Haywood the author has done) to their own advantage, while also being aware of it for their own protection. Highlighting the problem in this way, Haywood alerts her readers to the obstacles inherent in any personal, legal, or sexual relationship. At the same time she implicitly acknowledges that she, as a writer of fiction, depends on that linguistic volatility and valence.

Haywood also highlights the discrepancies within culturally inscribed texts through Clitander's critiques of certain cultural institutions. Indeed, the novel as a whole is concerned with the difference between appearance and reality. For example, until the death of her sister, Miranda lives in "perfect Amity and uninterrupted Chearfulness" (15). Her ignorance about her actual situation prompts the Narrator to ask: "So much is the World, and even our selves deceiv'd by Appearances; and how little are we capable of distinguishing the real Felicity for the Shadow of one?" (15).[52] Similarly, Clitander persuades Althea that the cultural expectations she perceives as natural are nothing more than artificial constructs: she "began to think, indeed, that what he said was just, and that those Laws which prohibited a free Commerce between the Sexes, were only the Boundaries of Policy, invented to keep Mankind in Awe, and restrain the Sallies of Nature, which otherwise wou'd involve the World in a general Confusion" (18). He alters her world view as he tries to author her existence. When he "read the State of her Mind" (19) and attempts to consummate the relationship, he appeals to Althea in terms ostensibly sympathetic to her position as a woman and a potential wife. He talks of "Marriage and the Unhappiness of that State" and bemoans the fact that "such a behaviour is too frequent" (20): "How much . . . shou'd I lament . . . shou'd I ever see you one of those complaining Wives, your Wit despis'd, your good Humour subservient to a lordly and imperious Husband's Rule, your Beauty, all that inestimable stock of Charms with which you are so divinely stor'd, unprais'd, unlov'd, and perhaps scorn'd even to your Face" (20). Clitander's description of the institution of marriage, which is consistent with other marital descriptions in Haywood, offers Althea a vision of its worst possible aspects. By making Clitander the source of such a description, so accurately critical of contemporary social practice, she can mark the utterance as illegitimate since it is made by an uncreditable subject. That technique allows her to interrogate an institution she finds problematic for women while distancing herself from such transgressive cultural critique.

Though Clitander questions cultural institutions and accepted narratives, they are what allow him to escape punishment for his crime. In a conversation with his wife, he attributes the noticeable change in Althea's behavior (stemming from their sexual relationship) to her allegedly overactive imagination and superstitious mind: "She will, in spite of me, indulge her Chagrin, and will give no other Reason for it, than that she had an ugly Dream last Night. *Miranda* laugh'd at this idle Superstition (as she call'd it) in her Sister" (25). After being poisoned, Althea realizes what has happened and she tells the apothecary she has been poisoned "by *Clitander*, that murderous Villain has kill'd both the Life and Honour of the lost *Althea*" (54). When an autopsy reveals her to be six months pregnant, Clitander plausibly suggests that she killed herself rather than have her condition revealed. He individually confronts each of his potential accusers and supplants their possible accusations with his own interpretation of events: "the Lady who had accus'd him . . . [was a] Lunatick for some Time before her Death; and besides it was wholly inconsistent with Reason to believe him both her Lover and her Poisoner; it seem'd more probable, that being with Child, to conceal her Shame she had taken something to destroy it, which work'd an Effect contrary to what she design'd" (61). He appropriates culturally inscribed narratives, the shame and hysteria of a pregnant unmarried woman, that provide him with credibility and enable him to remain unpunished for his deed.

The only remaining text that reveals Clitander's crime is the packet of his letters to Althea ("an undeniable Witness of his Guilt") that Miranda discovers with the body: "She keeps them by her, and daily reads them over, to preserve in Memory his Offences and prevent his Artifices from the Success he aims at" (62). Living with Miranda in that situation causes Clitander "Apprehensions of Danger" although he is never punished by law (62). Ironically, the packet of letters Miranda keeps and reads (which, like a Haywood novel, fits in a pocketbook) ultimately functions in the way Haywood hopes many of her texts would: as an antidote to predatory men; as primer for the obstacles women confront in society; as a model of sexual, financial, and social behavior. By gaining a familiarity with literary, cultural, and economic narratives, Haywood's readers can achieve a better understanding of how to interpret, construct, and ultimately revise the multiple texts they must negotiate within a patriarchal culture.

*   *   *

These two novels from the most prolific period in Haywood's career represent accurately the concerns and issues she consistently confronted in her work. Providing alternative models of behavior and sexuality for her female readers was, in part, what caused Haywood to be perceived as threatening within the literary marketplace and within culture more broadly. She frankly discussed female desire. She interrogated the cultural construction of gender and institutions such as marriage in a way that potentially enabled women readers to negotiate their social interactions more successfully. She provided women with strategies for using and obtaining various types of social, sexual, and financial capital, and she balanced the tension between credit and property in her own work. These narrative representations reconfigured a world of greater possibility for women. As such, they implicitly (and at times explicitly) questioned the existing gender hierarchy, and the popularity of such narratives enabled Haywood to erode the existing hierarchy within the print trade as well. The emphasis on redefinition, self-empowerment, and change appealed to the reading public, and contributed to Haywood's ability to create a community of (primarily female) readers whose sustained interest in her texts enabled her to publish steadily during the first ten years of her career. And of course, the process of continued reading changed her readers and potentially contributed to a more profound (if more prolonged) process of transformation within the community of reading female subjects. Her narratives, by virtue of their form and content, responded to a desire for texts that engaged the readers imaginatively, embraced the newly available socio-economic opportunities (real or imagined), and stimulated fantasies about the future. Her popularity with readers enabled her to accrue increasing amounts of "paper credit" yet it also fixed her in a specifically defined cultural position. Despite the multiple positions she occupied within the economic, literary, and gendered economies of eighteenth-century culture, she is often represented – and operates – as the monolithic persona of the scandalous female writer. As the next chapter discusses, Haywood, dependent on the marketplace, attempted to complicate and in a way distinguish among the multiple positions, and thus revise or at least manipulate her authorial persona and expand her role in the material production of texts as she sought to sustain herself in a changing literary milieu.

CHAPTER FOUR

The (gender) politics of the literary marketplace

In the 1740s, Eliza Haywood's position within the culture of professional authorship changed as a result of what Richardson termed the "new species" of fiction, as well as Haywood's attempts to operate less as a woman writer dependent on male publishers and booksellers, and more as a literary entrepreneur acting with some agency within the marketplace.[1] Capitalizing on her experience with a reading public, Haywood tried to use her connections within the trade to negotiate and reinvest her cultural currency in a material sense. Catherine Gallagher suggests that female authors writing in the eighteenth century "commonly figured their labor as the accumulation of credit rather than the production of property."[2] The previous chapter illustrates how the tension between credit and property informed Haywood's professional activities in the early decades; she published at a rapid rate and received various kinds of "paper credit" but only limited financial remuneration. The credit she earned earlier in her career had little value in the material world of the print trade. Although Haywood struggled to establish herself as a producer of texts as physical rather than imaginative commodities, her efforts generally failed to provide the autonomy or control she sought.

A concurrent shift in her literary persona proved equally difficult. The multiple subject positions Haywood occupied in the 1720s and their place within the various economies in which she circulated were often read singly under the rubric "scandalous woman writer." Such a monolithic reading of Haywood, which reflected and perpetuated the constructed literary hierarchies, hindered her ability to reconfigure her position within the marketplace. She could not escape the cumulative weight of her previous literary activity. While there was a certain inevitability (and at times benefit) in the circulation of Haywood's established authorial persona, she simultaneously sought to resist and complicate that construction in fundamental ways. Her professional activities as early as 1731, but primarily during the 1740s, reveal episodes in which Haywood tried not only to establish new positions for herself (for example dramatist or book-seller), but also to distinguish among the various subject positions she already occupied (novelist, actress, woman). To do so altered her relationship to sources of literary and cultural power, and her ability to circulate within the multiple economies that shaped her existence. Haywood defied her dominant authorial construction by actively mediating the diverse roles of author, playwright, actress, bookseller, and woman. Her experience suggests how simultaneously fluid and absolute those cultural positions were and how profoundly they were informed by the overarching construction of gender.

Haywood's letters to potential patrons in 1728 and 1729 demonstrate the skill with which she tried to create and then capitalize upon these multiple cultural positions.[3] Haywood frames her letters with reference to the difficulties of being an author: "Precarious as the condition of a person is whose only dependence is on the pen, to the name of Author." Detailing how monetary inspiration influences writers, she claims: "Encouragement, S^r, is the Sun by which poets thrive, and unless I am very dull indeed to receive it from Your Honor, must certainly inspire my Genius with some more worthy performance." "We are," she humbly asserts, "indebted for the privilege of imploring the protection of the great and good."[4] She casts herself as an impecunious author. Yet she also highlights her status as a widow in an appeal for increased sympathy and the possibility of financial support: "the Inclinations I ever had for writing be now converted into a necessity, by the Sudden Deaths of both a Father, and a Husband, at an age when I was little prepared to stem the tide of Ill fortune." She describes how an "unfortunate marriage" has forced her to support herself and "two children, the eldest of whom is no more than 7 years of Age."[5] Where in the early 1720s she professed "fame" as her desire, Haywood now modifies her ambitions; she claims to write simply because of "the melancholy necessity of depending on my pen." She assumes a doubly subordinate position: failed writer and impoverished widow. In doing so, she converts possibly negative categories (woman and writer) into valorizing markers in an effort to tap into another type of gendered currency.[6]

These letters appear at a time when Haywood began to explore discursive options other than the novel. The failed production of her 1729 tragedy, *Frederick, Duke of Brunswick-Lunenbergh*, which had only two performances, prompted Haywood to lament the "indifferent Success this Tragedy met with (not withstanding my great expectations)."[7] She dedicated the play to Frederick Lewis, Prince of Wales, himself Electoral

Prince of Brunswick-Lunenbergh, in a transparent (and unsuccessful) attempt to gain additional patronage or a royal appearance. In a sense, Haywood also signaled her political alliances by dedicating the text to the Prince of Wales, since he was quite public in his disdain for Robert Walpole. Her theatrical efforts in the 1730s marked her attempt to create a new role for herself as an actress and dramatist, while retaining the inescapable associations of her previous literary experience. Haywood made "use of her reputation as a writer," suggests John Elwood, "to interest the public in her stage appearances," indicating the double bind she was in.[8] Her attempts to reinvent herself often depended upon the well-known persona she tried to obscure. Haywood played a series of characters that offered an audience the opportunity to see her represent passionate women like those that populate her novels. In the advertisements for these productions, she frequently received one of the top billings and was often listed as "Mrs. Haywood, the Author" or "Mrs. Haywood the Muse, Author of Love in Excess, and many other entertaining pieces."[9] This appositive characterization "Eliza Haywood, the Author" can simultaneously refer to Haywood as *an* author or as *the* author of the text performed, and underscores the multiple positions she assumes.

Even dramatic pieces by others reinforced the cultural construction of her as a novelist. At Little Haymarket, for example, Henry Fielding capitalized on Haywood's reputation by satirizing her in the character of Mrs. Novel in his very successful play *The Author's Farce* (1730); like Pope, Fielding profited from Haywood's accumulation of cultural credit.[10] The literarily and sexually avaricious character of Mrs. Novel depended on audience recognition of the literary type – woman writer – if not the specific model – Eliza Haywood.[11] *The Author's Farce* opened on Monday March 30, 1730 and ran as a main piece through Friday May 8. The only break in this initial run at Haymarket occurred with the April 8 and 9 performances of William Hatchett's *The Rival Father; or, the Death of Achilles*, in which Haywood played Achilles' abandoned lover Briseis. While Charles Woods dismisses this coincidence as only a "curious fact," it seems instead to underscore the multiple and often conflicting roles Haywood had as an author, as a public figure, and as an "actor" on diverse stages. She was character and subject.

In a theatrical milieu marked by a performative intertextuality, Haywood demonstrated an understanding of how symbolic and literary economies function with the borrowing and accumulating of cultural capital. Haywood's successful *Opera of Operas* had its genesis in Fielding's farce, *Tom Thumb; or Tragedy of Tragedies* to which Haywood, William

Hatchett, and Thomas A. Arne added thirty-three songs.[12] The piece appeared at the Little Haymarket on May 31, 1733 and had thirteen performances until it "deferr'd playing on account of the excessive heat of the weather" on June 27.[13] It continued to have performances as both a main piece and on a double bill through the end of the year. The theatrical effort received the royal support Haywood sought previously. The Duke of Cumberland and Princess Amelia attended on June 4, 1733; the Prince of Wales "with a vast Concourse of the Nobility and Gentry" appeared on June 6; and the Earl of Egmont, the two youngest princesses, and Conde de Montijo, the Spanish ambassador, were among the others who saw the piece.[14]

Just as *Opera of Operas* gave Haywood a modest theatrical success, her professional participation in a cultural space that served as the locus of the discursive and performative political opposition helped develop her abilities as a political writer.[15] Fielding's Little Haymarket capitalized on the widespread desire for political satire as "The Grand Mogul's Company of Comedians" performed relevant, subversive, and profitable entertainment. Haywood, with her anti-Walpole pieces such as *The Adventures of Eovaii* (1736), imitated the topicality and innovation of Little Haymarket.[16] She exploited the perceived desire for political material, a marketing strategy that obviously motivated her pamphlets and periodicals in the 1740s.

Haywood's involvement in Little Haymarket may have provided a measure of financial stability, but it also made her particularly vulnerable to the effects of the Theatre Licensing Act of 1737. While the constricting measures of the Licensing Act affected a whole profession, they were particularly devastating to those, like Haywood, who were more peripherally involved. The Licensing Act may also have finally disappointed her hopes in the arena that seemed most elusive. In the "Authors of the Town," Richard Savage describes Haywood as someone for whom theatrical success was all: "A cast-off Dame, who of Intrigues can judge, / Writes Scandal in Romance – A Printer's Drudge! / Flush'd with Success, for Stage-Renown she pants, / And melts, and swells, and pens luxurious Rants."[17] Not actress enough to be with a patent company, not playwright enough (or, in the new repressive era, perhaps conformist enough) to be produceable, Haywood was forced again to reinsert herself into a changing literary marketplace that must have seemed increasingly distant and uninviting for a writer interested in more than just translations and literary piecework.

In the decade beginning in 1740, Haywood became involved in the circulation and sale of material texts. By 1742 she had opened her own bookseller's shop at the Sign of Fame in Covent Garden. Her choice of shop sign instantiated Haywood's career-long association with the negative aspects of fame for a woman. Like Behn's Angellica, Haywood advertised the characteristics that defined her existence and marked her as a public woman during a period that increasingly privileged the proper woman writer. Unfortunately her "fame" was largely behind her, for she kept the shop less than a year.[18] Her subsequent position as something akin to a mercury at the peripheral, and certainly unprestigious, edges of the print trade was followed by a steady decline in her ability to participate with any real agency within the production and sale of texts. During the 1740s, Haywood sought to secure literary and financial "success" (clearly a relative term) as she repeatedly tried to penetrate the print trade as something *other* than a novelist. Yet she was always slightly behind the power curve, imitating, appropriating, scrambling to maintain a foothold in the profession, and ultimately unable to gain access to the machinery of print culture. She achieved the lingering notoriety but only the fleeting financial rewards of someone always skirting the centers of power as she failed to shift from a producer of imaginative to a producer or distributor of tangible commodities.

In addition to attempting a new role in the material production of the print trade, Haywood also tried to reconfigure the elements of her authorial persona. She recontextualized her reputation for "inappropriate" professional and personal actions in a way that enabled her to meet the demand for didactically oriented discourse. For example, in the first book of *The Female Spectator* (1744–46), modeled on the introduction of the *Spectator*'s narrator, Haywood exploits the associations of two decades of writing to heighten interest in her as a literary figure and to prove her credibility as an advisor on a variety of women's personal, social, and financial situations.[19] To justify readers' involvement in her text, Haywood provides select details about herself. "[N]ever a beauty," Haywood claims her life "was a continued Round of what I then called Pleasure, and my whole Time engrossed by a hurry of promiscuous diversions" (5). "I have run through as many Scenes of Vanity and Folly as the greatest Coquet of them all" (4). Though this conduct has resulted in "Inconveniences" for Haywood, she consoled herself "to think that the Publick may reap some Benefit from it" (5). While the gesture pretends to reveal Haywood to her readers, it effectively functions to stabilize, control, and ultimately obscure her. It is, of course, as strategically constructed a "Haywood" as Pope's "Haywood" in the *Dunciad*. She provides the calculated version of her life that attempts to supplant other, less flattering portraits. Her later efforts to obfuscate intentionally her personal history similarly deny others the opportunity for interpretation. (Indeed, in *Biographia Dramatica* [1764] David Erskine Baker recounts that Haywood, "from a supposition of some improper liberties being taken with her character after death, by the intermixture of truth and falsehood with her history ... laid a solemn injunction on a person, who was well acquainted with all the particulars of it, not to communicate to any one the least circumstances relating to her" (216). Thus "[a]s to the circumstances of Mrs. Heywood's [*sic*] life, very little light seems to appear," largely through her own efforts.)

In a gesture of apparent conformity, Haywood, as the "female spectator," recuperates the transgressive elements of her past to secure her position as an instructor for women, and to control her dual commodities: the periodical and the narratable elements of her life. Similarly, she ostensibly adheres to the requirements of the prevalent literary marketplace with overtly didactic texts such as *The Fortunate Foundlings* (1744) and *Life's Progress through the Passions* (1748). Haywood published every year between 1740 and her death in 1756; clearly she was able to meet reader expectations and arouse some interest from an audience (no matter how limited). Despite her seeming concession to conformity, Haywood operated concurrently in a more subversive and marginal position as an author and as a member of the print trade. With texts like *Anti-Pamela* (1742) and *The History of Miss Betsy Thoughtless* (1751), she simultaneously supported and critiqued the dominant ideology inscribed in social, economic, and discursive practices. She also, of course, acted in a more unauthorized manner (as evidenced by her 1749 arrest) with her political texts about the Pretender and, more subtly, her actions that reveal the politics of the print trade.

This chapter explores three specific moments that illustrate the collision of conformity and subversion and the financial and literary obstacles often present for a woman writer trying to conserve or invest her paper credit. *Anti-Pamela*, one of the texts Haywood wrote and sold at her own shop, interrogates the generic expectations a novel like *Pamela* imposes on a reading public and on subsequent fictional narratives. Part literary satire, part cultural critique, *Anti-Pamela* explores the gendered conflict between business and pleasure, and refutes the consolidation of feminine virtue *Pamela* seems to endorse. Haywood's publication and subsequent arrest for a pamphlet on the Pretender, *A Letter from H— G—g, Esq. ... to a Particular Friend* (1749), reveals the categorical instabilities that plagued a literary market and a culture still assimilating the powerful role of the printed word. This episode, and the details about Haywood's marginalized production and distribution activities, illustrates how she breached the professional hierarchies of the print trade in a material sense in an attempt to create a new position for herself. Finally, *The History of Miss Betsy Thoughtless*, often considered Haywood's best novel, appears to observe the didactic and moral requirements of the newly reconceived genre. However, *Betsy Thoughtless*, like *Anti-Pamela*, tests generic and gendered expectations as it attempts to reconstitute the experience of the novel.

I

In 1741/42, Haywood began selling books at the Sign of Fame in Covent Garden, perhaps in an effort to control the means of her own production and to make a profit, or a least to support herself with something other than her writing alone. She probably functioned in a manner similar to a mercury, a category of bookseller between a full-scale bookselling shop (for which Haywood would have obviously lacked the start-up capital) and a hawker, who would sell or "hawk" pamphlets, newspapers, and prints within a prescribed area.[20] "Hawkers," writes Henry Atherton, "among them many women, belonged to the lowest caste of the trade: peripatetic sellers who carried their printed wares of ballads, broadsides, pamphlets and prints about the city" (2). Similarly, mercuries, as David Foxon describes, "seem to merge into the category of stall-holders or those who kept pamphlet shops."[21] The more marginal and precarious categories of booksellers were forced to accommodate a wider range of products and responsibilities. Haywood clearly sold some texts, including *The Busy Body; or the Successful Spy* (1741), *The Virtuous Villager; or Virgin's Victory* (1742), and her own *Anti-Pamela* (1742). She also relied on her own translations during this period, perhaps in an attempt to keep her shop supplied or to earn money to supplement her shop's earnings. Various printed material was probably only one facet of her venture, however. Paul Langford details how bookstalls or small pamphlet shops usually depended on "stationery or other commodities" to supplement their income: "Not a few made their profit from the patent medicines whose sale depended so much on shrewd publicity."[22] This situation was particularly true for women who, C. J. Mitchell asserts, not only handled other printed material, distributed newspapers, and received subscriptions for papers or books, but also sold items from quite distinct trades. "Shops had to stock a wider range of goods, and the line becomes blurred between the book trades and others," she suggests, at times defying precise description.[23] Regardless of the level of Haywood's operation, the business of selling texts (of whatever form) introduced her to the world of the print trade as something other than a novelist and, as a result, potentially provided her with the ability to operate as a member of that trade, albeit in an increasingly marginalized and often invisible manner until her arrest in December 1749.

One of the first texts Haywood advertised was her own writing, *Anti-Pamela*, which best captures the essence of her commercial and literary activity at this time. She attempted to increase her own marketability (which acquired an even greater urgency with her bookselling venture) while subverting the larger morality and didacticism that increasingly characterized the novel. *Anti-Pamela* tried both to devalue and capitalize on Richardson's success and, as the title indicates, obviously relied on the market value of the *Pamela* craze.[24] Ironically appropriating Richardson's text to serve her own satiric ends, Haywood tried to profit in both a financial and literary sense. She implicitly comments on Richardson's construction of female virtue and its role in *Pamela*, while she also interrogates that novel's didactic and generic expectations as well as its depiction of the relationship between morality and economy. She renegotiates (or reconstructs) Richardson's apparent lesson in the economy of virtue and the financial rewards of morality to represent more accurately the dynamic between sexuality and finance. She illustrates how a woman, if careless, can be (too) successful in the business of (sexual) pleasure without positioning herself to enjoy the pleasure of (financial) business.

Anti-Pamela details the adventures of the fifteen-year-old Syrena Tricksy, a serving girl who, with her mother's guidance, attempts to profit from her various relationships with men. Syrena had been "bred up" in the notion "that a woman who had Beauty to attract the Men, and Cunning to manage them afterwards, was secure of making her Fortune."[25] She understands the business of pleasure. Beginning with the son of the first house in which she works, Syrena successfully engages a succession of men and acquires (and then immediately spends) a great deal of money, often to a man's (near) financial ruin. Yet she fails to marry any of her "suitors" or secure any sort of financial stability for herself. She takes no pleasure in business. Consequently, at the end of the novel, Syrena is sent to Wales to earn her living again as a serving girl. On one level, the text serves as an antidote to *Pamela*; if Richardson's novel threatens to make all the servant girls in England pine after their masters, then *Anti-Pamela* teaches those masters how to resist such advances (and perhaps instructs serving girls how to dissemble even more effectively). Much as Fielding's *Joseph Andrews* (1742) expresses a concern for "male virtue," *Anti-Pamela*'s title page advertises

the text as "Publish'd as a necessary Caution to all Young Gentlemen":
"A Narrative which has really its Foundation in Truth and Nature; and at
the same time that it entertains ... arms against a partial Credulity, by
shewing the Mischiefs that frequently arise from a too sudden Admiration."
Men "ought to be warn'd" when "they enter into any Engagements with
Women, whose Principles they are not acquainted with; and not ... be
beguiled and ruin'd by a fair Face and seeming affection ... For in
corrupted Morals, no Sincerity can be expected, and the sacred Names of
Love and Friendship, are but prophan'd and prostituted for the basest
ends" (168). But Haywood is not really interested in didacticism or
admonishments for overly eager men. While *Anti-Pamela* certainly instructs,
it offers lessons in the appropriate use, circulation, and distribution of the
currency available to women. Haywood teaches economics, not morality.

Syrena Tricksy is the ideal subject for Haywood's discursive agenda.
Syrena possesses the beauty and cunning to attract men, and she clearly
understands the concept of exchange central to her ambitions: "he gave
his gold, and Syrena her Person" (114). Yet Syrena understands *only*
exchange and she lacks the financial acumen either to invest her money
speculatively or to consider other long-term arrangements. The text does
not condemn Syrena and passes no moral judgment on her actions or her
motives. Indeed, the text tacitly approves of Syrena's attempts to gain
increasing amounts of money as she recognizes how profitable a business
pleasure can be. However, Syrena allows her own desires to interfere with
her work, and she squanders her sexual and financial currency; the pursuit
of her own pleasure repeatedly conflicts with her business.

At multiple points in the text, Syrena accumulates enough money to
support herself indefinitely but she and her mother exhaust her funds
"indulg[ing] themselves in everything they liked" (144). Syrena's profligacy extends to her sexual capital as well. Unsatisfied, her "headstrong
and ungoverned appetites" (231) prompt her to seek sexual pleasure
beyond the boundaries of her business relationships, a pursuit her mother
warns is not "a true friend to interest" (205). Her resources are doubly
misdirected as her desires lead her astray. Syrena wastes what she should
conserve. She spends what she should save. She buys what she already gets
for free. She circulates her sexual commodities without remuneration and
even pays to support a satisfying lover. Though Haywood condemns
Syrena's lack of thrift, she also critiques the naturalized construction of
gender that enables men to indulge their desires in ways that women
cannot. For Syrena, the pleasure of business and the business of pleasure
are two mutually exclusive categories. Her business of seducing and

securing men, though in some cases "pleasurable," is work; her personal desires distract her from the business at hand and cause her to misdirect her resources.

Syrena's relationship with a Mercer demonstrates her inability to capitalize financially on the opportunities offered. She meets the Mercer through their commercial transactions; while Syrena looks at cloth in his shop, he "pulled down several pieces of fine Brocade, under the Pretence of tempting her to buy; but in reality, only to have the Pleasure of detaining her as long as he could" (154). For the Mercer, business begets pleasure. In order to make herself available to him, Syrena invents a liminal position for herself: "I am a wife and no Wife" (158), claiming her wealthy husband's family demanded a separation after only three days of marriage. Significantly, Syrena initially establishes an intimacy with the Mercer's wife, prompting him to claim, "if she were a Man, she should not approve of the Affection his Wife had for her . . . he merited something from her in compensation for robbing him of so much of his wife's company" (160). The compensation materializes in the form of a sexual relationship through which Syrena knew "she should henceforward have the command of his Purse" (161). They embark on a "guilty commerce" (172).

Taken with (and by) Syrena, the Mercer does not limit his gifts. "His lavish love bestowed so much upon her, that had she liv'd in any frugal decorum, she might have sav'd sufficient to have made her easy for a long time." However, Syrena cannot plan ahead, "having nothing now to think on, farther than indulging every Luxury." Too much a consumer, she is intent on immediate gratification, diversion, pleasure, and entertainment. (She resembles nothing so much as the presumed reader of Haywood novels as constructed by someone like Pope.) She utterly lacks thrift or frugality and depletes the currency she most needs to conserve when she falls "into an Adventure which was not a little expensive to her" (161). Syrena meets a man "of as amorous a Constitution, as her vicious Desires had made her languish for" who arouses her sexual desire, "something she had never felt before." Recognizing Syrena's inclination, the Gallant "was pretty secure . . . that she would be no manner of Charge to him, but on the contrary, he should be able to render his Acquaintance with her servicable, as well to his Interest, as he had found it to his Pleasure" (162). Like all men Syrena meets, the Gallant's interest and pleasure are mutually reinforcing as his pleasure begets interest. Syrena never meets him without taking "care to put more money in his Pocket, than the Charges of the Day could possibly amount to . . . never any Man . . .had more reason to be satisfied" (164). Initially her liaison with the Gallant "did not make her negligent in preserving her Interest with the Mercer" (164); nor does it prompt her to manage her money any more effectively.

Sharing Syrena's profligacy, the Gallant is soon imprisoned for debt. Syrena's own extravagance prevents her from having ready money for his bail. Because she "could not bear the loss of a Lover, so well qualified to please her" (166), she claims her mother is imprisoned for debt and receives two £50 bills from the Mercer. Attending the arraignment with a colleague to whom the Gallant owed the money, the Mercer sees Syrena and immediately recognizes bills he had just given her, "the Number of which he knew, paid as traceable so much Money to his Friend" (168). Bills of exchange, bank notes, and other kinds of paper money could be identified due to what James Thompson describes as their "individualized nature." Typically numbered, bills "not only held the name of the drawer and the bearer, but often a number of intermediary bearers who had endorsed the bill."[26] The bill allows the Mercer to construct a narrative about Syrena's relationship with the Gallant and, in turn, his own relationship with Syrena. Syrena fails to understand the kinds of narratives negotiable paper creates and requires. Indeed, her inability to see a profit stems from her ignorance about the possibilities (and limitations) of paper credit. She is concerned with immediate gratification, exchange, and tangible goods. She cannot make the imaginative leap to a world of investment, credit, or her own financial future.

Syrena's unremunerative sexual circulation ultimately destroys her last opportunity for financial security when she becomes the housekeeper and later fiancée of Mr. W—, who ultimately serves as the text's model of economy. A former merchant, with "sufficient for his contentment" (185), W— has done precisely what Syrena should do – make a fortune, invest wisely, and then retire. His fiscal economy is matched by his sexual restraint and he is unwilling to consummate the relationship until after their marriage. He does not circulate unadvisedly. Though his restraint might be read as virtue, it actually reveals his keen insight into symbolic economies and personal commerce. He believes male–female relationships are based inherently on exchange: "that Passion that makes us so liberal, makes us also desire something in return – we cannot content ourselves with rendering happy the Object of our Affections, but languish for something more than Gratitude ... as charming as you are, you will never find a Man who loves you for your own sake alone" (194). W—'s restraint with Syrena also stems from his belief in her virtue and economy. Syrena and her mother feign thrift and frugality which act as markers of feminine decorum, modesty, and virtue. Ostensibly Haywood reaffirms the very gendered construction of female domestic virtue; but she more profoundly demonstrates the superficiality and meaninglessness of those markers – they are hollow signifiers that can be appropriated and used at will.

Syrena's (pretended) duty provides the opportunity to meet a new lover after she becomes engaged to Mr. W—. Claiming to nurse her sick mother, Syrena repeatedly leaves the house to meet her new lover. Despite her mother's warning: "you were never in so fair a way of making your Fortune as at Present ... [do] not do anything that might even give a Possibility of reversing it" (205), Syrena acts extravagantly to indulge the "pleasure which attends the gratification of any Passion whatsoever" (210). As Syrena discovers on the eve of her wedding, the lover turns out to be Mr. W—'s son, prompting the cancellation of the wedding and the expulsion of Syrena from the household. Syrena's failure lies not in her unfortunate choice of lovers (although certainly that is part of it), but in her inability to practice economy. She cannot save for the future. When imagining her success, Syrena betrays the inevitability of her failure. The moment she mistakenly sees as the culmination of her ambition, her approaching marriage to Mr. W—, is one in which she envisages business enabling rather than prohibiting pleasure: "O! How I shall roll in Riches and Plenty – How I shall indulge every Wish – enjoy every Pleasure and despise all Restraint ... I'll make him settle a jointure upon me, get possession of his Plate and Jewels, turn them into ready money" (218). Even when she fantasizes about her moment of achievement she reveals the seeds of her destruction – jewels and goods of value will be exchanged for "ready money" easier to spend and squander. Syrena will not invest, conserve, or exercise restraint.

Syrena, like all financially failed characters in the text, puts pleasure before business or interest. Thus with *Anti-Pamela*, Haywood offers not simply a sexual model for women, or an educational text for men to help them avoid the snares of unsavory women. Instead she depicts a more inclusive economic model designed to help all readers avoid the pitfalls of immediate gratification and capitalize on the opportunities of paper credit and other kinds of imaginative, intangible property. While Haywood's previous fiction suggested that women should avoid the "inadvertencies" or sexual transgressions that can jeopardize their future, this text concerns a much more broadly based system of restraint – one removed from abstract notions of morality and repositioned in a world of economics and interest. The only morality *Anti-Pamela* privileges is success: a success Syrena easily could have achieved. By shifting the frame of her examination from morality to economy Haywood not only suggests the limitations of absolute notions of virtue but also recognizes the more pressing financial realities women regularly confront.

2

Haywood did not sustain her bookselling venture for more than a few months, though she clearly maintained her ties with the print trade. She continued to write for other booksellers during this period, but did not extricate herself completely from the production and distribution activities of the trade.[27] Her undefined though readily apparent participation, coupled with her earlier political writing and notoriety, may have contributed to her 1749 arrest for the publication and sale of a "seditious" pamphlet on the Pretender. The information revealed during the official examinations of a number of booksellers and of Haywood herself suggests she continued to imitate and appropriate, remaining in a rather marginalized position in relation to the print trade as a whole. It appears that she acted as a kind of distributor of texts; not a mercury who would sell from one place, or a hawker who would cover one region. She acted as more of a holder or even "text launderer" who would assemble and distribute texts to preserve the anonymity of the printer or author (in this case herself) but retain a willful ignorance about the related activities. This situation, as Foxon details, increased an individual's vulnerability to official scrutiny. Haywood, near the bottom of the bookselling hierarchy, was susceptible to government harassment, interrogation, and arrest. The entire episode surrounding this 1749 pamphlet provides insight not only into Haywood's activities within the print trade and the hierarchy of that commercial milieu, but also into her attempt to capitalize on what she perceived as a popular demand for political writings.

In December 1749, a pamphlet entitled *A Letter from H—G—g, Esq. . . . To a Particular Friend* appeared in various print shops in Fleet Street, Charing Cross, and Peacock near Temple Bar. Bearing no publisher's imprint, the pamphlet is marked as "Printed, and sold at the Royal-Exchange, Temple-Bar, Charing Cross and all the Pamphlet-Shops of London and Westminster." The absence of the names of specific booksellers' shops suggests the pamphlet's ephemeral nature and, of course, its political subject matter; publishers and booksellers want to avoid a direct association. *The Monthly Review*, which published a notice of the arrest of "the noted Mrs. H—d, author of four Volumes of novels well known, and other romantic performances," describes the pamphlet as "privately conveyed to the shops" since there was "no publisher caring to appear in it: but the government, less scrupulous, took care to make the piece taken notice of, by arresting the female veteran we have named."[28] Haywood, the alleged "Author, Printer and Publisher of [the] Scandalous Seditious and Treasonable Pamphlet," was taken up and held for "some weeks" by the messenger Nathan Carrington.[29] Booksellers John Jolliffe, Charles Corbett, John Barnes, and Henry Chappelle, as well as Elizabeth Woodfall, wife of printer George Woodfall, and Haywood's servant Hannah Stredden, were all examined by Lord Stanhope on December 12, 1749.[30] Haywood, previously excused because of "illness," was interrogated a month later, on January 14, 1749/50; yet, from all available evidence, she was never prosecuted.[31]

The text details the Young Pretender's journeys with his companion Henry Goring following his departure from the papal province of Avignon on February 28, 1749.[32] Combining romantic fiction and loosely written political philosophy, the pamphlet exudes a rather reverent attitude toward the Young Chevalier and, at times, levels thinly veiled criticism at George II. Despite its obviously political tone and potentially provocative subject matter – the travels of Bonnie Prince Charlie – the text as a whole is not necessarily inflammatory. Nevertheless, it raises questions about Haywood's generic and discursive practices as well as her political affinities and motivation.

The narrator of *A Letter from H— G—g* claims to have inadvertently received "an extraordinary packet" which was a letter from Henry Goring. In the preface, the "editor" explains that he lives in an apartment formerly occupied by the intended recipient (a man "of almost the same Name with myself, a single consonant making all the difference" [3]). Hesitant to make "so bold with what was none of my own," he initially resists revealing what was "never intended for the Press," yet feels compelled to publish "in order to gratify the Curiosity of the town, which I observe has been raised pretty high" (3). The "high curiosity" describes a political environment in which news about the Pretender is desirable and thus marketable – Haywood's primary motivation. Written as a personal letter from Henry Goring (H— G—g), the piece describes the Pretender in both public and private terms, and presents him as a "natural" monarch whose nobility transcends mere political position. Haywood combines the stylistics of her earlier amatory fiction with almost journalistic descriptions of the Pretender's journeys on the Continent. Consequently, the text, like its subject, is a generic hybrid. Haywood constructs the Pretender as a civic humanist who conforms to a social (and fictional) ideal of aristocratic honor; she makes him a personally desirable, romantic character to increase his political viability.

Significantly, Haywood uses a moment of sexual continence to exemplify his regal nature and altruism. In a display of self-restraint atypical for a Haywood hero (or even for contemporaneous fictional characters like Lovelace) the Pretender resists sexual opportunities available to him. When he sees a house on fire, he rescues a beautiful young woman (in the requisite state of dishabille) from her bed and takes her to safety. While the prolonged scene is written like (and mistaken for) a seduction (for the woman is sexually vulnerable and emotionally grateful), the episode becomes an example of virtue and sexual restraint:

> I am not a Stoick ... but I have been always taught that Pleasures, how pardonable soever they may be themselves, become highly criminal when indulged to the prejudice of another. – The Lady I have just parted from is young, beautiful, and I believe innocent; – She may make some deserving Man extremely happy. – It would then have been an Action unworthy of my real character under a feigned Name, to rob her of her Innocence; to ruin, and then to abandon her for ever; for you well know it suits not with the circumstances of my condition to enter into any Engagements of that Tender Nature she has a Right to expect. (25)

In a manner reminiscent of Richardson's *Pamela* (or perhaps even the fire scene in *Clarissa*), Haywood titillates her reader but rather than punctuate the moment with a lesson about female morality, she uses the opportunity to discuss personal and political virtue. H— G—g observes that the Pretender's abstinence is another example of his "proving those Virtues, which, though most admire, few are able to imitate" (18); " Ah! How fit is he to govern others, who knows so well how to govern himself" (26).

The Pretender's personal economy underscores his circumspect political philosophy, presented informally as a series of private conversations. Haywood addresses topical issues central to governing and uses many standard tropes of contemporary political discourse. The Chevalier details a distrust of governmental ministers consistent with the "common tradition of seeing British monarchs as misled or controlled by their minister," as Vincent Carretta describes.[33] He condemns "encroachments" upon liberty and the use of "arbitrary power" (15), a concern in a country increasingly repressive after the '45. He argues for fiscal conservatism, "A King ... can never be ... too frugal with the Publick [money]," a sly way to attack Hanoverian extravagance. Haywood's technique enables her to address a range of political issues in a narrative (rather than polemical) manner she perhaps thought would protect her from prosecution.

Though the pamphlet emphasizes general political philosophy rather than specific political situations, it does describe the possible return of the Pretender to the throne, a potent image for a culture disparately fearful of and anxious for such an event. The Chevalier admits that should "the Bulk of the Nation ... grow desirous of a Change ... I am not so old as to despair of enjoying in my own Person the Fruits of such a Change" (47). Goring reiterates the point by assuring his audience that "thoughts of filling the throne of his Ancestors ... with the Consent of the People, is the first and dearest view of his Soul" (48).[34] Haywood's pamphlet capitalizes on a perceived and mutually reinforcing political and generic instability, by representing (relatively) provocative political statements within domestic or romantic discourse. While Haywood may have believed such generic instability, coupled with a convoluted distribution system and obscured chain of accountability for the pamphlet itself, would protect her and the booksellers, the result was sharply different. Everyone involved was taken up and questioned shortly after the pamphlet appeared.

The four male booksellers questioned by Lord Stanhope (Barnes, Chappelle, Corbett, and Jolliffee) all claimed that twenty-five copies of the pamphlet were left at their shop when they were not there. Though these pamphlets were left anonymously, the men seemed certain they were from Haywood and suggested that an established professional relationship existed. While Chappelle and Jolliffee refused to elaborate, Corbett and Barnes indicated they were "accountable" or "indebted" to Haywood for the pamphlets and claimed they typically settled their financial accounts with her at the end of the month. Although Corbett had not seen Haywood for four years, he, like the other booksellers, had previously operated under this standard method of distribution and repayment before. Corbett said "he has sold several things wrote and published by the sd. Mrs. Haywood and has paid her servant Maid for them." He observed that "she has been the author of many things which she publishes in the same manner she has published this."[35] Corbett also expected to get the book "under the price it is published" because "to persons in the same trade a shilling pamphlet is always sold for nine pence and that he was to pay himself nine pence each to Mrs. Haywood."[36] He clearly identifies Haywood as some sort of colleague, a person of the trade.

Elizabeth Woodfall, wife of printer George, acknowledges her year-long acquaintance with Haywood, and notes that her "Husband employed Mrs. Haywood to write a book entitled Dalinda or the Double Marriage." She adds that Haywood's maid-servant, Hannah Stredden, "came very often from the sd. Mrs. Haywood with the proof sheets."[37] This observation might suggest Haywood's fairly high level of involvement with the production of her works. "Some women authors were closely associated with the production or marketing of their work," notes C. S. Mitchell, "[and] knew how to correct proofs and complained ... [about] poor type or coarse paper" (36). Given Haywood's intensive and extended involvement in all facets of book production, such an association seems possible if not likely. Elizabeth Woodfall also seems to suggest that some type of professional courtesy was extended to Haywood when she observes that Stredden "frequently comes to the shop of the Examt.'s Husband for the Evening papers for her Mistress to read and bring them back again." Woodfall said that forty-four copies of the pamphlets sold in approximately three weeks but claimed she did "not know who is the author or printer thereof." Fewer than 100 copies of the pamphlet sold altogether (something Haywood attributed to the recent City elections).

The examination of Haywood's servant Hannah Stredden suggests Haywood operated under a very limited means of production marked by instability, marginalization, and localized distribution. Although Stredden claims not to know the author or printer of the pamphlet, she describes how "a large quantity of said pamphlets" appeared "in sheet" at Haywood's lodging, and that Stredden herself "stiched the said sheets into books and by the Directions of her Mistress, delivered them to the shops ... [and] left word at those places where she came from and where they might have more."[38] The gathering, folding, and stitching of printed sheets could be, and often was, performed by women (Mitchell, 35), although the image of Haywood and Stredden performing those activities in Haywood's lodgings depicts a fairly low level of production. If the *Penny Post* is correct in calling Haywood author, printer, and publisher of the pamphlet, it suggests that she attempted to retain (or was forced to perform) all aspects of that trade (including distribution) herself.[39] Though her 1741/42 foray into the bookselling business would certainly qualify Haywood as the "person from the trade" Corbett describes, it seems increasingly apparent she had a more complicated relationship with other booksellers. She worked for Corbett and Woodfall as an author (they both also sold *Dalinda* in 1749), a relationship that would continue into the fifties. But it is also clear that she functioned as a printer-cum-distributor of texts, potentially a more difficult and precarious role. The eagerness of all the booksellers to identify Haywood as the distributor of this pamphlet might suggest she had operated in this way since the closing of her own print shop; or it might indicate that Haywood, for this particular publication, was the agreed-upon scapegoat or fall guy. Either scenario places her squarely within the operations of the print trade.

When finally examined in January, Haywood attempts to dissociate herself from most of the activity surrounding the text. She claims that 750 pamphlets were left at her lodgings about two months earlier and that she had her servant distribute them. She denies responsibility for authorship or production, and she observes that this sort of thing happens to her often:

frequently ... pamphlets have been left at her lodgings and she has not known from whom they come and ... she has Distributed them at the shops and Received the money from them and ... in about a month the proprietor came and the examinant accounted with him for the sale; but says that no body has yet demanded an account of her for the said pamphlets nor does she know who she must account to.[40]

Haywood may be describing a scaled-down version of her previous attempts at a bookseller's shop; she has kept her ties to printers, but only in a rudimentary way. She no longer sells these things on her own, but, now a notch lower in the print trade, acts only to distribute the texts that others have written and/or printed.

Haywood may also be describing a more intentionally obscured position. She casts herself as a holder and distributor who screens the actual participants, profits only in the most minimal way from labor very much not her own, and remains ignorant about related activities. She defines herself as largely uninvolved and uninformed. Of course, Haywood's ignorance seems by design. As Foxon reminds us, "'the anonymity conferred by the use of publishers and mercuries was only achieved at the expense of their being frequently arrested and interrogated" (8). Any profit Haywood might realize from this effort would perhaps be for her intentional obliviousness as much as for her efforts in the production and distribution of the text. A tone of ambiguity and a lack of specificity or accountability suffuse all the depositions. Booksellers are conveniently absent when the pamphlets arrive, no printer or author is given, the number of copies sold is indefinite. No one can offer any precise information. Even the parties involved change within each deposition. Although Corbett and Barnes both mention William Hatchett, Haywood's longtime companion who allegedly monitored the distribution and sale of the pamphlets, Haywood and Stredden skillfully avoid mentioning him.[41] Even Haywood's claim that she had "lost her Eyesight about six months and kept to her bed above two months" metaphorically defines her basic function. While various medical reasons exist to explain temporary blindness, Haywood lived in a professional world where intentional "blindness" to certain activities could be a great asset.

Equally significant, perhaps, is Haywood's claim that "she has been an author many years but never wrote anything in a political way." This appeal, like her plea of blindness, was a common one in attempts to avoid prosecution or seek lenience. For example, hawker Daniel Lynch, arrested in December 1749 for selling obscene pamphlets, sought the government's "levity" since "he has never sold anything of a political nature, but always refused to do so, tho often entreated to sell them."[42] Unfortunately, Haywood's claim was less compelling. Attempting to assert her own innocence in this instance, Haywood denies a body of work that many would read as primarily political: her periodicals *The Tea Table* (1725) and *The Parrot* (1725) both deal on some level with political issues. One of her most pointedly anti-Walpole pieces, *The Adventures of Eovaai* (1736), was reprinted in 1741 as *The Unfortunate Mistress, or the Ambitious Statesman.* Jerry Beasley believes this indictment of Walpole is "as complete and as savage as anything to be found in the opposition press."[43] Its reappearance, especially when Haywood was also selling pamphlets, might have created some irritation or produced unwanted attention. Her 1746 periodical, also titled *The Parrot*, specifically addressed the political and topical concerns of a post-rebellion audience and depended on the political context for interest and marketability.[44]

Haywood's denial of political writing, given the amount of her work that could be considered political, might prompt us to reexamine the uses of that term and the commercial opportunities afforded by such a generic instability. Haywood may have had a fairly strict understanding of "political" as referring perhaps to something specific in its details, intention, or style. For the most part her work lacks what Ballaster terms "the 'insider's' knowledge that made Manley's work so threatening."[45] Most of Haywood's texts that we might now consider political are marked by a hybridization which complicates their generic categorization. Her periodicals contain vast amounts of fiction, her political satires use romantic tropes, and her novels describe political situations. In practical terms, this hybridization may have enhanced Haywood's ability to avoid prosecution until the 1749 pamphlet. In generic terms, it enabled her to present a broadly political message, but in a self-conscious manner that almost enabled a type of meta-commentary on both her own work and the subject at hand.

Her 1746 periodical *The Parrot* contains threads of the multiple discourses. An obvious attempt to capitalize on the continuing preoccupation with the

Jacobite Rebellion of 1745 and the public fascination with the Young Pretender, *The Parrot* depended on its political context for both its relevance and its commercial appeal. Published for nine weeks between August and October 1746, *The Parrot* addressed current events and offered a section called "A Compendium of the Times," a weekly summary of "Occurrences as appear Worthy Attention," primarily details about the trials of the participants in the '45. The material is presented with a tone of political consequence designed to meet what Haywood perceived as the market's desire for news, however speculative, about the Pretender and his followers. By contributing to and perhaps fueling that interest Haywood makes her periodical seem topical, lively, and cloaked in a mask of insider knowledge. However, she really only "parrots" commonly known information about trials, executions, and appointments that she could have collected from other publications.

Haywood presents the "news" in a non-journalistic style accessible to those who do not normally read political material and she typically highlights the personal aspect of an event.[46] For example, in the first issue of *The Parrot*, she describes the "true" story of an execution with hyperbolic language reminiscent of her romantic fiction. When Mr. James Dawson's fiancée finds he was to be executed on the previous Wednesday at Kennington-Common for High Treason, she suddenly dies. "That Excess of Grief ... it is thought, put a stop to the vital Motion, and suffocated, at once, all the animal Spirits." Haywood highlights the gossipy nature of her text by claiming the narrative, which "very much affected me," will similarly touch the reader and "all who hear it" – either through reading her text or through the subsequent oral transmission by those who read it there first.

Her informal, subtly oral tradition continues with her discussion of the Pretender himself. Haywood retells all the stories of the Pretender's escape from England, which have a topical appeal. But her rhetorical maneuvering renders her text multivalent and ultimately uninterpretable in terms of her own political affiliations. Everyone *except* Haywood is a source for this information. She highlights the untraceable, unsubstantiated, and ultimately insupportable assertions from disparate sources:

Some will have it that he is escaped to France; others that he went in an open Boat from one of the Islands of the Hebrides to the Coast of Norway; many will have it that he perished in that Attempt; and more that he was killed at South-Ulst; but our last Accounts tell us, that at present he is in the Isle of Sky, disguised in Women's apparel ... However that be, his Party is all defeated, so that we may be entirely easy as to that Point. (xx)

She simultaneously arouses her readers' interest with information about the Pretender's daring escapes while ostensibly disguising any danger he represents. Similarly she explains her consistent attention to the effects of the rebellion ("Northern Intelligence") by claiming that "loyal" subjects would want to be fully informed: "I know you have too loyal a heart, and too sound a Judgement, not to interest yourself more deeply in what is doing there [in the North] for the preventing all future disturbances, than for anything else I could present you with." Though "loyal" subjects might have an interest, the information may be even more gratifying to readers with Jacobite sympathies. With this technique, Haywood writes to two audiences simultaneously.

Haywood employs similar strategies with her overly enthusiastic praise of George II. She claims that the current Sovereign stands "in no need of . . . a Monitor," for he

centers all his Wishes in the Peace, Opulence and Glory of his Subjects . . . loves us as his children, and is so far from encroaching on our Rights, that he is himself the best Guardian of our Laws and Liberties . . . We know the Blessings we enjoy, and want not to be told any thing would diminish our content. Far be it from the Parrot to attempt it.

Such praise, while appropriate to the anxious atmosphere of a post-1745 environment, does not really bear intense scrutiny. The idealized paternalistic role she accords the monarch (consistent with Country Party ideology) borders on hyperbole suggestive of parody and indicates a potentially excessive amount of monarchical power. Statements such as "all statesmen are patriots," so obviously and recently disproved, suggest Haywood's ironic distance from her own language. She simultaneously indemnifies herself from prosecution by effusively praising George II, and sends out the thinly veiled or coded message that this praise represents an ideal which the monarch definitely does not fulfill. When she asserts he does not need a monitor, she strategically introduces the possibility that he does.

In appealing to a multiple reading public's political allegiances and consumer desires, Haywood also imitates and appropriates the generic expectations of the periodical (much as she does with *The Female Spectator*) in a way that subtly questions the politics of genre. *The Parrot*'s title indicates the unfailingly imitative nature of the publication and in a sense Haywood's broader actions in the marketplace – she is imitative by "parroting" both the rumors floating around her and the style of other periodicals. But it is only through parody, at this point, that she can confound the construction of her authorial persona. Her texts and her material actions "parrot" others in a manner that complicates her position in relation to the discursive community. She seems to be simultaneously engaging in an attempt to secure a commercial success (and ongoing periodical) while disengaging herself (and her own voice) through her imitative and repetitive gestures. (She also parrots herself as an embedded fictional story retells the same plot that she conveyed in *The Mercenary Lover*, complete with a suitor who encourages an innocent woman to read lascivious material.) In some ways, *The Parrot* anticipates *Betsy Thoughtless* in that both use to their own ends a popular or profitable genre in which Haywood wants to write but to which she is not fully committed. As a result her work seems slyly subversive or at times parodic. In *The Parrot*, her narrative technique potentially speaks not to her lack of specific knowledge about politics (although that is probably a factor) but to fundamental generic instabilities that characterize this literary period – was fiction "political"? was political writing "fictional"? To ensure the broadest consumer appeal, Haywood's dominant concern, she attempts to respond to multiple strains of discourse and thus disparate and potentially new readers.

Regardless of the generic categorization, political writing – of even this broad a nature – was commercially desirable and, in the case of Haywood, the "authenticity" of her political voice is really not the salient issue. Her narrative technique and multivalent voice locate the text within consumer culture and highlight the connection between politics and commerce, and the commercialization of political discourse. Haywood simultaneously exploits that connection with her pseudo-political discourse and criticizes those who attempt to profit from others' political misfortunes. The executions of the rebels "at present ... engross the Attention of the Town," creating new commercial opportunities but also diverting people from the usual pursuits of consumer culture. To compensate for the diversion, Haywood repeatedly puffs now-neglected goods or services for sale. She tells of "a certain English Lady of Quality" so taken with "the Person and Deportment of the Lord Kilmarnock at his Trial" that she has avoided all company since his death. Consequently, she has abandoned all social activities, including cards, "to the great mortification of Mr. Hoyle, who has long been her Master in the Art and Mystery of the Game of Whist." She distinguishes her presentation of political events from her literary competitors for, unlike "little Authors – Hackneys for the Publishers of Newspapers," she claims not to exploit the political passions of others or to "influence the low and unthinking Part of ... Readers." She criticizes other profit seekers who advertise their homes to individuals "desirous of beholding the executions." Both landlord and (temporary) tenant "would better have ... employed their Time and Money in a different manner." Of course Haywood herself depends on a reading public willing to spend "their time and money" to learn more about (indeed "behold") the executions through her periodical.

The Parrot's rhetorical and political ambiguity as well as its overtly commercial interest may be what allowed it to be produced and sold without any governmental attention. Although the level of concern for any sort of treasonable words, actions, or publications had been very high immediately following the rebellion of '45, Haywood's periodical avoids any inflammatory gestures and might seem particularly mild for the time. Yet her pamphlet, with its adoring representation of the Pretender, appeared when the government was increasingly concerned with publications that in any way tended to "disquiet the Minds of his Subject, hurt publick Credit, and diminish the regard and duty which they owe" the monarch.[47] Accordingly, the printers and publishers of *The London Evening Post* were investigated and prosecuted in November 1749 for printing "false news" about the king:

seditiously ... intending to insinuate and make it be believed and thought as if our said present Sovereign Lord the King was in an extreme bad state of Health and so ill that his life was greatly despaired of and that his Death would be a matter of great Joy to the Publick and more especially to all the subjects of the Kingdom having a right to vote in the election of Members to serve in the Parliament of this Kingdom.[48]

Attention was also focused on texts that were considered obscene; John Purser, publisher of *Ancient and Modern Pederasty Investigated and Exemplified*,[49] and Ralph Griffith, printer and publisher of "a scandalous and obscene Book entitled Memoirs of Fanny Hill," were both prosecuted.[50] There appears to have been a shift in interest toward the moral rather than political dangers of print, as well as a greater interest in publications that reported "facts" rather than fictionalized accounts of a political figure. The government action (or inaction), like Haywood's pamphlet, reveals the generic instabilities that still challenged authors and cultural perception more broadly.

Though considered a "person from the trade," Haywood clearly did not enjoy a great measure of success. Her inability to secure a foothold in the material production and sale of texts seems in one way a function of her class and relative lack of status rather than her gender. But gender cannot be ignored when we consider the more intangible (and perhaps more meaningful) relationships individuals have to sources of power. A month after the initial examination of the booksellers taken up for handling Haywood's text, one bookseller, John Jolliffe, wrote a letter to an unnamed government official in which he attempts to extricate himself from any involvement with Haywood's pamphlet.[51] In his letter he reveals that, if he "could produce a line from" this individual, Lord Stanhope would be persuaded to "erase [his] name" from the incident. Additionally, Jolliffee has applied to Lord Trentham, for whom he printed handbills in the last election. Lord Trentham, in turn, spoke to his Grace of Bedford on Jolliffee's behalf. The letter subtly reveals how a bookseller like Jolliffee could attempt to insulate himself from legal ramifications through a network of connections – Trentham, Stanhope, Bedford – in a way that someone like Haywood could not because of her fundamental lack of access to the mechanisms of power as well as the imbalance of economic power between the sexes.

Equally important, perhaps, is Jolliffee's attempt to distance himself from his association with someone as clearly peripheral to and low on the professional hierarchy as Haywood. He does not want to "erase his name" for purely legal reasons; he is concerned with his reputation, status, and prestige within the trade. As Terry Belanger suggests, the book trade "carried on its business largely by means of such interlocking sets of personal relationships" among a variety of publishers and, in this case, between a client and printer.[52] Jolliffee doesn't want to upset the (potentially delicate) relationship with a nobleman who has already employed him to print his handbills for his victorious election campaign. Nevertheless, Jolliffee's access to the lines of power, like his position within the trade, seems as clear as Haywood's does undefinable.

This entire incident underscores the varied, indeed hybrid, nature of Haywood's involvement with the print trade. The ambiguous nature of the pamphlet on the Pretender, like Haywood's multiple roles within the print trade, complicates and at times defies categorization. As a female author, she writes fictionalized political pieces that attempt to titillate, educate, and persuade. As a member of the trade, she performs (or delegates) duties of bookseller, printer, and author. However, she assumes no responsibility for those actions. She is everywhere, yet her presence is unmarked. As one bookseller admits, he "believes" Haywood is responsible for the pamphlet, "tho he has no ... reason for his belief." This episode seems almost a materialization of a recurring literary practice; Haywood touches every aspect of the creation and production of this pamphlet, just as in the 1720s she exerts a profound influence on contemporaneous and subsequent prose fiction. Nevertheless, she repeatedly fails to gain lasting currency in the material or symbolic economy of the literary marketplace.

3

With the 1751 novel *The History of Miss Betsy Thoughtless*, Haywood strives to improve her own marketability by ostensibly conforming to the desire for increasingly didactic fiction.[53] Beginning with the popularity of *Pamela* (1740) and the subsequent success of *Joseph Andrews* (1742), *Clarissa* (1747–48), and *Tom Jones* (1749), the decade of the 1740s saw what William Warner terms "the reformed novel" irrevocably change "the set of cultural practices called 'reading novels.'"[54] As literary historians have observed, the discursive construct traditionally recognized as "the novel" often involved the (typically instructive) adventures of a fictional subject in a series of romantic and social interactions frequently concluding with a marriage.[55] Haywood's text appears to follow that formula by providing the story of a young lady's (often precarious) entry into the world. Betsy confronts obstacles to her virtue, makes an ill-advised first marriage to Mr. Munden, and perseveres to be rewarded at the end with marriage to her appropriate match, Charles Trueworth. Despite its apparent conformity, *Betsy Thoughtless* shares its discursive agenda with a text like *Anti-Pamela*, which, with its parodic form, makes a cultural as well as literary critique. Both texts emphasize the inadequacy of the novel to represent the material conditions women confront in their own lives and the need for women to control any capital available to them. The texts' sexual and financial currencies complicate the construction of value, worth, and virtue, and affirm a woman's need for specific economic skills. *Betsy Thoughtless* interrogates and ultimately offers an alternative to the conventional morality that characterizes the novel. Through her skillful manipulation of generic expectations Haywood not only offers a critique of the novel's increasing didacticism, but also the ideology implicit in that genre. She resists the domesticated and domesticating female subjects prevalent at this time.[56] Instead, with a character like Betsy, she presents with great specificity a subject who negotiates a culture defined by material and symbolic economies.

Haywood avoids a predictable narrative trajectory and highlights the originality of her text. For example, the subheading to volume One, chapter I conveys the air of narrative uncertainty that pervades the whole novel. Haywood observes that it "Gives the reader room to guess at what is to ensue, tho' ten to one but he finds himself deceived" (9). She subtly asserts her authorial control while cultivating an ironic distance from her own text. At the beginning of each chapter, Haywood offers a preview of the contents with a subheading that provides a narrative guidepost.

Occasionally she hawks or puffs a chapter, assuring that it "will not tire the reader" or "let the reader fall asleep." Frequently she directs the reader's attention to important sections of the novel: volume Three chapter LI "Seems to be calculated rather for the instruction than entertainment of the reader" (308). Volume Four chapter LXXII "Contains among other particulars, certain bridal admonitions" (434). When approaching a particularly challenging chapter crucial to the plot, Haywood warns the inattentive reader that the section "Seems to demand, for more reasons than one, a greater share of attention than ordinary, in the perusal of it" (438). At one point she suggests, "If it were not for some particulars, [this chapter] might as well be passed over as read" (303).

Though Haywood's tone here and throughout emphasizes the fictionality – the "unrealness" – of the novel, she grounds her narrative in specific details of material culture. The price of clothing, carriages, food, and other consumer goods is discussed with great specificity. The first time Betsy spends money for clothes independently, the fabrics, style, and colors are described in a detailed manner that emphasizes not only the importance of the consumer goods but Betsy's understanding of their ability to enhance her desirability as a type of commodity: "As she was extremely curious in every thing relating to her shape, she made choice of a pink coloured French lustring, to the end, that the plaits lying flat, would shew the beauty of her waiste to more advantage" (41). Public entertainments, parks, streets, and pubs in London are recognizable. Characters arrange to meet at White's coffee house, Green Park, "the habit-shop, in Covent-garden" (27), or "at General Tatten's bench, opposite Rosamond's pond, in St. James's Park" (264). At certain points even specific addresses are given; Betsy calls for Miss Forward at "the house of one Mrs. Nightshade, in Chick-Lane, near Smithfield" (75). She can later be found at "Mr. Screener's, the very next door to Linko's Head, in Tavistock-street, in Covent Garden" (171). Haywood's specificity provides the opportunity for her well-known attack on Fielding's "scandal shop" stemming from Betsy's complaint about the absence of "public diversions worth seeing" (45). "There were no plays, no operas, no masquerades, no balls, no public shews, except at the little theatre in the Hay-Market, then known by the name of F—g's scandal shop; because he frequently exhibited there certain drolls, or, more properly, invectives against the ministry" (45).[57] The legal system – courts, types of lawsuits, punishment – is explored with careful attention.[58] All the characters demonstrate a keen knowledge of their financial situation. When Lady Mellasin's "stolen" necklace is pawned, its price of "a hundred and thirty guineas" is detailed (106). The debt she runs up, and for which Mr. Goodman is later arrested, is noted as "two thousand, five hundred, and seventy-five pounds, eight shillings" (218).

The myriad details Haywood provides contrast sharply with the text's obvious, almost parodic use of names: "Trueworth," "Goodman," "Chatfree," "Forward," and of course "Thoughtless." In the context of such cultural detail, these names underscore the genre's inability to be both didactic and "real." Haywood expresses a similar concern with the moral issues central to a didactic novel when she uses negative models to instruct the reader. Miss Forward illustrates the dangers of sexual promiscuity; she speaks plainly of her unwanted pregnancy, her search for an abortion, her activities as a prostitute, and her ultimate decline into debtors' prison. Haywood foregrounds such issues to illustrate material realities typically ignored or discussed obliquely in contemporaneous fiction.

By interrogating some of the generic characteristics of the novel, Haywood reveals the ideological structures that dictate those conventions. The most striking example is her treatment of marriage. Haywood frustrates readers' expectation that novels will conclude with a romantic union. Betsy's unromantic, ill-fated marriage to Mr. Munden enables Haywood to explore the cultural construction of marriage in contrast with its social practice. In presenting the series of problems in the Munden relationship, Haywood details the cumulative domestic abuses and subtle exertions of power that can render marriage intolerable. Before the wedding, Betsy wonders "what can make the generality of women so fond of marrying? ... [is it] not a greater pleasure to be courted ... by a number, than be confined to one, who from a slave becomes a master, and, perhaps, uses his authority in a manner disagreeable enough" (431). Although aware of the potential shift in control when a suitor becomes a husband, Betsy is unprepared for Munden's behavior. He denies her even limited power and, consistent with the cultural expectations for the institution, "he considered a wife no more than an upper servant, bound to study and obey, in all things" (448). Appropriate to Haywood's emphasis on economy, money becomes one of the primary problems in Betsy's marriage. Munden accuses his wife of being a "bad oeconomist" and reminds her that, to his mind, one of her main duties is "to be frugal with her husband's money" (440–41). He begrudges her pin money, "since a woman ought to have nothing apart from her husband," and wants her to use it to defray household expenses (442). Her confidante Lady Trusty, with advice consistent with conduct books, urges her to "behave, as if entirely unconcerned, contented, and easy ... let every thing you urge on this occasion, be accompanied with all the softness it is in your power to assume" (445). By reiterating social expectations for the appropriate behavior of a wife and then, in turn, demonstrating their damaging conse- quences, Haywood highlights the discrepancy between theory and practice. Despite Munden's escalating abuse, until he boards his mistress under the same roof as his wife, Betsy lacks a socially sanctioned reason to leave him. Legally, Munden retains control over Betsy, forcing her to escape to the country where he cannot find her; even then he threatens to exercise his rights, send a constable after her, and confine her in his home. Betsy's experience implicitly critiques the generic and ideological expecta- tions of novels which represent marriage as a triumphant conclusion rather than a problematic beginning.

In addition to reflecting on these conventions, Haywood comments on her own literary past when she devalues the language and characteristics of her fiction popular in the 1720s. Early in the text Betsy assumes that a suitor's failure to appear at the appointed time signaled his demise: "Death only she thought could be an excuse for him, and had that happened she should have heard of it" (30). Like Arabella in *The Female Quixote*, Betsy applies fictional models to her own life; and like Charlotte Lennox, Haywood wants to undermine the potency of those models. For example, the letters of F. Fineer, a valet masquerading as a baron, are filled with the romantic hyperbole that earlier Haywood characters use with regularity:

I am grieved to the very soul, to hear you have any subject for affliction; but am very certain, that in being deprived of your divine presence, I endure a more mortal stab than any loss you have sustained can possibly inflict. – I am consumed with the fire of my passion: – I have taken neither repose, nor food, since first I saw you: I have lived only on the idea of your charms: – O! nourish me with the substance! – Hide me in your bosom from the foul fiend despair, that is just, ready to lay hold on me. (298)

Though typical in a Haywood novel of thirty years earlier, such language has no value in this text and its use signals Fineer's low social class and sinister intentions. (It is as though he is thirty years behind in his reading and participating in a plot with completely different narrative conven- tions.)

Haywood consciously departs from the linguistic characteristics of her earlier fiction, though she continues to depict the dual economies of finance and sexuality in which a woman must circulate. From the perspec- tive of her guardian and her brothers Betsy is a commodity on the market to be purchased by the highest bidder. Betsy, however, does not have the same expectations. In both the lived material economy of consumer

culture and the symbolic economy of sexuality and marriage Betsy wants
to be autonomous. An avid consumer, she desires free access to the marketplace and control over any monetary or sexual capital she possesses.

Betsy initially signals her desire for control by demanding to handle her
own money while still under the protection of her guardian, Mr.
Goodman. Unhappy with the silk Goodman's wife Lady Mellasin selected
for her, Betsy requests

that out of the income of my fortune, thirty pounds a year should be allowed for
my board, twenty pounds for my pocket expenses, and fifty for my cloaths, I think
I ought to have the two latter entirely at my own disposal, and to lay it out as I
think fit, and not be obliged, like a charity-child, to wear whatever livery my
benefactor shall be pleased to order. (40–41)

Goodman gives Betsy the money she requests, but requires the guarantee
of fiscal responsibility: "You shall have the sum you mention, Miss Betsy
. . . but I would have you manage with discretion, for you may depend, that
the surplus of what was at first agreed upon, shall not be broke into, but
laid up to increase your fortune, which, by the time you come of age, I
hope, will be pretty handsomely improved" (41). Ready cash, consumerism,
and Betsy's desire to "lay out" her money contrast sharply with
Goodman's demand that she "lay up" investments and leave the principal
untouched.

Betsy's consumer impulses also take control in the symbolic though
equally manifest economy of heterosexual relationships. Circulating in
that economy, Betsy implicitly markets her sexuality to acquire power over
men which, she believes, will give her the ability to make better decisions
about her future. Though an eager participant in that economy, she lacks
the ability to discriminate among suitors; she fails to discern the relative
value of an individual: "Pleased with the praise, she regarded not the
condition or merits of the praiser, and suffered herself to be treated,
presented, and squir'd about all public places, either by the rake, the man
of honour, the wit, or the fool, the married as well as the unmarried, without distinction, and just as either fell in her way" (35–36). Women like
Betsy, who take a quantitative perspective, value themselves on "the
number and quality of their lovers, as they do upon the number and rich-
ness of their cloths, because it makes them of consideration in the world,
and [they] never take the trouble of reflecting how dear it may sometimes
cost those to whom they are indebted for indulging this vanity" (115). Men
function like any other consumer good one has the capital to purchase.
Although Trueworth declares himself as Betsy's suitor (and her fiancé
if she would accept him), she resists losing her ability to operate in an

economy which she believes requires nothing from her, but which repeat-edly affirms her value and worth: "to become a matron at my years is what I cannot brook the thoughts of; – if he [Trueman] loves me, he must wait, – it will be sufficient to receive the addresses of no other; but then how may I refuse those who shall make an offer of them, without giving the world room to believe I am pre-engaged?" (178). Avaricious in "affairs of love," Betsy wants to continue to circulate – socially, physically, geographically – without restraint.

Although Betsy wants to participate in a heterosexual economy, she refuses to acknowledge the terms of exchange it ultimately demands: "unreasonable, and indeed unjust, was she in the affairs of love: – in all others she was humane, benevolent, and kind; but here covetous, even to a greediness, of receiving all, without any intention of making the least return" (303). Betsy's quantitative fervor and her desire to accumulate rather than expend contributes to her inability to understand what her own behavior signifies. She fails to recognize what she might "owe" or "earn" from a lover as a result of her actions within the established dis-course of sexual courtship. For example, early in the novel, Betsy flirts with Mr. Gayland to make her first suitor, Saving, jealous. She intends only to exercise her power over both men by provoking their emotional reaction, but Gayland interprets her seductive demeanor as a specific sexual overture:

Dear Miss,

I must certainly be either the most ungrateful, or most consumedly dull fellow upon earth, not to have returned the advances you have been so kind to make me ... I have found out a way to pay you the whole sum with interest; – which is this: You must invent some excuse for going out alone, and let me know by a billet directed for me at White's, the exact hour, and I will wait for you at the corner of the street in a hackney coach, – the window drawn up, and whirl you to a pretty snug place I know of, where we may pass a delicious hour or two, without a soul to interrupt our pleasures. (22–23)

He believes he "owes" Betsy, and she him, and expresses his willingness to pay "the whole sum with interest." He delights in the perceived terms of the agreement. Betsy, though newly conscious of "having, by a too free behaviour toward him, emboldened him to take this liberty" (23), does not alter her behavior.

When visiting her brother in Oxford with Miss Flora, she again places herself in a situation where she is expected "to pay the [sexual] debt, which love, and youth, and beauty challenge" (51). Similarly, Betsy's behavior and association with Miss Forward cause Sir Basil Loveit to mistake Betsy for a prostitute and offer her specific remuneration for sexual favors: "I will make you a handsome present before we part, and if you can be constant will allow you six guineas a week" (204). As a result of her vanity and her acquisitiveness, Betsy repeatedly finds herself owing men sexual currency she is unwilling (and often unaware of needing) to pay.[59] Her guardian Mr. Goodman is concerned that Betsy will circulate to the point that she loses her value within a heterosexual economy, that she will, "as the old saying is, out-stand her market" (108). In fact, Betsy's experiences prompt Trueworth's withdrawal of his marriage offer, resulting in her union with Munden.

However, marriage does not diminish Betsy's wish to inspire desire in men. In fact, her vanity places her in a compromising position when she is approached by a potential patron of her husband's. Smitten with Betsy, Lord — writes her a letter that indicates the sexual nature of his interest. "[H]er vanity was delighted with the conquest she had made," although her pride and virtue recoil at the "audacious" manner he uses; nevertheless she believes it in her power to avoid "receiving any farther insults from him" (480–81) upon his invitation to dinner. When he sends her husband out on a feigned errand and traps her alone in his house, she faces the most clearly defined exchange in the novel. Claiming her "generous consenting to reward my passion" would cement the union between him and her husband, Lord — attempts to coerce her into sex by appealing to her husband's financial interest: "I should then love him [Munden] not only for his own, but for your sake also, and should think myself bound to stretch my power to its extremest limits to do him service: – be assured, my angel, that in blessing me you fix the happiness of your husband, and establish his future fortune in the world" (511). Lord — insists that he "could name some husbands, and those of the first rank, too ... who, to oblige a friend, and for particular reasons, have consented to the complaisance of their wives in this point" (487). Betsy resists his advances, but when she describes the encounter to her husband, he demonstrates a greater concern for his financial situation than for her sexual or moral one. To Munden's mind, Betsy's sexual modesty is merely another example of her unwillingness to pay what she owes him or Lord —.

Though Betsy's refusal to pay manifests itself in specifically sexual ways, she often becomes indebted in terms of common courtesy or established courtship rituals. For example, she acquires an "immensely rich" suitor in Captain Hysom, who has "twenty-five years in the service of the East India Company" (104). Captain Hysom possesses the wealth but not the social position to make him an appropriate suitor or spouse for Betsy (to her mind). She encourages his addresses, as she does all others, out of vanity; but her unwillingness to make a commitment or "close the deal" elicits a violent response from the Captain, for whom courtship is another type of business. His inability to obtain a commitment – or even any attention – from Betsy prompts him to visit her persistently. Betsy accuses him of talking "in an odd manner" and causing other suitors present to "think I have out-run my income, and that you come to dun me for money borrowed of you" (119). She conflates the practices of the sexual and financial economy. Dunning for money or for an emotional commitment are indistinguishable. Hysom's reply indicates he regards courtship no differently than any other business and, to his mind, Betsy has been acting in bad faith: " '[M]adam, I should be glad to know some answer to the business I wrote to you upon' – 'Lord, sir!' replied she, 'I have not yet had time to think upon it, – much less to resolve upon any thing.' " He can't wait for her to decide because "I have a great deal of business upon my hands . . . all the morning I am engaged either at the India-House, or at 'Change" (119). For a businessman like Hysom, time is money and to woo someone without the possibility of marriage is a bad investment.[60]

The one exchange Betsy is willing to make anticipates her eventual union with Trueworth. She eagerly pays for a miniature portrait of Trueworth commissioned for his fiancée, Harriet Loveit. When Betsy's brother "cursorily mentioned" having seen the finished portrait, Betsy wants to be "the mistress of what she so much desired" (393), just as she does another suitor: "she longed to have in her possession so exact a resemblance of a man, who had once loved her, and for whom she had always the most high esteem" (393). Though she had earlier refused Trueworth's offer of marriage, her feelings for him were rekindled when he rescued her from the attempted rape of "Frederic Fineer." Rather than carry the portrait as a token from a conquest, Betsy wants it as a reminder of the debt she is unable (but willing) to assume: "the obligation I have to him, – I might forget it else" (393). At the painter's shop, she has the opportunity to acquire the portrait without actually purchasing it, for the artist assures her "I shall see Mr. Trueworth again" (395). In a departure from previous behavior, however, Betsy refuses to "take it without paying" and reckons the 10 guineas well spent. "[T]he success of her enterprize elated her beyond expression" (395). Ironically, Trueworth's portrait, by design, functions literally in the way Betsy regards all men metaphorically: as an ornament, a possession designed to adorn or enhance her appearance. At this point, Betsy can have Trueworth only in that abstract way, although the miniature acts as the device that reunites the two lovers. Later, when the widowed Trueworth discovers Betsy crying over his portrait (which she carries at all times), he realizes the nature of her feelings, and marries Betsy one year after her husband's convenient death.

Rather than diminishing her worth, Betsy's failed marriage, like her mishaps with other men, increases her value within the novel's larger economy. The last sentence of the text reminds us that "the virtues of our heroine (those follies that had defaced them being fully corrected) at length rewarded with a happiness, retarded only till she had render'd herself wholly worthy of receiving it" (568). The experiences provide the sobriety, maturity, and modesty Betsy needs. She retains her frugality while tempering her consumerism to become the good economist she always claimed to be. The comic resolution, the idealization of Trueworth, and the self-conscious (at times parodic) moral platitudes are among the characteristics that make the text consistent with the tone and temper of the reformed novel. Yet, as the previous section suggests, Betsy's vanity, poor judgment, and disastrous marriage allow Haywood to critique the emergent novelistic conventions and offer an alternative model of fictional practice and social action.

Though *Betsy Thoughtless* is significantly more complicated in terms of plotting, character development, and social commentary than Haywood's earlier fiction, like most of her work, it illustrates how a woman must negotiate the play of power in the sexual, social, and financial economies of eighteenth-century England. She discursively revises the culture's construction of gender and suggests ways women can control the currency available to them as they act as economic and political subjects. Producing texts that simultaneously conform to and subvert the increasingly codified conventions of the bourgeois novel, Haywood also attempts to control her own currency – her paper credit – through a carefully shaded relationship with her professional contemporaries within an imaginative and material literary economy.

Haywood's cultural significance seems, at this point, undeniable. An exploration of her complicated, unorthodox, indeed hybrid professional life highlights both the possibilities and limitations of paper credit. Her previously unknown activities as a producer and distributor of material texts force us to reconsider the hierarchical structure of the print trade. While, in part because of class and gender, she was unable to combine the production of literary texts and material commodities as someone like Richardson could, her experience illuminates our reading of his professional activities. Similarly, detailed reconsiderations of her extremely popular fiction prove her to be a novelist who records and, in turn, contributes to, the texture of subtle social interaction. Yet her personal notoriety alternately hindered and enhanced the reception and circulation of her fiction among her contemporaneous, if not our contemporary, critics. Despite Haywood's attempt to establish a significant presence within eighteenth-century culture and to complicate her literary persona, until recently she has remained known primarily for her amatory fiction, her representation in the *Dunciad*, and her allegedly scandalous personal history. Her position as an author engaged in complex narratives about sexual and financial economies has often gone unnoted. Her texts, as her return to the novel with *Betsy Thoughtless* indicates, marked an important and sustained development in the discourse of popular fiction. And, as the next chapter's discussion of Samuel Richardson suggests, it is apparent we can no longer write the literary history of this period without acknowledging her distinct presence and her inventive, if not always successful, use of paper credit.

CHAPTER FIVE

Samuel Richardson and the domestication of paper credit

At the beginning of Samuel Richardson's *Pamela; or Virtue Rewarded* (1740), Pamela sends her parents four gold guineas she has received from Mr. B, advising them to put half of it toward their "old debt" and the other half toward their "comfort."[1] When she discovers they have "laid it up in a rag among the thatch," because of their concern for the origin of that money, Pamela chides them for hoarding it and urges them to "make *use* of the money" (29, emphasis mine). While Pamela's specific instructions are consistent with a dutiful daughter interested in her parents' welfare, they more strikingly reveal her approach toward economics. Money, property, and capital, in any form, are, to Pamela's mind, designed to be put to use, to be invested for a profit, to bear some form of interest. She recognizes the need to circulate and invest rather than just save one's capital. Many scholars have observed Pamela's preoccupation with money, a trait consistent with the stereotypical habits of a mercantile middle class; indeed, one critic describes Pamela's letters as a "bourgeois autobiography."[2] Certainly we see numerous examples of her accounting abilities, her shrewd financial assessment of other (often male) characters, and her recognition that most aspects of the socio-cultural world are determined by the absence or presence of money. But Pamela is not simply thrifty or desirous of accumulated goods. Her more pressing concern is with a type of speculative investment that makes her, in essence, a domestic stock-jobber. During the course of the novel, she departs from the material world of real, tangible goods (for which she never loses interest) as she becomes increasingly fascinated with the imaginative world of paper credit and the possibilities it holds. Though Pamela lacks access to public financial opportunities like investment in a joint-stock company, she constructs a domestic speculative economy that allows her to produce, manipulate, and ultimately profit from her own paper credit.

Though the suggestion that Pamela is a "domestic" stock-jobber is, perhaps, metaphorical on one level, it is also much more than that. *Pamela,* with its representation of paper credit and speculative investment, functions as a vehicle for transformative cultural practice. Despite the title page's reference to Pamela as "a beautiful young damsel," a gesture removing her from the "real" world, the language of Richardson's novel locates his female subject firmly in a material culture preoccupied with credit, speculation, and intangible forms of property. The key terms of speculative finance (credit, interest, project) appear in Richardson's novel and indicate the inextricable connection between the practices of divergent domestic and financial spheres. We cannot remove such a popular fictional text from the public field of cultural discourse; the material and symbolic practices of the novel and the activities of Exchange Alley are connected and mutually informing, both circulating within a relationally configured culture. *Pamela*, deeply embedded in the newly dominant economic practices, vividly illustrates the relationship of an emergent "economic" subject to the financial, social, and political structures in which she lives.

Like a stock-jobber in Exchange Alley, Pamela speculatively deals in symbolic instruments of exchange on her own account. She transforms the good opinion and fine reputation she has within the household (a measure of her worth based on past behavior) into a growing source of credit (faith in her future value and performance). She further invests in her self for herself by creating her own negotiable paper or "paper credit," letters and a journal which act as an indicator of her worth. When placed in circulation – with her parents, Mr. B, or Mr. B's social circle – Pamela's written accounts of her relationship with B provide her with a growing amount of imaginative "capital" with which to trade or invest within the closed economy of the novel. This production of symbolic capital would have no value if Pamela did not recognize a potential investor in Mr. B, and her letters and journal act as an *ad hoc* stock prospectus. B already understands and participates in the speculative financial economy, having invested "large sums in government securities, as well as in private hands" (392); he proves equally willing to participate in Pamela's speculative domestic economy. Pamela simultaneously jobs her paper credit while acting as a projector for her own stock scheme: Pamela as joint-stock company. Finally, however, she uses her accumulated interest to translate the credit she has accrued (a term with significance within an economic system or marketplace) into virtue, a concept whose meaning extends beyond the domestic stock exchange Pamela creates, and gains currency within the (idealized) moral economy represented by Mr. B. As Pamela transforms Mr. B's estimation of her from that of a "saucebox" to his "own true virtuous Pamela," by presenting her virtue as a textual construction within an imaginatively understood value system, she implicitly invites Mr. B and the reader to invest in her accounts.

The emergent practices associated with speculative investment achieved an expanding cultural dominance that *Pamela* records and sustains. The manipulative pattern of ascent Pamela follows, when practiced by a stock-jobber or a woman with the means to invest speculatively, was at one time a source of profound cultural anxiety. As chapter 1 details, participants in the new financial activities were represented as emotional, frequently hysterical, creatures susceptible to the vagaries of the marketplace. Women investors were depicted as sexually and financially avaricious subjects whose pursuit of "pleasure" and "business" was often mutually reinforcing. The figure of the female investor, or even the feminized economic man, circulating within the public economic sphere created apprehension about the erosion of always tenuous cultural distinctions. The ease with which individuals could acquire and manipulate credit – and by extension the cultural markers of class it afforded – bespoke what Michael McKeon terms the "status inconsistency" so disturbing to Augustan critics.[3] The hierarchical categories of class, property, and even gender potentially suffered a fundamental instability. Of course *Pamela* engendered criticism with its representation of a penetrable class hierarchy, a representation that replicated the type of social mixing resisted by members of the gentry and aristocracy. Yet, by making the transgressive individual a beautiful young serving girl and, in turn, by containing the site of class disruption within B's household (and within romantic fiction), Richardson strategically deflects the anxiety about the practices associated with speculative investment and, thus, uses *Pamela* as a vehicle for the domestication of paper credit.

The system of financial speculation Pamela's ascent exploits has its origins in the new financial practices of the 1690s which introduced England to the possibility of different forms of property.[4] As discussed in previous chapters, the innovations of credit and speculative investment – a constellation of economic activities now referred to as the "financial revolution" – represented a stark departure from the relationship between the citizen and the state fostered by the idealized tradition of civic humanism which located the foundations of citizenship in the owning of land. From participation in a system of landed property, the citizen not only constructed a public personality, but also achieved virtue – "civic virtue" – that influenced his actions. Unlike land, the new forms of property – stocks, lottery tickets, all forms of negotiable paper – were inherently intangible and seemingly not grounded in "real" things. Such property had an imaginary basis, and the relationship between sign and signified, between stock and value, depended on the fluctuations of the market-place.

Originally, resistance to "paper credit" arose in part because of its fundamental insubstantiality. It represented only a promise, not a tangible good.[5] Repayment of any investment, whether in a joint-stock company or government stock, was constantly deferred to a future moment that could only be imaginatively conceived, never actually reached.[6] Investors pay for the opportunity to profit (potentially) from intangible, indeed imaginary, possibilities. Consequently, speculative investment essentially required participation in a fictional narrative about the continuing worth of a stock or company; it relied on fantasy rather than reason and stimu-lated the passions, emotions, and imagination of the individual investors. The initial desire with which an investor participates had to be sustained – and its consummation deferred – indefinitely. The prolonging and pre-sumably heightening – the arousing and deferring – of desire was what enabled the continued process of investment. A stock-jobber had to make an emotional as well as economic investment to sustain the financial narrative in which he or she chose to participate. The "economic man" who participated in this kind of financial narrative privileged his imagina-tion, emotions, and desires, and resided in a world of inherently unstable values such as opinion and credit. "Investing men were now expected to be obsessed with what others thought, or might think of them," observes J. G. A. Pocock. "The creature of the credit mechanism must be a creature of passion, fantasy and other-directedness."[7] The emotional aspects of this persona, seemingly "natural" to a teenage girl like Pamela, also con-tributed to the perception of this figure as "feminized."

While speculative investment and the intangible nature of credit caused conservative cultural critics to view the practices associated with Exchange Alley as potential for social disruption, by mid-century the figure of the moneyed or "economic" man, like the forms of negotiable paper with which he dealt, was gradually assimilated into a larger system of national interests.[8] The increasing dependence on and connection with credit and investment by both the aristocracy and the middle classes made it necessary to recuperate, as far as possible, the symbolic and material practices associated with speculative finance. The aristocracy recognized the need to diversify investments, and the opportunity to capitalize on the new financial instruments proved, for many, irresistible.[9] Similarly, the middle classes wanted to legitimize and thus stabilize their position by combating their connection with the more speculative and passionate aspects of trade. This move was motivated, in part, by a Whig desire to accommodate innovative finance with the language of traditional cultural ideals as credit was translated into a new kind of virtue.[10] Instead of being a marker of aristocratic status or referring to "civic virtue," virtue assumed a more practical and practiced existence and now relied on industry, "talent, frugality and application."[11] Isaac Kramnick observes that "self-centered economic productivity, not public citizenship, became the badge of the virtuous man."[12] The redefinition of the concepts of virtue, independence, and citizenship changed the terms of the evaluative discourse. This transformative process not only elevated the status of the economic man, but also solidified the connection between credit and virtue. Just as one could redirect one's passions into interests, the cultural mechanisms also existed to turn one's credit into virtue. Passions and the desire for credit they aroused, previously seen as self-directed and residing in the imaginary realm, were converted into a type of virtue and an interest for the whole of society, indeed the nation.

Translating passions into interests and credit into virtue contributed to eighteenth-century culture's assimilation of the concept of paper credit. It also marked an increasing understanding of and participation in the narrative possibilities, similar to those on which the novel as a genre relied, demanded by speculative investment. Investing in a stock or reading a fictional narrative depends on needs, desires, and fantasies, just as an understanding of Pamela's writings demands an investment in both the romantic fiction she creates and the volatile paper credit that comprises her virtue. *Pamela* explores the cultural use of narratives to make meaning, create value, and, ultimately, construct virtue. The text illustrates fictional or financial narratives' power to entrance, indeed seduce, a willing reader or investor. Its preoccupation with investing and ultimately profiting from different forms of property also provides economic models for its readers. The "ideal" reader would learn to recognize and use wisely her sexual, financial, and textual capital. By illustrating the power of participation in constructed narratives, whether literary or financial, Richardson's novel records and advances the process of cultural transformation similarly enabled by speculative investment.

This chapter explores how *Pamela* contributed to the cultural "domestication" of paper credit and the narrative demands of speculative investment. The first section discusses Richardson's dual role as a printer and a novelist. His texts' engagement with economy, credit, and speculative investment stems in part from Richardson's own extensive participation in the new financial structures. As a printer, he understood and benefited from many of the innovations created by the new financial instruments and the expanding system of credit. As a novelist, Richardson invested in the constitutive power of (credit-able) narratives to construct and transform reality. Indeed, as the second section argues, by representing Pamela as a successful "domestic stock-jobber," Richardson discursively recuperates the more unstable elements of speculative investment.

I

Richardson operated in a culture irrevocably altered by the social and economic changes introduced by the financial revolution. His printing and his writing were two mutually enabling activities inextricably linked to and dependent on paper credit, and they allowed him to exploit the economic and symbolic value of his involvement in print culture. He and his own rise to prosperity suggest the broader cultural transformation *Pamela* illustrates. Richardson translated a profession (both printing and writing) and product (texts as imaginative and material commodities) based on inherently unstable signifying systems into a tangible (and certainly profitable) commodity. His professional life was defined by various types of speculative activities ranging from his role as a shareholder in the English Stock to his primary concerns for the commercial success of the texts he printed. Richardson benefited from the increasing mobility and economic openness that characterized his social milieu as he transformed himself from an industrious apprentice suffering from, in his own words, "narrowness of fortune ... his situation for many years producing little but prospects of a numerous family," into one of the leading printers of his time.[13] Richardson believed in the value of investing in himself, and in the perceived rewards of frugality, and moral and financial self-management – his position was defined by the expanding notions of virtue he presents in *Pamela*.[14]

Richardson's profession and the activities in his printing shop located him at the nexus of numerous social, commercial, and financial interactions. As a clearing house for various goods, his shop, perhaps like the tavern or coffee house, emerges as a site for diverse exchanges.[15] His advertisements in *The Daily Journal* seek the return of lost or stolen goods and list disparate consumer items including "a hundredweight of raw coffee, five yards of cambric, two yards of muslin, a canvas bag, a fiftypound bank note, an old blue grogam gown, and two ells of new Holland."[16] If Richardson's daily interactions introduced him to heterogeneous commercial activities, his involvement with the Stationers'

Company and its joint-stock company, the English Stock, inextricably connected him with speculative financial activities. The Stationers' Company was the livery for individuals such as printers, booksellers, bookbinders, or papermakers who participated in the authorized production and sale of books. The company was unique among liveries because it supported itself with what was essentially a joint-stock company, the English Stock.[17] Chartered in 1603 and operated from Stationers' Hall, the English Stock was a book-producing and book-wholesaling organization that derived its profit from the company's monopoly rights on almanacs, psalms, Psalters, and primers, all perennially popular and profitable texts. Once admitted to the livery, members could be voted the right to purchase stock in an amount predetermined by their rank within the company. Dividends on this stock were high, 12½ percent, and holding shares conferred not just prestige within the livery but real economic rewards. Consequently, the "business of the English Stock and the business of the Company were difficult if not impossible to keep separate," suggests Cyprian Blagden.[18] Stock-holders at all levels of the trade wanted the dividend to remain constant so they might reap the financial benefits, and the financial structure fostered the lesser members' support of their superiors.

In one sense, the existence of the English Stock and the ambition to purchase gradually larger shares when available complicated the professional pattern of stationers. The individual voted the opportunity to purchase a share and possessing the start-up capital could dramatically change or improve his path within the company. Not every member of the company could hold shares. The number of shares remained relatively constant while the number of members did not – in fact, the Stationers' Company experienced more growth than any other livery in the eighteenth century. Consequently, keen competition for shares existed among liverymen.[19] The distribution of shares was further complicated by the fact that widows of liverymen could collect their annual dividend until they remarried. Although the difference between those who could and could not hold shares created a gap within the livery, those who did not yet own shares, or as large a share as they wished, were still implicated in the cycle of investment as all members strove to be participants in the English Stock. Holding stock offered further financial opportunities since, as liverymen discovered, one's holdings could be mortgaged to raise additional capital if needed.[20] Shares in the English Stock provided a type of built-in credit.

Most significant, however, is the position in which the English Stock placed liverymen in terms of eighteenth-century culture. Not only were members of the trade concerned with the daily operations of their own mercantile existence (whether the sale of books and paper, or the printing of a text), they also participated in the financial narratives necessarily demanded by all speculative investment. The financial structure of the livery relied on an ability to envisage the improvement, enhancement, and, most important, continuation of the English Stock in which they had an emotional and financial investment. At a fundamental level, the Stationers' Company, the authorized organ of the print trade, depended upon, invested in, and was epistemologically attuned to the narrative and imaginative prerequisites of speculative investment.[21]

As a highly ranked member in the livery, Richardson benefited considerably from the opportunities afforded by the English Stock. His rise through the Stationers' Company was steady but by no means meteoric. At the beginning of his career in 1727 he was elected renter-warden (or steward) of the company. Although the position had no real responsibility, aside from collecting fees from liverymen and contributing financially to the banquet on Lord Mayor's Day, it provided a certain prestige and enabled Richardson's initial investment in the English Stock. After his election in 1727, he was, in February 1731, voted a £40 or half-yeomanry share in the English Stock. During the next twenty years, Richardson gained progressively larger holdings in the English Stock until, as the senior member of the court of the assistant, he was voted the largest possible share, £320, which provided annual interest of £40.[22]

Participation in the English Stock, coupled with Richardson's numerous other investments, exposed him to the cultural practice and financial possibilities of speculative investment. What little is known about Richardson's financial situation also suggests that he invested in government securities and various annuities. His business activities, like his personal finances, which included the continued renting and improvement of various properties, indicate his reliance on and profit from the economic framework established by the financial revolution. In his edition of *Aesop's Fables* (1739), he describes how he witnessed "the South-Sea Project, the Bank Contract, the Charitable-Corporation Bubble, and twenty others that might be named in this Age so fruitful of such Projects" absorbing the possibilities and consequences of new financial schemes.[23] Richardson's actions within the marketplace as both a printer and a novelist demonstrate his understanding of the literary text itself as a type of speculative commodity. For example, his considerable copyright holdings indicate his ability to recognize the immediate and long-term benefits of a publication and regard it as another type of investment.[24] The copyright itself, like a piece of stock, is intangible, a somewhat imaginary concept – the possession not of a material object but of the right to reproduce an imaginative property in the future. Richardson capitalized on the financial (and later aesthetic) possibilities of a text, the interests and concerns of a disparate reading public, and the potential long-term profitability of both.[25] Richardson was also the printer for a number of the congers, associations of booksellers or wholesalers who largely controlled the production and distribution activities of the trade. Through his careful alliances with congers, "Richardson made most of the profit that did not come to him as an author or printer."[26]

In addition to understanding the financial implications of copyrights and calculated business connections, Richardson was also clearly very attuned to the dangers of governmental scrutiny, the strategies of protection against official harassment, and the cycles of the commercial marketplace. Early in his career, he published a series of often political newspapers such as *The True Briton* (1723–24); printing newspapers was typically a financially advantageous venture. In this publication and others, Richardson strategically avoided putting himself at risk, especially early in his career, and he shielded himself from government harassment or prosecution. "Richardson's name never appears on the colophon of any newspaper, even of those he was certainly printing," note Eaves and Kimpel.[27] Instead he often used the name of less respectable printers for he possessed the status and power to hire others as professional scapegoats (much as Haywood was used for the pamphlet on the Pretender).[28]

Richardson also had a well-documented flair for marketing and self-promotion. In fact, McKillop asserts that Richardson's connections in the trade gave *Pamela* unusual advantages in advertising that might have contributed to the text's overwhelming popularity. He had "to his credit a large stock of goodwill in the commercial sense . . . [and] . . . the book was published under conditions much more favorable than those usually enjoyed by works of fiction."[29] Richardson also inserted "puffs" in the prefaces he wrote for the books he published as a subtle form of advertising that kept his name in the commercial discourse. For example, in the fourth edition of Defoe's *Complete English Tradesmen* (1737/38), Richardson recommends the *Plain Dealer* ("an excellent collection of papers") which he published, and *The Apprentice's Vade Mecum*, "a little Piece . . . which, besides some other very needful things, contain[s] general Rules and Directions for a Young Man's Behaviour in his Apprenticeship."[30] After the publication of *Pamela*, "a curious attempt was made for a time to attract attention" to Richardson's edition of *Aesop's Fables* (1740) "by advertising it as the edition of Aesop quoted in *Pamela*."[31] And of course the succession of revised editions and supplementary texts following the first edition of *Clarissa* enabled him to remain visible in the literary marketplace. Like other publishers, Richardson also understood the significance of a book's date and season of publication. If he published something late in the fall, he would usually date the imprint a year ahead to increase its timeliness and sense of freshness or innovation. As Sale notes, he also had a "dislike of publishing before the sitting of Parliament in the autumn, or after the rising of Parliament and the emptying of the town in the spring."[32] While Richardson operated at a (slightly) higher, more prestigious level, his manipulation of the marketplace resembled the actions of someone like Edmund Curll. Richardson's moral, cautious, and typically bourgeois publications distinguish them from the more sensational and prurient texts published by Curll, but Richardson depended no less on the commercialization of literature, the profession of authorship, and the reconfiguration of literary hierarchies.

As significant, perhaps, as Richardson's manipulation of the legal and commercial aspects of the marketplace was his understanding of the ideological implications of imaginative narratives at this particular moment in eighteenth-century culture. His professional ascent suggests his personal investment in the idea of social mobility, personal improvement, and economic advancement. But in a way, his profession as a printer and novelist depended on a belief in the possibility for such advancement specifically through the production and consumption of (often fictionally oriented) symbolic instruments – texts in various forms. For example, he represented the conduct book – the self-help manual – as integral to the rise of the individual, and he profited from the public's increasing faith in such a text's ability to provide information that could improve or alter one's life. "The growth of the primer, the educational aide," writes J. H. Plumb, "enabled any earnest apprentice to struggle up the ladder of self education in his leisure hours."[33]

Richardson recognized and profited from potentially dynamic social interactions and his first two non-fiction publications, *The Apprentice's Vade Mecum; or Young Man's Pocket-Companion* (1734) and *Familiar Letters on all Occasions* (1741), exploited the public's desire for a seemingly easy formula for social and professional improvement, for emulative behavior. In *Familiar Letters*, Richardson constructs textual self-representation – i.e. an individual's credit on paper – as determinant of an individual's success in personal or professional relationships. Designed for the nascent letter writer of a middling state, the text ideally provided both the appropriate epistolary form and moral thought processes. Richardson noted that "the forms . . . [and] what is more to the purpose . . . the rules and instructions contained in them, contribute to mend the heart, and improve the understanding."[34] The most striking aspect of these texts, however, is Richardson's emphasis on the future, the implicit belief that present action determined future success, and the certainty that both could be influenced by the power of a text. *The Apprentice's Vade Mecum* addresses its tone and subject to "Youth of tender Years, who are to be dictated to in a plain and easy manner, and considered as Persons just stepping out into Life."[35] The preface reiterates the text's goal to teach apprentices "how to behave in this their first Stage of Manhood and Business, on which the Whole of their future Good generally depends" (vi). The text urges apprentices to imagine the future, to create a narrative about their existence which they could then fulfill in a consistent and meaningful way. This type of text appealed to a segment of the population for whom such self-improvement was a relatively new concept, one arising, in part, from the emerging economic and social opportunities. Just as Elizabeth Molesworth exclaimed in 1720 that the possibility for investment in the South Sea Company was an opportunity likely never to happen again, by the 1740s the culture was seemingly teeming with multiple opportunities (however illusory). The development of a consumer society and expanding commercialization of leisure and litera-ture, writes Plumb, "required men and women to believe in growth, in change, in modernity; to believe that the future was bright, far brighter than the past; to believe, also, that what was new was desirable."[36]

The quest for the "new" and thus commercially desirable contributed to innovations in fictional texts and what Richardson termed "a new species of writing." In a 1741 letter to Aaron Hill, he expressed his thought that certain stories, "if written in an easy and natural manner . . . might possibly introduce a new species of writing, that might possibly turn young people into a course of reading different from the pomp and parade of romance-writing, and dismissing the improbable and marvellous, with which novels generally abound, might tend to promote the cause of religion and virtue."[37] Richardson carefully distinguishes his work from "romance writing" and the "novel." He wants to produce texts of greater morality, didacticism, and cultural authority. Yet the so-called "new species of writing," which helps Richardson accrue cultural credit in terms of both popularity and profit, relies on his appropriation of the narrative and stylistic conventions developed by Eliza Haywood. Margaret Doody has recorded specific instances where Richardson seemingly appropriates large sections of Haywood's work and transplants them into his fiction.[38] Doody's analysis is quite acute, and I believe even more instances of appropriation exist. But in some ways the implication of the gesture is more significant than a list of specific examples for it reshapes our understanding of the novel. Though Richardson always claimed that *Pamela* emerged "naturally" out of his work on *Familiar Letters on All Occasions*, it is readily apparent that he wrote within the existing fictional discourse produced by Eliza Haywood.

Although he is not using the cultural weight of Haywood's authorial persona, Richardson, much as Pope does in the *Dunciad*, draws on her recognizable narrative tradition and manipulates it to fit his own aims. In doing so, he achieves the cultural currency and financial remuneration to which Haywood aspired unsuccessfully. Richardson effectively subsumes the work of his predecessors as he revises the generic expectations of the novel and to a certain extent its social and cultural legitimacy. Though he tacitly acknowledges the power of Haywood's previous novels, he consistently marks himself as different to give his novel what William Warner terms "a higher cultural calling," a gesture that makes the novels of Haywood appear low or "immoral" in contrast.[39] Richardson's metaphorical and material appropriation of Haywood's texts acts as a kind of financial speculation.[40] Richardson acquires "stock" in Haywood's literary tradition by investing in her style, language, and seductive fictional situations. However, to increase the value of his product, Richardson reconstructs these characteristics by emphasizing the didacticism that makes them more palatable to readers from the middle classes. This gesture diminishes Haywood's cultural currency (and potential marketability as suggested by the subsequent changes in her own fiction), while creating a privileged space for Richardson and the newly re-formed novel.

Just as Richardson domesticates the instabilities of paper credit, in a sense he "domesticates" the more extreme elements of Haywood's fiction such as "natural" feminine discourse and titillating descriptions of physical intimacy.[41] He simulates the unmediated feminine discourse that distinguished Haywood's novels, but he detaches himself from the source of the emotion. He creates authorial distance and avoids the appearance of deliberate fiction by posing as the editor rather than author of the published letters, a gesture that allows him to assume the voice of rational, masculine, and editorial authority. While Haywood's effusive emotionalism and extreme passion are dismissed as instinctual or overly sentimental, Richardson's more (artificially) distanced handling of the same emotions is heralded as natural, the striking effect of "writing to the moment."

Similarly, Richardson's depiction of physical situations, presented in a style consistent with Haywood's, is framed by overt didacticism. When half-clothed bodies appear in Richardson's texts (the fire scene in *Clarissa*, Mr. B's search for Pamela's letters), they are female bodies lacking sexual desire. Clarissa and Pamela do not experience the passions of a Haywood heroine, which allows them more readily to act as vessels for Richardson's didactic message.[42] Any potential sexual encounter only evinces the heroine's unshakable virtue or illustrates her ability to finesse a potentially disastrous erotic situation.[43] Richardson drains his female characters of their emotional and physical responses, and places the overwhelming passion that distinguishes Haywood's female characters in a man of a higher social class.[44] With this gesture, Richardson attempts to translate an impulse read in Haywood as extreme and transgressive into a normative male–female relationship. As a result, he constricts the boundaries of female sexuality and resists Haywood's more empowering construction of gender. Of course Pamela's seeming absence of sexuality contributes to her success as a domestic stock-jobber. She directs her desires primarily toward her own advancement within the domestic speculative economy.

Richardson also attempts to stabilize the volatile generic aspects of the novel. Although he benefited from and exploited the opportunities provided by the dynamic of paper credit, he also seemed to understand – and at some level combat – the fundamentally speculative nature of the fictional narrative. Unlike history, which was perceived by many as objective or "true," the novel retained its association with unreliability, fantasy, and the imagination – a discourse of intentional deception. Richardson's pose as the editor of "real" letters makes claims for a certain "reality." The public preoccupation with *Pamela*, fed by a feverish production of consumer goods connected with the text,[45] often demonstrated a slippage in terms of the distinction between "fact" and fiction that Richardson himself attempted to elide. The oft recounted incident of the ringing of the church bells at Slough captures the mood of a culture eager to believe in, if not Pamela herself, then the cultural pattern her narrative offered.[46] Richardson writes of the powers of transformation found in various types of self-construction and self-actualization. He argues not just for the importance of a serving girl's virtue, but for himself, his sense of class, and his genre.[47] The text's overwhelming popularity suggests the cultural predisposition for narratives of social and economic elevation available through the manipulation of paper credit.

2

Pamela lives in a world defined by the financial and fictional narratives she creates and interprets. She recognizes the importance of investing in the future and cultivating her value. When the novel begins, she has already earned a certain amount of credit within the household and, like a trader in stocks, she scrupulously guards her reputation; she refuses to "forfeit [her] good name" (28). Capturing the favor of Lady B, Pamela acquires clothes, social skills, and an education; her ability "to write and cast Accompts" (25) distinguishes her from the other servants and marks the slightly higher station from which she originally came. In true Richardsonian fashion, Mr. B encourages Pamela to "look into any of her [ladyship's] books to improve yourself." As a result of her accomplishments, Pamela is a valued member of the household who has the good opinion or "good word" of her employers and fellow servants.

Despite all the credit she accumulates within the household, Pamela lives with the specter of her debt and worries about returning her parents to (and maintaining her own) financial solvency. In the novel, the Andrews' attempt to start their own school has failed, leaving them financially ruined and lowering their social position. They are burdened by their "old debt," to which Pamela refers at the beginning of the novel. In a 1741 letter to Aaron Hill, Richardson claimed that this aspect of the novel was based on the true story of a daughter whose parents were "ruined by suretiship,"[48] a contractual obligation that makes one legally responsible for another individual's debt. Similarly, Mrs. Jervis, who becomes Pamela's surrogate mother-cum-silent partner, has also been forced into service to pay "old Debts for her Children that were extravagant . . . This, tho', was very good in her" (76). Like Pamela, she is "a Gentlewoman born, tho' she has had misfortunes" (30).

Pamela clearly understands what it means to be legally indebted, and she repeatedly expresses her refusal to incur new debt and her desire to keep her accounts in order. When she owes John some favors she wants to erase the "debt" monetarily: "John is very good, and very honest; I am under great obligations to him. I'd give him a guinea, now I'm so rich, if I thought he'd take it" (87). She resists borrowing from the other servants: "though I warrant I might have what I would of Mrs. Jervis, or Mr. Jonathan, or Mr. Longman; but then how shall I pay it? you'll say: And, besides, I don't love to be beholden" (70). She maintains a keen awareness of the importance of maintaining at least the appearance of financial solvency: "money runs a little lowish, after what I have laid out; but I don't care to say so here" (70). Pamela appraises individuals in terms of their potential economic usefulness. For example, she reflects on the possible advantages in her relationship with "kind and civil Mr. Longman our steward": "He said once to Mrs. Jervis, he wish'd he was a young Man for my sake, I should be his Wife and he would settle all he had upon me on Marriage, and, you must know, he is reckon'd worth a Power of Money" (51). She reveals an awareness of her attractiveness to Longman, and the potential profit of that attraction. She makes this observation in the context of a longer letter that suggests her potential for advancement with Mr. B, as well.

Her preoccupation with debt suggests not only its prevalence given the economic realities of the time, but also Pamela's resistance to incurring any new debt or obligation – moral, sexual, or economic – that would force her to squander her capital. Yet for a woman in her position there is often a fine line between liabilities and assets. Pamela understands the possibility for advancement and failure within the social realm: "I have liv'd above myself for some Time past" (28). Her refusal to be "quite destitute *again*" (25, emphasis mine) indicates her awareness of the vagaries of the market-place. She realizes her options are limited because she has, in a sense, over-capitalized – she has "qualifications above [her] degree" (25); her extra-ordinary skills have made it more difficult for her to move within the servant class: "Much I fear'd, that as I was taken by her Goodness to wait upon her person, I should be ... forc'd to return to you and my poor Mother, who have enough to do to maintain yourselves ... it would have been no easy Matter to find a Place that your poor Pamela was fit for" (45). The inability to secure employment would necessarily cause Pamela to become beholden to someone – her parents, a husband, or a prospective employer.

Immediately after Lady B's death, Pamela receives a crucial piece of advice from Lady Davers that provides her with a potential model for avoiding debt and illustrates the law of supply and demand. Observing that Pamela is "a pretty wench" with "a very good character," she advises her to "take care to keep the fellows at a distance; and said, *that* I might do, and be more valu'd for it, even by themselves" (29). She is advised "to keep myself to myself" (29) and not to circulate unadvisedly. While Lady Davers intends this information to be used with other servants or neighborhood boys, rather than her brother, Pamela lets this principle guide her inter-actions with Mr. B. Pamela mirrors the actions of a clever stock-jobber – one who buys low and sells high; she demonstrates her credit and her worth, cultivates Mr. B's interest (both romantic and economic), and then raises the price of her stock by keeping him "at a distance" and introducing the concept of virtue.

To succeed, Pamela must maintain her own credit (and credibility), as well as that of her potential investors; thus when Mr. B approaches her sexually, she initially describes those encounters as threatening to her credit and reputation, not necessarily to her virtue. When B kisses Pamela's hand, she complains it "would ruin his credit as well as mine" (30). She worries Mr. B has "undervalued himself, as to take notice of such a poor girl as I."[49] Early in the novel, Pamela balances this concern for credit and appearances with her desire for immediate profits in the form of material goods. She keeps delighted accounts of the clothing she acquires from Mr. B, and her letters resemble a ledger of sorts: "he has given me a Suit of my old Lady's Cloathes, and half a Dozen of her Shifts, and Six fine Handkerchiefs, and Three of her Cambrick Aprons, and Four Holland ones" (30). She later counts gifts of shoes, buckles, and stockings with equal interest and specificity: "Two Suits of fine *Flanders* lac'd Headclothes, Three Pair of fine Silk Shoes ... Four Pair of fine white Cotton Stockens, and Three Pair of fine Silk ones; and Two Pair of rich Stays" (31). Pamela demonstrates the stereotypically bourgeois concern with the accumulation of goods.

When Pamela decides to leave B— Hall, she claims she will leave all these clothes behind, "as he expected other Returns for his Presents, than I intended ... to make him; so I thought it was but just to leave his Presents behind me when I went away: for, you know, if I could not earn his Wages, why should I have them?" (53). Yet she clearly indicates the success of her "project" to have the clothes sent after her when she leaves:

I hear nothing of my Lady's Clothes, and those my Master gave me: For I told Mrs. Jervis, I would not take them; but I fansy, by a Word or two that was dropt, they will be sent after me. Dear sirs! what a rich Pamela you'll have, if they should! But as I can't wear them, if they do, I don't desire them; and will turn them into Money, as I can have Opportunity. (87)[50]

She relies on the "word" in the marketplace, on the rumor and opinion she hears; she tells one thing but intends another. She doesn't desire the actual clothes, she prefers to have the profit she can get for them.

The clothes allow Pamela to adorn and thus enrich herself but they also represent potential capital – she can put them to use by converting them to money. While these gifts represent an initial payment to Pamela (or, perhaps, the interest she gains from the principal of her beauty), she recognizes that such non-negotiable goods are, in fact, less useful than actual currency. To her parents she expresses her wish that "it was no Affront to him to make Money of them [the gifts], and send it to you: it would do me more good" (30). Her desire for currency allows her to rationalize her acceptance of money indirectly given by Mr. B: "he has this Moment sent me five guineas by Mrs. Jervis, as a Present for my Pocket: so I shall be very rich; for as *she* brought them, I thought I might take them" (87). She balances fiscal responsibility and social decorum. She boasts about her plans or projects to sell her clothes and her ability to save money for future investment: "You'll say, I was no bad Housewife to have sav'd so much Money" (53). She is already beginning to cultivate and advertise the values of industry and frugality that will become part of her virtue.

Pamela's preoccupation with appearance also causes her to remake herself in rustic dress enabled by the conversion of clothes into money and herself into a country maid. She decides to abandon the luxurious clothes she received from Mr. B in favor of dress "that will be fit for my condition" (52), both to maintain her reputation and to give heightened credibility to her textual accounts. In anticipation of returning to her parents, Pamela procures "rustic" clothes, appropriate for her life away from B—Hall. She expresses her anticipation of them in a way that suggests their ability to disguise and transform: "I long to have them on. I know I shall surprise Mrs. Jervis with them; for she shan't see me till I am full-dress'd" (59). The new rustic attire represents Pamela as she wants to be seen – as an innocent young girl – and, more important, allows her to control how she is seen. This is the first of many times she remakes herself through her own "projecting" (77); she uses her own "industry" (76) and her buying power to acquire the humbler clothing. (Although Pamela's description of her rustic clothes suggests they are not truly humble, rather "ordinary I mean to what I have been lately used to" [60].) The rustic dress acts as another symbolic instrument that Pamela creates and places into circulation. It materializes the fruits of her labors and suggests the transformative power of paper credit. In the most fundamental way it conflates the multiple meanings of *investment* – not only is Pamela investing in her future with her narrative construction of virtue, she is literally "in-vesting" herself with the material signifiers of the persona she wishes to present to B. She has clothed herself in her virtue (as she will do later when she literally wears her letters on her body) to increase her credibility in a way that makes her simultaneously impenetrable and even more desirable. The episode also indicates how easily Pamela, in a world of fundamentally ambiguous signifiers, can recreate herself: "Oh the pleasure of descending with ease" (60). Pamela's declaration "I never liked myself so well in my life" seems rooted in her perceived success at self-fashioning; she is "metamorphosed" (60).

When Pamela descends the stairs having "tricked [her]self up" in her new clothes, Rachel "did not know her" nor did Mrs. Jervis, who observes "I never knew the like of thee" (61). Pamela is different from all the other servants and also fundamentally unknowable. In light of the profound (and literal) impenetrability of Pamela, Mrs. Jervis's admonition "pray don't reveal yourself till he finds you out" (61) has meaning beyond Pamela's seeming disguise and speaks to her inscrutable nature throughout the novel. Her attempts at self-empowerment pervade the whole scene since once she dons her rustic gown she, like the economic man, invokes the role of Fortuna: "Let Fortune's Wheel turn round as it will" (60).[51] The invocation to Fortuna, traditionally viewed in opposition to virtue and often regarded as a marker of an individual's ambition beyond his or her degree, further allies Pamela with the uncertain world of trade, specula- tion, and commerce, and intensifies the understanding of her virtue as a primarily textual construction.[52]

Such language and the entire episode with rustic clothing underscores the larger element of masquerade and disguise that pervades the whole novel in a pattern allusive of previous cultural discourse about the dangers of paper credit. When B encounters Pamela, he claims she has intention- ally tricked him: "so you must disguise yourself to attract me" (62). Yet she asserts she has been "in disguise, indeed, ever since my Good lady your mother, took me from my poor parents . . . and . . . heaped upon me rich clothes and other bounties" (62). Although Pamela considers the rustic dress her "own self" it really acts as another in a series of disguises in the novel.[53] This transformation is, of course, regarded as an intentional trick by Mr. B, who says he has been "robbed" (63); it has caused him to lay out an excess of capital in terms of revealing his own desire. He reacts in the slightly scattered, somewhat frenzied manner of a stock-jobber indecisive about an investment: "I can neither bear nor forbear her. But stay; you shan't go! – Yet begone! – No come back again" (62). This instance is the first in a series of moments where B's own behavior metaphorically mirrors that of the new economic man in a manner appropriate to his role as an "investor" in Pamela. Like Exchange Alley, B— Hall becomes a site of social mixing with the removal of the signifying codes of previously established cultural classifications.

Pamela worries that this incident has "cost" her place and that she will suffer an immediate loss of credit and perhaps financial remuneration. As Mr. B's pursuit of her continues, however, Pamela sacrifices her opportu- nities for immediate short-term profits in hopes of a greater long-range return. Her resistance to Mr. B's advances, and her dutiful recording of them, provide her with credit from B and her parents which contributes to her virtue. Early in the novel, B offers Pamela a verbal contract with a *quid pro quo* arrangement: "I tell you I will make a gentlewoman of you if you be obliging" (35). Pamela rejects such an offer outright both because it relies on B's word rather than a documented exchange and because it is not the best deal for her. She resists being seen as tangible property that can be easily bought; in fact, she repeatedly refers to her "very worthless body" (151, cf. 138). She realizes that gifts and coins, while immediately gratifying, ultimately have limited value for her. They establish a system of exchange in which she will probably lose. The real potential for financial rewards exists in shifting the relationship and the terms of the exchange from the culture of material goods (kisses for stockings) to an imaginatively based economy of speculative investment and negotiable paper.

From the beginning of the novel, Pamela is always writing, manipulating paper, exercising her imaginative powers in the creation of an intangible set of values offered in her narrative. Once she is taken to the Lincolnshire estate and imprisoned, writing becomes Pamela's full-time job; she rarely does anything else. "I Have so much Time upon my Hands, that I must write on to employ myself" (134). She understands that her writing is an investment in her future. Her imaginative and textual creation of self represents her unwavering investment in her virtue – a completely intangible construct that determines the course of the relationship with Mr. B. Pamela's virtue is a commodity the reader and Mr. B receive only on paper. Like the projected return on an investment in stock, the real value of her virtue will never appear; the moment when B gains material proof of her virtue – her virginity – it of course ceases to exist. Virtue is a purely verbal construct that gains currency within the self-enclosed financial system Pamela establishes. By calling her virtue a product of her imagination, I do not mean to suggest (as Fielding or Haywood do) that Pamela is somehow not virtuous. Rather, her discourse provides the only real value her virtue has. Her paper credit, like a stock, composes a narrative that seeks and ultimately receives an emotional and financial investment from Mr. B as he becomes increasingly involved in the fiction that constitutes her virtue.

Pamela's text also exploits B's appetites, passions, and emotions, while it records and creates his desire to invest in her. Her story increases his desire by offering a textual account of the arousing experiences he has already had; in a sense, she places him in a perpetual cycle of desire. Pamela's mirroring of text and experience, or read and lived encounters, heightens B's desire while simultaneously deferring its consummation. The only "satisfaction" B achieves is his possession of the letters themselves, what he terms a "pretty story in romance" (42). Yet Pamela's "pretty story" also has a price. Her fictional and financial narratives are inextricably linked and mutually informing. Investment in the one necessarily requires investment in the other. When she first recognizes Mr. B's attraction to her, she admits she has "read of things almost as strange, from great men to poor damsels" (74), indicating her familiarity with romance. He realizes the power of Pamela's tale despite its fundamentally intangible basis: "you may as well have *real* Cause to take these Freedoms with me, as to make my Name suffer for imaginary ones" (41). At times she resorts to the lines she has read as the basis for her verbal defense: "O how I was terrify'd! I said, like as I had read in a Book a Night or two before, 'Angels, and Saints, and all the Host of Heaven, defend me!' " (41). Initially B locates her protestations of virtue in that tradition: "You have a very pretty romantic Turn for Virtue, and all that" (71). He uses the same attitude with Goodman Andrews, claiming, "I think thou hast read Romances as well as thy Daughter, and thy head's turn'd with them" (93).

While the abduction to Lincolnshire fits into the plot of a romance, it forces Pamela to reassess her situation and reestablish her credit. She has a new set of individuals with which to deal and she has to make appropriate adjustments. When Pamela first arrives at Lincolnshire, she evaluates the potential usefulness of the people around her, determining they are all "strange creatures, that promise nothing" (105). She is tricked out of the only coins she has to prevent her from making a "bad use of it" and corrupting Nan "with money or fine things" (121). In the absence of actual currency, Pamela attempts various other "projects" that depend on the strength of her cunning and B's attitude toward her. For example, she attempts to win Mrs. Jewkes's confidence by showing her a letter from Mr. B:

I thought, when I had written this Letter, and that which he had prescrib'd, it would look like placing a Confidence in Mrs. Jewkes, to shew them to her; and I shew'd her at the same time, my Master's Letter to me; for I believ'd, the *Value* he expressed for me, would give me *Credit* with one who profess'd in every thing to serve him right or wrong. (110, emphasis mine)

She hopes his letter will act like a letter of credit from a bank allowing Pamela to borrow on the good opinion B has of her. She similarly tries to get Williams to participate in her project to escape, but he proves to be a bad risk; he lacks the guile necessary to service her plans: "His oversecurity and openness have ruined us both" (148).

Lincolnshire also signals a slight shift in Mr. B's attitude as well. He is transformed from a member of the landed elite, disdainful of Pamela's scribbling, to a frenzied, slightly feminized economic man eager to invest in her scheme. Initially, like a conservative ideologue, Mr. B repeatedly complains that Pamela never does any "real" work: "This girl is always scribbling; I think she may be better employed" (34). This is of course the same criticism leveled against stock-jobbers, who earn their money through the artificial inflation of stock prices rather than any real (e.g. manual) work or labor. B later calls her an "idle girl" and claims she minds her "pen more than [her] needle" (59). He continues to observe that he doesn't want such "idle sluts" in his household, linking virtue with the middle-class conception of industry and chastity. Certainly he is bothered by Pamela's apparent lack of tangible product for her efforts, but he is also nervous about her textual creation of self and the negotiable paper she produces. He resists her rejection of the world of tangible goods, where he has more power, for the imaginatively conceived world of virtue and paper credit. He laments that "pride of birth and fortune" cannot "obtain credit" with Pamela (82). That type of authority can't buy him anything, even though he loves Pamela to "extravagance" (116).

Mr. B also questions the value of Pamela's reputation, and by extension her credit, and its relationship to his own world. He tells Mrs. Jervis: "I know Pamela has your good Word; but do you think her of any Use in the Family? ... Why that Word Virtuous?" (39). He is suspicious of her possible plans for other servants: "but 'tis my Opinion, she is an artful young Baggage; and had I a young handsome Butler or Steward, she'd soon make her Market of one of them, if she thought it worth while to snap at him for a Husband" (39). Nevertheless, her text plays on B's appetites, passions, and emotions. He is beguiled by the notion of investing in Pamela (instead of bartering for her as he initially intended). Consequently he abandons his aristocratic demeanor (peering through keyholes and rifling through her letters) in his pursuit of her. Perhaps the fullest example of this abandonment occurs when B disguises himself as Nan in order to trap Pamela in her bedroom. Wearing Nan's "gown and petticoat" with "her apron over his face and shoulders" (175), B observes Pamela from a chair. When Nan/B comes to bed, Pamela expresses concern that her breathing was "all quick and short" (176) and she "quiver'd like an Aspin-leaf" (176). B literally changes gender signifiers in an attempt to gratify his overwhelming desire for Pamela. Led by his passions and emotions, he, like the economic man, becomes a feminized creature. He abandons all sense of class distinctions. Similarly, he now places increasing importance in Pamela's reputation and credit. As he learns Mrs. Jervis's estimation of Pamela and the general opinion of the other servants within the household, he gains a renewed interest in "investing" in Pamela:

All the Servants, from the highest to the lowest, doat upon you, instead of envying you; and look upon you in so superior a Light, as speaks what you ought to be. I have seen more of your Letters than you imagine, (This surpriz'd me!), and am quite overcome with your charming manner of Writing ... all put together, makes me, as I tell you, love you to Extravagance. (83)

B's inability to penetrate Pamela and his recognition that he must look to her paper credit rather than her physical body for worth causes this change in his approach. When Mr. B wants to escalate the relationship to another level of physical intimacy by making Pamela his mistress, he sends her an elaborately written proposal detailing the economic benefits to her. Nancy Armstrong suggests that "[w]hile Mr. B offers money in exchange for her body, she maintains that her real value does not derive from her body; she is not, in other words, currency in a system of exchange among men."[54] Armstrong attributes Pamela's value to her gender, her "female subjectivity," and her language, and reads her resistance throughout the novel as the triumph of the modern self over traditional forms of political power. While Pamela's maneuvers certainly are political in that they involve the play of power, her rejection of B's proposal is a profoundly economic act. She will not allow herself to be used as currency in a system of exchange among men because she has already constructed an alternative financial model. Pamela wants Mr. B to invest in her, not buy her outright. He must recognize and believe in the potential returns (moral, sexual, economic, domestic) she has to offer; he cannot be diverted by his desire for immediate gratification.

Although his written proposal indicates his belief that his relationship with Pamela has long-term potential, he wants to test it, to borrow against rather than invest in the future. B introduces the possibility of marriage in Item VII: "if your Conduct be such, that I have Reason to be satisfied with it, I know not (though I will not engage for this) that I may, after a Twelvemonth's Cohabitation, marry you" (167). With this statement, he unwittingly causes his terms necessarily to be rejected. Pamela is a much shrewder negotiator than B and she recognizes that marriage is in fact a possibility; she has "undervalued" her stock, so to speak. If she accepts these terms, she will sell at too low a price, and also lose the credit she has already established. Her rejection under the guise of virtue and propriety only further increases her value; B insists:

I would divide with all my Soul, my Estate with you, to make you mine upon my own Terms. These you have absolutely rejected; and that, tho' in sawcy Terms enough, yet, in such a manner, as makes me admire you more ... And I see you so watchful over your Virtue, that tho' I hop'd to find it otherwise, I cannot but say, my Passion for you is increas'd by it. (183–84)

Indeed, Pamela has done precisely what Lady Davers initially suggested; she has held B at a distance and made herself more attractive and thus valuable as a result. Through resistance and shrewd negotiation, Pamela is able to achieve the end she wants and to transform her credit into virtue.

Before Mr. B ostensibly sends Pamela away to marry Williams, he reads her journal and letters, which he describes as a "fond folly [that] ... cost me so dear" (213). His reading or "borrowing" of her paper credit only prolongs the negotiation and increases her value: "Your Papers shall be faithfully return'd you, and I have paid so dear for my Curiosity in the Affection they have rivetted upon me for you, that you would look upon yourself amply reveng'd, if you knew what they have cost me" (214). Pamela extracts her fee and the "cost" to Mr. B is his increasing affection; he is ready to invest in Pamela. He has nothing tangible, save Pamela herself, on which to base his good opinion; his infatuation and commitment to her in the form of marriage is ultimately speculative. His final agreement to marry her represents his emotional and economic investment in her imaginative narrative. The pretty romance B complained Pamela was writing becomes a story he accepts as true.

The discussions of the marriage illustrate how Pamela's paper credit, transformed into virtue, constitutes a completely negotiable, albeit intangible, property within the economy of the novel. On the eve of her wedding, Pamela imagines how Mr. B would be concerned with the legal preparations if he were marrying a "lady of birth and fortune": "all the Eve to the Day, would be taken up in reading, signing, and sealing of Settlements, and Portion, and such-like" (282). She observes "how poor is it to offer nothing but Words for such generous Deeds !" (283). Mr. B assures her that what she brings to the marriage is equal to any dowry: "To all that know your Story and your Merit, it will appear, that I cannot recompense you for what I have made you suffer ... who shall grudge you the Reward of the hard-bought Victory" (283).[55] Yet the victory is one fought over intangible values for very tangible goods. The terms have now completely shifted − B hopes *he* has enough credit to ensure the maintenance of Pamela's virtue. Mr. B claims to "have no business of equal value to [Pamela's] company" (311). Pamela has been his business and the process of negotiation, investment, and capitalization has been as elaborate and intricate as any in Exchange Alley.

Once married, Pamela uses her paper credit to convince Lady Davers and others of her worth. When Lady Davers arrives unexpectedly to find Pamela, now Mrs. B, alone she harasses the former servant and refuses to believe a legitimate marriage has taken place. She will not take Pamela's "word" for it. The spoken word or Mr. B's letter to Pamela have no credit; even Mr. B's later pleas for Pamela's new status go unheeded. Only her written account will convince Lady Davers of her worthiness: "I can find, by your Writings, that your Virtue is but suitably rewarded" (374). Pamela agrees to circulate her letters, "not doubting your generous Allowances, as I have had his [Mr. B's]" (375). Although Lady Davers can only provide social acceptance in contrast to Mr. B's financially oriented "allowances," "the sight of [Pamela's] papers" (375) persuades her that she has the necessary virtue for her new station. Lady Davers, like B, makes a social and emotional investment and, through the process of narrative involvement, imaginatively transforms Pamela's textual account into proof of her virtue.

As Mrs. B, Pamela translates her considerable financial abilities to an expanded domestic economy. Mr. B puts her in charge of her own accounts, 200 guineas a year. He insists that she not be uneasy about the amount since, in addition to his prosperous estate, he lays "up Money every Year, and have besides, large Sums in Government and other Securities" (306). While he expects "no Account" for the money, by placing the distribution of the sum in the context of his other financial dealings handled by Mr. Longman, he implicitly characterizes Pamela as another in a series of investments. In the final recuperation (or perhaps reinvestment) of her assets, Pamela translates the accounting skills that enabled her success into expert household management, a domesticated virtue. Yet she is still determined to put her money to use:

I am resolv'd to keep Account of all these Matters, and Mr. Longman has already furnish'd me with a Vellum-book of all white Paper; some Sides of which I hope soon to fill, with the Names of proper Objects: And tho' my dear master has given me all this without Account, yet shall he see, (but nobody else) how I lay it out from Quarter to Quarter; and I will, if any be left, carry it on, like an Accomptant, to the next Quarter, and strike a Ballance four times a Year, and a general Ballance at every Year's End. (387–88)

Pamela's new financial ledger, described in great detail, is as intimate a journal as the one she kept during her captivity. Moreover, she will use this new ledger to maintain her credibility with Mr. B. She will show these accounts (an *ad hoc* investor's report or an annual summary), like her personal writings, to her "beloved master . . . (but nobody else)."

With her marriage and her absorption into B's economy, Pamela fully translates her credit into virtue, a virtue proved or maintained by a show of financial solvency. However, she does not lose her concern with turning a profit, and she conflates the aristocratic ideal of the moral economy and good deeds with the new economic man's understanding of investment. She asks her parents for a "List of the honest and worthy Poor" (408) so she might carefully dispense her money among them and put it to use: "[F]or the Money lies by me, and brings me no Interest. You see I am become a mere Usurer; and want to make Use upon Use" (409). Appearing in the last letter of the novel, this passage most accurately characterizes Pamela's attitude toward capital, investments, and profit. Like the new economic man, Pamela is endlessly concerned with getting a return on her investment, on making her sexual, financial, and fictional capital work for her – whether that capital is self-generated paper credit or her annual allotment of pin money. When she calls herself a "mere usurer" she, in fact, identifies her guiding principle through the book. Like a usurer, she has lent her capital – journal, letters – to Mr. B and allowed it to be circulated, but at a very high rate of interest. With a verbal, imaginatively conceived account of her experiences – with her paper credit – she gains a profitable marriage and an annual allowance. By using an alternative form of currency and determining her own rate of exchange, Pamela (at least in Part 1) temporarily transcends the patriarchal economy of exchange in women and creates her own domestic economy in which Mr. B must invest.

3

Pamela's preoccupation with investment, credit, and the construction of virtue is consistent with the cultural anxiety about a woman's use of her sexual, financial, and textual capital – an anxiety informed by the changing notions of property. It also suggests an increasing desire for discursive evidence of inherently intangible things. While *Pamela* contributes to the recuperation of paper credit and speculative investment, it by no means stabilizes those concepts completely, although other types of cultural texts emerged that attempted to continue that process of recuperation. The week of January 8, 1750, an advertisement for *The Lady's Compleat Pocket-Book* appeared in *The Penny London Post; or the Morning Advertiser*. For one shilling, this conveniently sized "pocket-book" claimed to provide women – for at least the year – with the most important information needed to negotiate the town. Like *The Apprentice's Vade Mecum: or the Young Man's Pocket-Companion*, the *Lady's Pocket-Book* provides rules and directions for all sorts of social and financial interactions. It offered everything from "rates, rules and orders relating to Coachmen, Chairmen, Carmen and Watermen, in order to prevent any Imposition offered to those who are unacquainted with the Town" to "Directions for dancing forty-eight new country-Dances compos'd for the present year." A woman could learn how to get around town and know what to do once she got where she was going. Most significant is the *Pocket-Book*'s promise to serve as a prefabricated vehicle for recording and reviewing one's life. It acts as a "Memorandum-Book for every Day in the Year, so dispos'd as to discover at one view, what Cash is received, what paid, What Appointments or Engagements are on Hand; and other occasional Business of Importance." The annual purchase (and subsequent preservation) of these "pocketbooks" – since they will "be continued every year" – will enable "any Lady to tell What Business she has transacted, and What Company been in every Day, during any Period of her Life." A woman will be able to reflect on past days or past years as time "well spent."

Like Pamela's "vellum-book of all white paper," the *Pocket-Book* offered a way for women to keep their accounts in order. It provided a potential journal of appointments, primer of dances and social rituals, and ledger in which to note "cash received" and "what paid." With such a volume, women will, in effect, be able to record the daily business of their lives, to create their own "paper credit." Like Pamela, these women can turn the "business . . . transacted" into a narrative that can demonstrate their fiscal responsibility, economy, and continued frugality – their attempts to act within the redefined parameters of middle-class values that increasingly define virtue. Ironically, though, this possible marker (or perhaps measure) of women's virtue and dutifulness now resides in the potentially unreal world of paper credit – as women "take stock" of their activities, gain "credit" for learning the latest dances, and learn how to act credibly with coachmen so as not to be financially gullible. Women invest in ways of investing in themselves. They are all potentially "domestic stock-jobbers."

Their presence in a *domestic* site is significant. The female subjects in Richardson's and Haywood's texts negotiate the sexual–financial economies in distinctly different locations. Pamela creates a private economy in which to circulate her paper credit, making her actions palatable to a culture increasingly seeking the domestication of women. Consequently, Richardson displaces the anxiety about paper credit, and also about a woman circulating in public. Pamela is never forced to negotiate the public sphere of Exchange Alley or a more "public" sexual economy that parallels and replicates the financial economy. (And when a subject like Clarissa leaves the private sphere, her disastrous experiences within an unfamiliar public prove fatal.) The previously discussed texts from the 1720s represent women actively seeking participation in various versions of the public – the City, Exchange Alley, and the attendant sites providing the pleasures of business. Richardson's text effectively eschews the public sphere while merging the characteristics of a stock-jobber with the notion of virtue. The concepts of speculative investment and paper credit are retained but refigured in a text that also signals a shift to a more contained, controlled – indeed virtuous – female subject. By locating Pamela primarily within the private sphere, Richardson anticipates her restricted agency within marriage and the cultural desire for a more restrained, contained, and thoroughly domesticated woman.

The preoccupation with the private sphere contrasts sharply with Haywood's representation of women. Haywood's texts, which largely replicate her own inevitably public existence, resist the domestic or private sphere – indeed, the private is typically a site of danger (seduction, submission, or abandonment) for women. Her female subjects act in a public economy with the new financial instruments; they gamble, acquire mortgages, understand stocks, shop voraciously, and generally immerse themselves in the pleasures of business in its multiple forms. They also circulate and often profit from a more "public" sexual economy as well. Though not always successful in pursuing the business of their own pleasure, Haywood's characters typically understand how to benefit from visibility in a competitive heterosexual market. Their mobility is enabled by their freedom from the constraints of virtue – it does not hold the high value it acquires in *Pamela* and in a changing cultural economy. Motivated by their own desires, they operate in a world where credit, reputation, and speculation have yet to be subsumed under the valorizing marker of virtue.

Read together, Richardson's and Haywood's fiction charts a distinct change in the cultural attitude toward expectations for women, the possibilities of financial instruments, and the expanding and incalculable power of texts. John Bender suggests that novels "may serve as a medium of cultural emergence through which new images of society, new cultural systems, move into focus."[56] Haywood's texts of the 1720s mark a world reeling from the effects of the South Sea Bubble; an environment in which women can explore new vehicles for social and economic improvement, exercise unrealized freedoms, and exploit the imaginative and material opportunities found during the contestation of social, sexual, and discursive models. The offering of *The Lady's Pocket-book* at the end of a decade in which *Pamela* appeared in five editions suggests the degree to which Richardson's novel contributed to a new way of thinking about virtue, narratives, and the use of paper credit.[57] *Pamela* addresses not only issues of social volatility, cultural capital, and speculative finance; it also indicates how fully eighteenth-century culture, informed by fictional and financial narratives, had embraced the act of writing, accounting, and investing as a means of self-actualization, if not transformation.

Conclusion: negotiable paper

Pope, Haywood, and Richardson wrestled with the problems and possibilities of the economy of professional authorship, and their individual strategies illuminate an often resistant acceptance of the power of paper credit. The gendered characterizations that variously informed the emergent culture of print and the attendant constructions of authorship compelled the acts of revision and publication by each author. They operated with an awareness of the dynamic of authorship, the power of authorial personae, and the potentially lasting weight of an *oeuvre*. To various degrees, each writing subject confronted the inevitable tension between writing for a place in an *ad hoc* (and ultimately imaginary) literary history – a comfortably static, authorized, and ostensibly "masculine" discourse – and the equally powerful demands of a feminizing and ephemeral literary marketplace. While success in the marketplace did not ensure a place in literary history (as Haywood demonstrates), without a commercial presence or an audience, a lasting professional reputation could prove elusive. Authors had to calculate their fluctuating values in both arenas. Notoriety did not provide fame, fame did not mean success, and commercial success did not guarantee the kind of permanent recognition sought by an author like Pope. A brief examination of each author's attitude toward the act of revision suggests how literary hierarchy, commercial pressures, and gendered considerations inform the ultimate gestures of these writers as they attempted to cash in their paper credit.

Pamela fundamentally changed the generic expectations and commercial possibilities of the novel. The text entranced a culture preoccupied with discourses that fueled and satisfied their desires. That impulse, so evident twenty years earlier at the time of the South Sea Crisis, contributed to a fascination with the multiply commodified versions of *Pamela* (and Pamela) – Pamela fans, prints, waxworks, poems, and opera. Readers turned consumers sought material reminders of Richardson's intangible narrative. Ironically, a text that helped "domesticate" the concept of paper credit revealed how unstable negotiable paper still was in a public, literary marketplace. In a sense, the commercial success of *Pamela* cost Richardson control of his own text.

The publication of *Pamela II* illustrated the problems an author faced in terms of controlling and maintaining the value of his paper credit. Richardson always claimed he would continue Pamela's narrative only if compelled by the threats of a spurious sequel. He feared a sequel planned by "those who knew nothing of the story, nor the Delicacy required in the Continuation of the Piece," would "ravish" the story "out of my Hands," and cause "my Characters [to be] depreciated and debased."[1] The subtly coded language of feminization privileging Richardson's "delicacy" and his fear of "ravish"ment captures the complicated and gendered dynamic of the market. While casting himself in a feminized position, Richardson nonetheless asserts an authority over his text and his fictional subjects. His desire for control, though articulated in a vastly different – and differently gendered – discourse, still echoes Pope's construction of good writing as the cultural performance of masculinity. Pope's rigorous dominance of his work, like the texts themselves, ignored the gendered ambiguities that marked his own existence; he tended and cultivated his texts like property, assuming a position of ownership and control (no matter how tenuous that position really was). By contrast, Richardson regarded his novel much as Pamela regards her virtue – as something that can be taken from him without his continued vigilance and the production of alternative versions. He tried to preserve his control, and by extension his masculinity, but he did so through emphasis on the inviolateness of his (ever multiply-ing) text. He needed to protect its purity in the face of the debasing, scandalous, and potentially feminizing effects of unchecked consumer desire, unmonitored readers, and enthusiastic competitors anxious to benefit from his original publication. Richardson's text must not circulate unadvisedly, unchaperoned, or too freely. To do so was to risk being used, exploited, or devalued like Haywood, or an ill-advised heroine from one of her novels.

Richardson did not want to appear overtly commercial, yet he also worried about public reception in terms of both sales and critical reaction. As he shrewdly noted, "Second Parts are generally received with Prejudice, and it was treating the public too much like a Bookseller to pursue a Success till they tired out the buyers."[2] Most troubling to Richardson, however, was the violation he felt when his narrative was appropriated and continued without his authorization. He lamented "the Baseness as well as Hardship it was that a Writer could not be permitted to end his own Work, when and how he pleased, without such scandalous Attempts of Ingrafting upon his Plan." While Richardson's subsequent prolixity in terms of commentary on and revisions of all his novels might make him sound ingenuous here, he articulated the inevitable consequence of the commercialized literary marketplace Pope envisaged in the *Dunciad*.[3] In the face of publishers who threaten to publish, in this case a sequel to *Pamela*, "still more and more Volumes ... so long as the Town would receive them," consumers would purchase and writers produce (or in Pope's words, "spawn") texts indefinitely. *Pamela* accorded Richardson a great stock of paper credit, cultural currency, and status within the dynamic hierarchy of the literary marketplace, but it also revealed his inability to control a momentum that originated with him. By placing the reader-consumer in the cycle of desire, Richardson must keep producing literary commodities to meet their needs and to assure the high value of his own negotiable paper.

This is not to suggest, however, that Richardson did not try desperately to maintain control of his texts. His ceaseless revisions indicate his recognition of the infinite mutability and interpretability of fictional discourse. He revised with an awareness of the volatility of paper credit. He also had the imaginative capability to realize the potential value of his private texts as well. After being approached in 1757 by Erasmus Reich, a Leipzig bookseller, about publishing a possible edition of his letters,[4] Richardson began editing the correspondence, recognizing its possible worth as a literary commodity if his family subsequently needed the money: "Should Calamities befall them (Who in this World is exempt from such?) and *proper Leave be obtained*, the Daughters of a Father, who never troubled the Public with levying a Subscription on it ... may, perhaps, if any thing be deemed worthy in his Part of the Collection, meet with Favour." He also relished the idea that his correspondence with Lady Bradshaigh "wd. make the best Commentary that cd. Be written on the History of Clarissa."[5] Revision – of published texts, of letters, of readers' interpretations – produces more negotiable paper and additional commodities.

For Pope, like Richardson, revision was a remunerative and an aesthetic act, one that provided the opportunity to increase profits by issuing subsequent editions of a work, while also continually refining his message or redefining his authorial position.[6] Pope's extensive revision of all his written texts – poems and letters – and his strategic publication of collected works demonstrates the concern for maintaining literary and cultural authority and constructing a place in literary history. His revisions ranged from correcting minute textual errors to composing completely new sections to poems like *The Rape of the Lock* or the *Dunciad*. Similarly, Pope published collected editions of his work, beginning in 1717 (as what Maynard Mack termed a "monument to vanity"), and punctuated his career with collected works at other strategic points (1735, 1741) to assert or reclaim his poetic position.[7] Though Pope rather off-handedly said, "I writ because it amused me: I corrected because it was as pleasant to me to correct as to write," his revision of his poetry allowed him to fulfill his dual desire for artistic and financial control (*Corr.* 1, p. 6). Pope's publication of his letters, as briefly discussed in chapter 2, was a similarly complicated process during which he manipulated Curll to obscure the supremely egotistical gesture of publishing his collected letters while alive. Pope actively revised the letters he offered for publication in an attempt to refine the image of himself consistent with his socio-poetic persona. As George Sherburn notes, "in publishing his letters Pope had recombined parts of two or three, had omitted passages, and had transferred some letters to correspondents to whom they were never sent."[8] He attempted to consolidate his poetic voice and aesthetic vision by making the public and the private mutually reinforcing (a gesture that Haywood's critics performed for her to a distinctly different end).

Richardson and Pope retained their ability to republish, revise, and profit, in part because they maintained the copyrights to their works and monitored the publication of their texts. Richardson's dual role as a publisher and printer facilitated his ceaseless process of revision. Similarly, Pope's marketing acumen and close relationships with his primary publishers allowed him to control the literary means of production (to the degree that was possible in an eighteenth-century literary culture marked by piracies and unauthorized editions). The process of revision and the publication of successive editions of an individual work contributed to the cultural currency an author derived. By revising their writing, their medium of exchange, Pope and Richardson revised the value of the text as both an immediate commodity and a subsequent object for literary history. They attempted to satisfy the demands of both arenas. Revision represented another investment in the principal of their literary fortune, another addition to the amount of capital earning interest.

In light of Richardson's copious revision of his own work, his attitude toward Pope's multiple editions of the *Dunciad* is telling. Richardson complains to Aaron Hill that "I have bought Mr. Pope over so often, and his Dunciad so lately before his last new-vampt one, that I am tir'd of the Extravagance; and wonder every Body else is not."[9] He concedes, however, that with these successive editions Pope potentially secured a certain amount of interpretative control:

Mr. Pope in the Height of his Fame, tho' he had made himself, by Arts only He (as a Man of Genius) could stoop to, the Fashion, could not trust his Works with the Vulgar without Notes longer than the Work, and Self-praises, to tell them what he meant, and that he had a Meaning, in this or that Place. And thus every-one was taught to read with his Eyes.[10]

In one sense, the observation reveals much about Richardson's interpretation of Pope's motive – a gesture of enforcement ("read with his Eyes").

Richardson's observation also provides insight into the relationship between the two men and their respective positions within the symbolic hierarchy of eighteenth-century literary culture. Pope's "Genius," as Richardson called it, cannot be trusted with the "vulgar," who may misinterpret the text without Pope's reading aids. His abilities exceed the capabilities of his audience. Yet, he suggests Pope has compromised his talents, and the skills of "Versification," by "s[i]nk[ing] so low. Has he no Invention, Sir, to be better employ'd about? No Talents for worthier Subjects?. . . what must then be the strength of that Vanity and of the Ill-nature that can sink such Talents in a Dunciad?" In language reminiscent of Pope's previous critics, Richardson marks him as a kind of hybrid – the man of genius who repeatedly yields to the impulse of vanity and ill nature (both feminized characteristics in Pope's lexicon).

Pope's lofty versification stands in stark contrast to Richardson's all too accessible texts and workman-like approach to writing. While Richardson shared Pope's difficulty controlling readers' interpretations, he was not separated from the "vulgar" but was inextricably linked to his audience (and thus potentially feminized as a result). Richardson was painfully aware of his lack of experience in the "high reaches" of society and the difficulty it created in his representation of upper-class characters. Lady Mary Wortley Montagu observed, " I beleive [*sic*] this Author was never admitted into higher Company, and should confine his Pen to the Amours of Housemaids and the conversation at the Steward's Table, where I imagine he has sometimes intruded, tho oftener in the Servant's Hall" (*Corr.* III, p. 96). His class was elided with that of his readers and fictional subjects. To Lady Bradshaigh, Richardson lamented his difficulty representing Harriot in *Sir Charles Grandison* and cast himself as a retiring individual with limited experience within the world.

How shall a man obscurely situated, never delighting in public entertainments . . . naturally shy and sheepish, and wanting more encouragement by smiles, to draw him out, than any body thought it worth their while to give him . . . How, I say, shall such a man pretend to describe and enter into characters in upper life? How shall such a one draw scenes of busy and yet elegant trifling?[11]

Richardson's fame could not erase his lack of formal education, his dedication to his printing trade, and his association with the middle classes. His social class was imbricated with his position in a literary hierarchy which despite its subtle reconfigurations still retained the influence of a dominant Augustan aesthetic.

Although Pope allegedly admired *Pamela* and, according to Aaron Hill could "not bear any faults to be mentioned in the story,"[12] in many ways Richardson's success with *Pamela* represented a cultural impulse Pope fundamentally despised.[13] The emergent cultural practices Pope resisted in the 1728 *Dunciad* – popular fiction, paper credit, imaginative narratives, the unstoppable production of texts – assume a position of dominant cultural authority with Richardson. Though taking a different form, *Pamela* served a cultural function similar to Haywood's novels: it stimulated the emotions, it appealed to disparate social groups with its accessible narrative, and it depended on the manipulations of paper credit threatening to a literary and cultural elite. Richardson aroused public sentiment, causing overly eager readers to obscure the difference between fact and fiction. Richardson's domestication of paper credit, which remains dynamic, makes central in cultural discourse those emotions, transgressions, and desires that mark the feminizing impulse.[14]

Richardson's ability to surmount and ultimately capitalize on this feminization stemmed from his authorized role in the print trade, his careful containment of the narrative patterns established by Eliza Haywood, and his position in a culture reconfiguring its literary and social parameters. Indeed, his success casts Haywood's failure in sharp relief. On a fundamental level Haywood, by virtue of her gender, her genre, and her work's low cultural status, never had access to the privileged mechanisms of the print trade. She never published a collection of her correspondence, she never revised the subsequent editions of her text, and she certainly never assured herself a place in literary history. The extant Haywood letters offer a testimony to her desperate straits, her perpetual penury, and her marginalized position; ironically, they document the existence she strove to eradicate. While two collections of her novels were published, their discontinuous pagination reveals their purpose was as much for selling remaining copies of her previous texts as it was for celebrating her body of work. The novels themselves were unchanged from their initial editions, a lack of revision consistent with her limited time and access to the production of texts (even after her experience in the print trade). As a commercial writer forced to produce texts quickly and frequently to earn a living, Haywood was primarily at the mercy of the booksellers. Though she wrote as steadily (if not as voluminously) as Pope and Richardson, her production served to sustain her viability within the marketplace – to create new negotiable paper, not to increase the value of her existing stock. Her negotiable paper, when placed in circulation, did little to assure her ascent or long-term success. Where Pope and Richardson maintained the copyrights to their own texts, Haywood, of course, did not.[15] Thus subsequently issued editions of her work not only failed to provide her with an opportunity for revision, they also probably failed to provide her with any additional income.

However, Haywood engaged in a broader type of revision during the course of her literary career. Not only did she reconstruct her authorial persona to attempt to remain current within the marketplace, she helped transform cultural expectations for women writers, the novel, and the female subjects to whom and about whom she wrote. Though, of these three authors, Haywood achieved perhaps the least tangible benefit from the opportunities introduced by paper credit in its literary and financial manifestation, she was arguably the subject for whom it was most important. The openness of the discursive field, the anonymity of paper credit, and the destabilized (and thus more penetrable) literary hierarchies created a situation in which Haywood could cultivate her unique narrative voice. Her representation and negotiation of a social milieu transfixed by the textual manifestation of its own desires introduced the discursive possibilities subsequently capitalized upon by Richardson. Her depiction of female subjectivity illuminated the situation for contemporaneous subjects of both genders. And her fictional texts with their emphasis on paper credit, speculative narratives, and alternative models of value capture the dynamics of sexual, social, and financial economies that increasingly marked early modern culture.

Notes

INTRODUCTION: PAPER CREDIT

1 See Catherine Ingrassia, "Women Writing/Writing Women: Pope, Dulness and Feminization in the *Dunciad*," *Eighteenth-Century Life* 14 (1990): 40–58.
2 This, numerically, meant anywhere from 176 women in South Sea stock in 1723 (after the crash) to 964 women in Bank Stock in 1724. The participation of women is discussed more fully in chapter 1. See P. G. M. Dickson, *The Financial Revolution in England: A Study in the Development of Public Credit* (New York: St. Martin's Press, 1967), table 38, p. 282.
3 Nearly one-third of the 391 titles listed in McBurney's *Checklist of English Prose Fiction 1700–1739* were written by women, with a large portion of those appearing in the 1720s. In *Living by the Pen* Cheryl Turner similarly notes the quantitative surge in fiction by women in the 1720s (figures 3–5, pp. 36–37) (William Harlin McBurney, *A Check List of English Prose Fiction 1700–1739* [Cambridge, MA: Harvard University Press, 1960]; Cheryl Turner, *Living by the Pen: Women Writers in the Eighteenth Century* [London: Routledge, 1992]).
4 *The Politics and Poetics of Transgression* (London: Methuen, 1986), 24.
5 J. G. A. Pocock, "The Mobility of Property and the Rise of Eighteenth-Century Sociology," *Virtue, Commerce and History: Essays on Political Thought and History, Chiefly in the Eighteenth Century* (Cambridge University Press, 1985), 114, 113.
6 For example, in *Economic Thought and Ideology in Seventeenth-Century England* (Princeton University Press, 1978) Joyce Appleby claims that "[b]y slighting the economic writings of the seventeenth century, Pocock claims for the Augustan period an undeserved priority in the discussion of market economics and political power" (p. 268, n. 61). Though Appleby questions Pocock's chronology (and some other minor points of his vast body of work), her study reveals a pattern of representation and cultural anxiety similar to the one Pocock discusses. In a footnote to a recent essay, Michael McKeon generally dismisses Pocock's discussion of the "feminized economic man" by suggesting that Pocock makes an "unwarranted inference (and generalization)" from the association between the pursuit of exchange value and the traits of imaginative fantasy, passion, and hysteria that were figured as female. McKeon's assertion (itself a generalization) ignores Pocock's elaborately developed argument leading up to that assertion and, more important, the extensive economic discourse of the early eighteenth century that consistently and repeatedly employs the pattern of representation Pocock uses. Indeed, as the next chapter suggests, the cultural anxiety about the feminized economic man and the activities of women in the financial marketplace may have been even more pervasive and potent an image than Pocock himself indicates. McKeon's otherwise useful essay on the relationship between sexuality and socio-economic relations too readily and

too uncritically dismisses Pocock's assertion in the service of his own discussion ("Historicizing Patriarchy: The Emergence of Gender Difference in England, 1660–1760," *Eighteenth-Century Studies* 28 [1995]: 295–322).

7 As Pocock observes, "there were no pure dogmas or simple antitheses, and few assumptions that were not shared and employed to differing purposes by the writers on either side" (*The Machiavellian Moment: Florentine Political Thought and the Atlantic Republican Tradition* [Princeton University Press, 1975], 446).

8 Alexander Pope, *Epistle to Bathurst*, in *The Poems of Alexander Pope Vol. III. ii, Epistles to Several Persons (Moral Essays)*, edited by F. W. Bateson (London: Methuen, 1961), 69–70. Subsequent references will be made parenthetically.

9 *TE* III. ii, p. 102, n. 142.

10 By the "financial revolution," I refer to the development of a flexible credit network, improved techniques of exchange, a Bank of England, and a growing paper economy introduced primarily in the 1690s that fundamentally altered the economy of Britain. The standard discussion of the financial revolution is Dickson, *The Financial Revolution,* chapters 5 and 6. J. G. A. Pocock extensively discusses the financial revolution and its effect on the relationship between virtue and commerce in much of his work (some cited below). His most concentrated discussions of the financial revolution and the issues addressed here include *The Machiavellian Moment,* chapters 8 and 9, and "The Mobility of Property." In *Bolingbroke and His Circle: The Politics of Nostalgia in the Age of Walpole* (originally published 1968; reprinted Ithaca: Cornell University Press, 1992), Isaac Kramnick discusses what he calls the "Economic Revolution" in similar terms (pp. 39–48, 65–70). John Brewer, *The Sinews of Power: War, Money and the English State 1688–1783* (New York: Alfred A. Knopf, 1989), looks at the relationship between commerce and war, and the transformation in the British government that enabled the development of the "fiscal–military state" (xvii). He also examines the importance of taxes in the financial revolution (chapter 4, and pp. 178–89).

11 These innovations arose, in part, from the government's need to retain economic viability and to finance prolonged foreign wars. Parliament lifted restrictions on trade and the formation of private companies to create a much more open economic system. Most important, the government devised a way to provide itself with a constant source of credit by establishing a number of financial institutions, like the Bank of England, started when a group of British and European investors with £1,200,000 simply assumed the government's debts. While the establishment of the national debt relieved the immediate financial demands on the government, it escalated the government's debt from £3.1 million in 1691 to £53 million in 1727, a debt owed to corporate creditors like the Bank of England, the South Sea Company, and the East India Company. To finance its increasing military expenditures, the government also held a series of national lotteries that essentially enabled the government to borrow quickly a great deal of money from its citizens with a deferred rate of repayment.

12 Joint-stock companies typically issued sequentially numbered bonds that

would be recorded as belonging to an individual investor. For example, the advertisements in *The London Gazette* frequently print notices of missing bonds, suggesting their primary function within the new economic interactions: "Lost or mislaid since the 9th of June, 1719, two South Sea Bonds, for 100 *l.* each, No. 13272, 12372, dated December 26, 1718, of no Use to any but The Owner, Payment being stopt" (*The London Gazette*, no. 5810, Tuesday December 22 to Saturday December 26, 1719). Numerous other examples exist in the pages of *The London Gazette*, and elsewhere.

13 *A Letter to a Conscientious Man: Concerning the Use and Abuse of Riches, and the Right and the Wrong Ways of Acquiring Them* (London, 1720), 22.

14 *The Spectator*, edited by Donald Bond, 5 vols. (Oxford at the Clarendon Press, 1965), 11, p. 249. In this quotation he is describing the effects of the lottery, considered another form of speculative investment, and uses similar language elsewhere to describe investment in the stocks.

   Peter De Bolla examines the discourse of credit and the "unreality" that pervades it. Speaking specifically of the national debt that accrued later in the century he observes "the necessity for a hierarchization of discourses, into a real and an imaginary, required in order to prevent the latter leaking into the former" (*The Discourse of the Sublime: Readings in History, Aesthetics, and the Subject* [Oxford: Blackwell, 1989], 136).

15 Sandra Sherman, "Credit, Simulation, and the Ideology of Contract in the Early Eighteenth Century," *Eighteenth-Century Life* 19 (1995): 86–102.

16 Obviously, various forms of symbolic property existed previously with financial instruments such as the international letters of credit used during the Renaissance. While those letters enabled individuals to obtain funds within a wide geographic area (although often individuals from a fairly limited segment of the population) they lacked the chronological dimension – the preoccupation with the future – that marks speculative investment and the financial instruments introduced by the financial revolution.

17 By emphasizing the imaginary elements of speculative investment I do not mean to suggest that *commercial* capitalism was not dependent on the arousal and deferral of various types of desires designed to place customers into a self-perpetuating cycle of consumerism. While consumer goods might arouse a certain type of acquisitive desire (which of course transcends a desire for the goods themselves) the consumer does purchase a product, a tangible commodity, that potentially sates his desire (while also striving to perpetuate it). The recent work on consumer culture in eighteenth-century England is considerable. For a good introduction, see Neil McKendrick, John Brewer, and J. H. Plumb, *The Birth of a Consumer Society: The Commercialization of Eighteenth-Century England* (Bloomington: Indiana University Press, 1982).

18 Of course, as chapter 2 discusses, Pope, as a Catholic, could not own land, which undoubtedly fueled his compensatory gesture and contributed to his characterization of "true" poetic ability as a distinctly masculine (and empowering) activity. For a discussion of the "real-estate" metaphor as applied to literary property, particularly by Pope, see Mark Rose, *Authors and Owners:*

The Invention of Copyright (Cambridge, MA: Harvard University Press, 1993), especially chapter 4.

19 Though obviously not the purview of my study, the period of the Interregnum, with its social and economic disruption and reconstructions, also offered opportunities to individuals typically barred from certain types of power and social authority.

20 Fredric Jameson, *The Political Unconscious: Narrative as a Socially Symbolic Act* (Ithaca: Cornell University Press, 1981). See also Louis Althusser, "Ideology and Ideological State Apparatuses (Notes towards an Investigation)," in *Lenin and Philosophy and Other Essays*, trans. by Ben Brewster, (New York: Monthly Review Press, 1971), 127–86; Terry Eagleton, *Marxism and Literary Criticism* (Berkeley and Los Angeles: University of California Press, 1976) and *Criticism and Ideology* (London: Verso, 1976); and Raymond Williams, *Marxism and Literature* (Oxford and New York: Oxford University Press, 1977).

21 Richard Johnson, "What Is Cultural Studies Anyway?" *Social Text* (Winter 1986/87): 45.

22 The terms "dominant," "residual," and "emergent" come from Williams, *Marxism and Literature*, 121–27.

23 Kramnick, *Bolingbroke and His Circle*, 4.

24 Indeed, the South Sea Bubble can be read as a type of popular "text" in the way Ronald Paulson describes it: one "read or seen by almost everybody . . . [one] part of the consciousness of the learned and educated as well as the uneducated" (*Popular and Polite Art in the Age of Hogarth and Fielding* [University of Notre Dame Press, 1979], x).

25 See M. M. Bakhtin, *The Dialogic Imagination*, edited by Michael Holquist, trans. by Caryl Emerson and Michael Holquist (Austin: University of Texas Press, 1981).

26 Albert O. Hirschman, *The Passions and the Interests: Political Arguments for Capitalism before Its Triumph* (Princeton University Press, 1977).

27 Some important studies include Bridget G. MacCarthy, *Women Writers, Their Contribution to the English Novel, 1621–1744* (Cork University Press, 1944); Elaine Hobby, *Virtue of Necessity: English Women's Writing 1649–1688* (London: Virago, 1988); Jane Spencer, *The Rise of the Woman Novelist: From Aphra Behn to Jane Austen* (Oxford: Basil Blackwell, 1986); Terry Lovell, *Consuming Fiction* (London: Verso, 1987). Elaine Showalter's *The Literature of Their Own: British Women Novelists from Bronte to Lessing* (Princeton University Press, 1977), while treating nineteenth- and twentieth-century authors, similarly uses a primarily recuperative model. An extreme (and unreliable) example of that type of work in eighteenth-century studies is Dale Spender's *Mothers of the Novel: 100 Good Writers before Jane Austen* (London: Pandora Press, 1986).

28 Margaret Doody, *A Natural Passion: A Study of the Novels of Samuel Richardson* (Oxford at the Clarendon Press, 1974), chapter 6.

29 Howard Erskine-Hill, *The Social Milieu of Alexander Pope: Lives, Example and the Poetic Response* (New Haven: Yale University Press, 1975); Colin Nicholson, *Writing and the Rise of Finance: Capital Satires of the Early Eighteenth Century* (Cambridge University Press, 1994).

30 Sandra Sherman, *Finance and Fictionality in the Early Eighteenth Century: Accounting for Defoe* (Cambridge University Press, 1996).

31 Jean-Christophe Agnew, *Worlds Apart: The Market and the Theater in Anglo-American Thought, 1550–1750* (Cambridge University Press, 1986); Kurt Heinzelman, *The Economics of the Imagination* (Amherst: University of Massachusetts Press, 1980); Walter Benn Michaels, *The Gold Standard and the Logic of Naturalism: American Literature at the Turn of the Century* (Berkeley: University of California Press, 1987); Marc Shell, *The Economy of Literature* (Baltimore: Johns Hopkins University Press, 1978) and *Money, Language, and Thought: Literary and Philosophical Economies from the Medieval to the Modern Era* (Berkeley: University of California Press, 1982); James Thompson, *Models of Value: Eighteenth-Century Political Economy and the Novel* (Durham, NC: Duke University Press, 1996). A work like Barbara Herrnstein Smith, "Contingencies of Value," *Critical Inquiry* 10 (1983): 1–35, also addresses similar issues and has informed my thinking.

32 Ian Watt, *The Rise of the Novel: Studies in Defoe, Richardson and Fielding* (Berkeley and Los Angeles: University of California Press, 1957); Nancy Armstrong, *Desire and Domestic Fiction: A Political History of the Novel* (New York: Oxford University Press, 1987); J. Paul Hunter, *Before Novels: The Cultural Contexts of Eighteenth-Century English Fiction* (New York: W. W. Norton and Co., 1990); Michael McKeon, *The Origins of the English Novel, 1660–1740* (Baltimore: Johns Hopkins University Press, 1987); John Richetti, *Popular Fiction before Richardson: Narrative Patterns 1700–1739* (Oxford at the Clarendon Press, 1969). Although Richetti's book was originally published in 1969, it was recently republished with little revision, making it still current in discussions of the eighteenth-century novel. Obviously this is by no means an exhaustive list of major work on the novel, but rather reflects the recent trends and influences in the field.

33 Janet Todd, *The Sign of Angellica: Women, Writing and Fiction 1660–1800* (New York: Columbia University Press, 1989); Ros Ballaster, *Seductive Forms: Women's Amatory Fiction from 1684 to 1740* (Oxford: Clarendon Press, 1992); Turner, *Living by the Pen.*

34 Catherine Gallagher, *Nobody's Story: The Vanishing Acts of Women Writers in the Marketplace 1670–1820* (Berkeley and Los Angeles: University of California Press, 1994); Laura Brown, *The Ends of Empire: Women and Ideology in Early Eighteenth-Century English Literature* (Ithaca: Cornell University Press, 1993). Mona Scheuermann's *Her Bread to Earn: Women, Money, and Society from Defoe to Austen* (Lexington: University Press of Kentucky, 1993) addresses the issue of women and economy, although, as discussed in chapter 5, n. 2, in a way that fundamentally differs from my own.

I WOMEN, CREDIT, AND THE SOUTH SEA BUBBLE

1 *Letters to and from Henrietta, Countess of Suffolk, and her second husband, the Hon. George Berkeley: 1712–1767*, in 2 vols., edited by J. W. Croker (London 1824), I, p. 55. The letter is dated June 25, 1720. Elizabeth Molesworth (d. 1725) was the daughter of

James Welwood, M.D., and the wife of Captain the Honorable Walter
Molesworth, fifth son of Robert, first Viscount Molesworth. Lady Sutherland,
formerly Judith Tichborne, was a friend and coat-tail relation. Her grand-
mother, Lady Tichborne, was also the grandmother of Mr. Molesworth and
Mr. Molesworth's sister had also married her cousin Captain W. Tichborne.
The information about Molesworth appears in Croker (55–56) and Lewis
Melville, *Lady Suffolk and Her Circle* (London: Hutchinson and Co., 1924), 145.

2 Corruption marked the South Sea Company from the beginning. Various
members of the government were bribed to facilitate the decision to allow the
company to convert the national debt. The company acted to drive up the
price of shares by illegally buying £332,350 of its own stock. And of course
after the collapse, while many individuals, including John Aislabie, Chancellor
of the Exchequer, were ostensibly punished, many were also shielded or
"screened" from prosecution. The most extensive and authoritative discussion
of the Bubble can be found in Dickson, *The Financial Revolution*, chapters 5 and
6. Two book-length studies of the South Sea Bubble are John Carswell, *The
South Sea Bubble* (originally published Stanford University Press, 1960; revised
edition, Dover, NH: Allan Sutton Publishing, 1993), and Virginia Spencer
Cowles, *The Great Swindle: The Story of the South Sea Bubble* (London: Collins
Press, 1960). See also Kramnick, *Bolingbroke and His Circle*, chapter 3; Larry
Neal, *The Rise of Financial Capitalism: International Capital Markets in the Age of
Reason* (Cambridge University Press, 1990), chapters 4 and 5; Nicholson,
Writing and the Rise of Finance, chapter 2; Pocock, *The Machiavellian Moment*,
chapters 8 and 9; and W. R. Scott, *The Constitution of English, Scottish and Irish
Joint-Stock Companies to 1720*, 3 vols. (Cambridge University Press, 1910–12).
John Sperling provides a bibliographic discussion in *The South Sea Company: An
Historical Essay and Bibliographical Finding List* (Cambridge, MA: Harvard
University Press, 1962).

3 The company was to have a monopoly of trade with the east coast of South
America, "from the River Orinoco to Tierra del Fuego" (Dickson, *The
Financial Revolution*, 65).

4 Ibid., 134–36.

5 Croker, *Letters to and from Henrietta*, 1, p. 56. Because subscriptions could be
bought on margin with only 10 percent of the price initially invested,
Molesworth had to seek only £50 from her father.

6 Ibid., 1, p. 55. Continuing the letter, Molesworth appears to suggest subtly that
perhaps Howard should lend her additional funds since Molesworth and her
husband lack the collateral to borrow from other sources:

> As greedy as I seem, I should have been satisfied if I could by any means have raised the
> sum of £500 or £1000 more, but the vast price that money bears, and our being not
> able to make any security according to the law, has made me regret a scheme I had of
> borrowing such a sum of some monied friend.

7 In light of the £43,126 profit realized by Aislabie, his claim that he did not act
deceptively rings somewhat hollow. The £43,126 is the amount the government calculated as Aislabie's profit and confiscated from him after the Bubble

collapsed. Aislabie purchased stock in the first three offerings or "subscriptions," purchasing a total of £13,000 valued at £900 at £117,000 (Dickson, *The Financial Revolution*, 110).

8 John Aislabie, *Mr. Aislabie's Second Speech on his Defence in the House of Lords, on Thursday, July 20, 1721* (London, 1721).

9 *A Letter to a Conscientious Man: Concerning the Use and Abuse of Riches, and the Right and Wrong Ways of Acquiring Them* (London, 1720), 22; William Rufus Chetwood, *The Stock-Jobbers: or, the Humours of Exchange Alley. A Comedy in Three Acts* (London, 1720).

10 The proliferation of speculative financial schemes was tremendous and numerous joint-stock companies, insurance companies, and private lotteries sprang up in a bid for investment monies. Many offered subscription lists without establishing any clear project or activity; others offered outlandish schemes (The Bleaching of Hair Company, a Company to Insure Marriages from Divorce). The schemes were designed to appeal to potential investors of all ranks. Other practices emerged that expanded the opportunities (real and suspect). For example, speculators trying to spread their risks would purchase batches of lottery tickets and then resell each ticket by dividing it into affordable shares that could be purchased for small amounts.

11 Dickson, *The Financial Revolution*, 267.

12 Obviously a figure like Defoe plays extensively with the permutations of female participation in multiple economies, both with his allegorical Lady Credit and with fictional subjects like Moll and Roxana. For sustained and insightful treatment of Defoe, see Sandra Sherman, *Finance and Fictionality*.

13 Pocock, *The Machiavellian Moment*, 109.

14 Thomas Gordon, *A Learned Dissertation Upon Old Women, Male and Female, Spiritual and Temporal, in all Ages; whether in Church, State or Exchange Alley* (London, 1720), 26. Jonathans was a popular coffee house adjacent to Exchange Alley that was the site of business transactions (and social gatherings) among the growing number of stock-jobbers.

15 Hunter, *Before Novels*, 99.

16 Pocock, *The Machiavellian Moment*, 431.

17 Steele, *The Spectator* no. 509, IV, p. 309.

18 As chapter 5 suggests, *Pamela* demonstrates the applicability of that comparison.

19 John Dennis, *An Essay upon Public Spirit; Being a Satyr in Prose upon the Manners and Luxury of the Times* (London, 1711), 15.

20 *Some Considerations on the late Mismanagement of the South-Sea Stock . . . in a Letter to a Friend* (London, 1721), 4.

21 *An Examination and Explanation of the South Sea Company's Scheme for taking in the Publick Debts* (London, 1720), 16–17.

22 For a discussion of the concept of luxury in eighteenth-century culture, see John Sekora, *Luxury: The Concept in Western Thought, Eden to Smollet* (Baltimore: Johns Hopkins University Press, 1977). For a discussion of women and luxury see Laura Mandell, "Bawds and Merchants: Engendering Capitalist Desire," *ELH* 59 (1992): 107–23.

23 McKeon, *The Origins of the English Novel*, 205.

24 For a further discussion see Paula R. Backscheider, "Defoe's Lady Credit," *Huntington Library Quarterly* 44.2 (1981): 89–100, and Gary Hentzi, "'An Itch of Gaming': The South Sea Bubble and the Novels of Daniel Defoe," *Eighteenth-Century Life* 17 (1993): 32–45.

25 Joseph Addison, *Spectator* no. 3, I, pp. 15–16. As Pocock observes, "like all these goddesses, Credit typifies the instability of secular things, brought out by the interaction of particular human wills, appetites and passions . . . in which she is shown operating malignantly and irrationally" (*The Machiavellian Moment*, 453).

26 Steele, *Spectator* no. 460, IV, pp. 121–22.

27 James Milner, *Three Letters Relating to the South-Sea Company and the Bank. The First Written in March, 1719–1720. The Second in April 1720. The Third in September 1720* (London, 1720). The Bank of England and the South Sea Company competed to see which would assume a larger portion of the national debt and thus receive a larger payment from the government.

28 John Aislabie, *Mr. Aislabie's Two Speeches Considered* (London, 1721), 12.

29 *The Battle of the Bubbles. Shewing Their Several Constitutions, Alliances, Policies and Wars . . . By a Stander-By* (London, 1720), 10.

30 Most of the prints surrounding the South Sea Bubble originated in Amsterdam or Paris, where the Tulip Scheme and Mississippi Land Scheme had an effect similar to the South Sea Bubble. The locations and names involved were altered to fit Exchange Alley and the personalities involved. The prints discussed here appear in *The Great Mirror of Folly [Het Groote Tafereel der Dwaasheid]* (1720), a collection of these broadsides. For further discussion of the assembled prints see Vincent Carretta, *The Snarling Muse: Verbal and Visual Political Satire from Pope to Churchill* (Philadelphia: University of Pennsylvania Press, 1983); Arthur H. Cole, *The Great Mirror of Folly: An Economic-Bibliographical Study* (Boston: Harvard University Press, 1949); and *The Catalogue of Prints and Drawings in the British Museum 1870–1954: Division I: Personal and Political Satire, vol. 2, 1689–1733* (London, 1873). For a discussion of the iconography of the petticoat see Erin Mackie, "Lady Credit and the Strange Case of the Hoop-Petticoat," *College Literature* 20 (June 1993): 27–43. For a discussion of male resistance to the petticoat see Kimberly Chrisman, "*Unhoop* the Fair Sex: The Campaign against the Hoop Petticoat in Eighteenth-Century England," *Eighteenth-Century Studies* 30.1 (1996): 5–24. Another important visual representation of the South Sea Bubble is, of course, Hogarth's *An Emblematic Print on The South Sea Bubble*. While Hogarth's print lacks a central female image, the detailed visual text supplies numerous markers indicating women's participation in the Bubble. Women wait on line to purchase tickets in a "raffle for Husbands with Lottery Fortunes" and they occupy many of the seats on the South Sea Company carousel. For discussions of the print see Ronald Paulson, *Hogarth: The Modern Moral Subject, 1697–1732* (New Brunswick and London: Rutgers University Press, 1991), chapter 3, and Sean Shesgreen, *Engravings by Hogarth* (New York: Dover Publications, Inc., 1973).

31 The scholarship addressing women's role in the new consumer culture is

extensive and includes most notably Laura Brown, *Ends of Empire: Women and Ideology in Early Eighteenth-Century English Literature* (Ithaca: Cornell University Press, 1993). See also Felicity Nussbaum, *The Brink of All We Hate: English Satires on Women 1660–1750* (Lexington: University Press of Kentucky, 1984), and Beth Kowalski-Wallace, "Women, China, and Consumer Culture in Eighteenth-Century England," *Eighteenth-Century Studies* 29.2 (1995/96): 153–68.

32 Dickson, *The Financial Revolution*, 267.

33 Peter Earle, *The Making of the English Middle Class: Business, Society and Family Life in London, 1660–1730* (Berkeley and Los Angeles: University of California Press, 1989), 173.

34 Carswell, *The South Sea Bubble*, 144.

35 Susan Staves, *Married Women's Separate Property in England 1660–1833* (Cambridge, MA: Harvard University Press, 1990), 152. Staves explores "why the legal changes allowing women to become autonomous owners of property did not empower married women" (222). See also Susan Moller Okin, "Patriarchy and Married Women's Property in England: Questions on Some Current Views," *Eighteenth-Century Studies* 17 (1983/84): 121–38.

36 For example, in *Epistle to a Lady*, Pope praises Martha Blount for her ability to maintain equanimity in the face of financial fluctuations or unlucky lottery tickets: "Let Fops or Fortune fly which way they will; / Disdains all loss of Tickets, or Codille" (*TE* III. ii p. 69: 265–66).

37 Croker, *Letters to and from Henrietta*, I, pp. 43, 36.

38 Ibid., 57, 60.

39 Carswell, *The South Sea Bubble*, 144.

40 For a discussion of the Duchess's considerable financial acumen during the South Sea episode, see Frances Harris, *A Passion for Government: The Life of Sarah, Duchess of Marlborough* (Oxford: Clarendon Press, 1991), pp. 227–31.

41 See Robert Halsband, *The Life of Lady Mary Wortley Montagu* (Oxford: Clarendon Press, 1956), 100–04, and *The Complete Letters of Lady Mary Wortley Montagu*, 3 vols., edited by Robert Halsband (Oxford: Clarendon Press, 1965–67), I, pp. 450–53; II, pp. 1–5, 14.

42 Carswell, *The South Sea Bubble*, 116.

43 William Rufus Chetwood, *South Sea; or, the biters bit* (London, 1720), 8.

44 Thomas D'Urfey, *The Two Queens of Brentford: or, Bayes no Poetaster ... With a Comical Prologue and Epilogue* (London, 1721), 11.

45 *Exchange Alley; or, the Stock-jobber turn'd Gentleman; with the Humours of our Modern Projectors* (London, 1720).

46 Chetwood, *The Stock-Jobbers*, 23.

47 Cited in Cowles, *The Great Swindle*, 43.

48 Sherman, *Finance and Fictionality*, 41.

49 "An Excellent New Ballad upon the Masquerades," in *Love's Invention: or, the Recreation in Vogue* (London, 1718), 6.

50 Terry Castle, *Masquerade and Civilization: The Carnivalesque in Eighteenth-Century English Culture and Fiction* (Stanford University Press, 1986), 224–25.

51 This print, like the others discussed, appears in *The Great Mirror of Folly* (1720) and the text quoted is located at the bottom of the print beneath the visual image.

2 POPE, GENDER, AND THE COMMERCE OF CULTURE

1 Lance Bertelsen, "Journalism, Carnival and *Jubilate Agno*," *ELH* 59 (1992): 358.
2 David L. Vander Meulen, *Pope's Dunciad of 1728: A History and Facsimile* (Charlottesville: For the Bibliographical Society of the University of Virginia and the New York Public Library by the University of Virginia Press, 1991), 23.
3 Paulson, *Popular and Polite Art in the Age of Hogarth and Fielding*.
4 Pat Rogers, *Grub Street: Studies in a Subculture* (London: Methuen; New York: Barnes and Noble, 1972).
5 Mikhail Bakhtin, *Rabelais and His World*, trans. by Helene Iswolsky (Bloomington: Indiana University Press, 1984). I don't mean to ignore the fluidity and mutually informing quality that Bakhtin's categories, in his discussion, necessarily suggest. But neither am I comfortable with the notion of authorized or "licensed" misrule that the inversion of categories allows. One of the most anxiety-producing aspects of Grub Street for Pope was his perception of it as un-"author"-ized in every sense of the word – a commercially driven site of transgressive cultural discourses in which classical authorship as Pope constructs it is replaced by anonymous and interchangeable professional writers.
6 Stallybrass and White, *The Politics and Poetics of Transgression*, 3.
7 Rogers, *Grub Street*, 280.
8 Montagu to Lady Bute, July 23, 1754, *The Complete Letters of Lady Mary Wortley Montagu*, III, pp. 68–69.
9 James Ralph, *The Case of Authors by Profession or Trade, stated, with regard to the Booksellers, the Stage, and the Public* (London, 1758), 8.
10 David Foxon, *Pope and the Early Eighteenth-Century Book Trade* (Oxford: Clarendon Press, 1991), 108.
11 *The Poems of Alexander Pope: Vol. IV, Imitations of Horace with an Epistle to Dr. Arbuthnot and The Epilogue to the Satires*, edited by John Butt (London: Methuen, 1953), Epistle II. ii, 68–69.
12 John Gay, *Letters*, edited by C. F. Burgess (Oxford: Clarendon Press, 1966), 43. For a discussion of Pope's experience in the South Sea Bubble see Howard Erskine-Hill, "Pope and the Financial Revolution," in *Alexander Pope*, edited by Peter Dixon (London: G. Bell and Sons, 1972), 200–29, Nicholson, *Writing and the Rise of Finance*, esp. pp. 63–68, and Laura Brown, *Alexander Pope* (Oxford: Basil Blackwell, 1985).
13 For another discussion of Pope, Gay, and the South Sea Bubble, see David Nokes, *John Gay: A Profession of Friendship* (Oxford: Clarendon Press, 1995), chapter 10, "Bubbled."
14 "Politicians, Peers and Publication by Subscription 1700–50," in *Books and Their Readers in Eighteenth-Century England*, edited by Isabel Rivers (Leicester:

Leicester University Press, 1982), 50. As A. S. Clapp describes, "the author or bookseller agrees to produce a book of specified content, size and quality, whose publication is financed by individuals, or subscribers, each of whom receives in return a copy or copies of the book" ("The Beginnings of Subscription Publication in the Seventeenth Century," *Modern Philology* 19 [1931–32]: 204, quoted in Speck, 48).

15 Nicholson, *Writing and the Rise of Finance*, 8. John Brewer observes a subscription of any kind "could liberate men from the client economy ... [because] it provided a degree of security in a period of change, enabling [the author] ... to move outside the protected realm of patrician patronage without being totally at the mercy of the open market's vagaries and whim" ("Commercialization and Politics," *The Birth of a Consumer Society*, 225).

16 Foxon, *Pope and the Early Eighteenth-Century Book Trade*, 52. For a discussion of Pope's acrimonious relationship with Madame Dacier see Claudia N. Thomas, *Alexander Pope and His Eighteenth-Century Women Readers* (Carbondale: Southern Illinois University Press, 1994), 49–52.

17 William Kurtz Wimsatt, *The Portraits of Alexander Pope* (New Haven: Yale University Press, 1965), 145. For an important discussion of how Pope manipulated verbal and visual representations of his body (by himself and others) see also Helen Deutsch, "'The Truest Copies' and the 'Mean Original': Pope, Deformity and the Poetics of Self-Exposure," *Eighteenth-Century Studies* 27 (1993): 1–26, and *Resemblance and Disgrace: Alexander Pope and the Deformation of Culture* (Cambridge, MA: Harvard University Press, 1996).

18 Samuel Johnson, *Lives of the English Poets* in 3 vols., edited by George Birkbeck Hill (Oxford: Clarendon Press, 1945), III, p. 197. While some critics, like Maynard Mack, argue that Pope's own marginality, as well as his close associations with women like the Blount sisters, increased his sensitivity to the limited opportunities for an eighteenth-century woman, the simplicity and essentialism of this approach ultimately limits its usefulness in a reading of Pope.

19 Alexander Pope, *The Correspondence of Alexander Pope*, edited by George Sherburn in 5 vols. (Oxford: Clarendon Press, 1956), I, p. 114. Subsequent references will be made parenthetically with reference to volume and page number. Pope wrote a letter to Martha Blount that expressed his resistance to marriage and his anxiety about infidelity. He describes how Lord Harcourt

> gravely proposed her [Mrs. Jennings] to me for a Wife, being tender of her interests and knowing (what is a shame to Providence) that she is less indebted to fortune than I. I told him his Lordship could never have thought of such a thing but for his misfortune of being blind, and that I never could till I was so: But that, as matters now are, I did not care to force so fine a woman to give the finishing stroke to all my deformities, but the last mark of a Beast, horns. (*Corr.* I, p. 431)

Many biographers discuss Pope's physical situation. See, for example, Maynard Mack, "'The Least Thing Like a Man in England': Some Effects of Pope's Physical Disability on his Life and Literary Career," in Mack's *Collected in Himself: Essays Critical, Biographical, and Bibliographical on Pope and Some of His Contemporaries* (Newark: University of Delaware Press, 1982), 372–92. The most complete discussion can be found in G. S. Rousseau and Marjorie Nicolson, *"This Long Disease My Life": Alexander Pope and the Sciences* (Princeton University Press, 1968).

20 *The Poems of Alexander Pope: Vol. I, Pastoral Poetry and An Essay on Criticism*, edited by E. Audra and Aubrey Williams (London: Methuen, 1961).

21 Ann Rosalind Jones, "Writing the Body: Toward an Understanding of l'Ecriture Féminine," in *The New Feminist Criticism: Essays on Women, Literature and Theory*, edited by Elaine Showalter (New York: Pantheon Books, 1985), 362.

22 Pope's rakish persona in his correspondence is explored in: Dustin H. Griffin, *Alexander Pope: The Poet in the Poems* (Princeton University Press, 1978), pp. 40–41; James Winn, *A Window in the Bosom: The Letters of Alexander Pope* (Hamden, CT: Archon Books, 1977); and James Grantham Turner, "Pope's Libertine Self-Fashioning," *The Eighteenth Century: Theory and Interpretation* 29 (1988): 123–44. For discussions of his correspondence with Lady Mary Wortley Montagu, see Patricia Meyer Spacks, "Imaginations Warm and Tender: Pope and Lady Mary," *South Atlantic Quarterly* 83 (1984): 207–15, and Cynthia Wall, "Editing Desire: Pope's Correspondence with (and without) Lady Mary," *Philological Quarterly* 71.2 (1992): 221–37.

23 *The Poems of Alexander Pope: Vol. II, The Rape of the Lock and Other Poems* (New York: Oxford University Press, 1942).

24 Ronald Paulson, *Breaking and Remaking: Aesthetic Practice in England, 1700–1820* (New Brunswick: Rutgers University Press, 1989), 51.

25 Catherine Gallagher, "Raymond Williams and Cultural Studies," *Social Text* 30 (1992): 87.

26 Despite a flurry of feminist treatments of the Augustans in the late 1980s, critics seemed to avoid the issue of Dulness's gender. Valerie Rumbold's *Women's Place in Pope's World* (Cambridge University Press, 1989) deals more with Pope's personal relationships with women, and does not discuss Dulness the woman. Laura Brown's new historicist treatment of Pope, *Alexander Pope* (Oxford: Basil Blackwell, 1985), provides a good discussion of Pope's representation of imperialism, capitalism, and the commercialization of culture, but she does not deal directly with the gendered implications of Dulness. In *The Brink of All We Hate*, Nussbaum focuses only briefly on Dulness in any way. Similarly, Ellen Pollak's *The Poetics of Sexual Myth: Gender and Ideology in the Verse of Swift and Pope* (University of Chicago Press, 1985) addresses only *The Rape of the Lock* and *Epistle to a Lady*. Penelope Wilson in "Feminism and the Augustans: Some Readings and Problems," *Critical Inquiry* 28 (1984): 80–92, describes Dulness as a "force of anti-creation" (81), but only in the context of her larger examination of Augustan misogyny and the critical problems it presents. Even Susan Gubar's interest in "The Female Monster in Augustan Satire," *Signs* 3.2 (1977): 380–94, focuses on Swift, giving little attention to Pope's Dulness. More recently Dennis Todd specifically discusses Dulness as a monster connected with the imagination, but only mentions her gender once in a footnote (*Imagining Monsters: Miscreations of the Self in Eighteenth-Century England* [University of Chicago Press, 1995]).

27 Andreas Huyssen, "Mass Culture as Woman: Modernism's Other," in *After the Great Divide: Modernism, Mass Culture, Postmodernism* (Bloomington: Indiana University Press, 1986), 53.

28 Thomas C. Faulkner and Rhonda L. Blair, "The Classical and Mythographic Sources of Pope's Dulness," *Huntington Library Quarterly* 43 (1980): 246, 215, 216. An exhaustive source study of Dulness and other figures in the *Dunciad*, this essay makes connections to a range of mythological figures including but not limited to Cybele, Ceres, Hecate, Circe, Cloacina, and Bellona: what the authors term "a very complex web of cross-associations" (216). Dulness is also a mock-Venus but quite the opposite of Lucretius' in the opening of *De Rerum Natura* who generates all life.

29 Faulkner and Blair, "The Classical and Mythographic Sources," 217.

30 Simone de Beauvoir, *The Second Sex*, trans. and edited by H. M. Parshley (1952; New York: Vintage Books, 1974), 193.

31 Ibid., 166.

32 *The Poems of Alexander Pope: Vol. V, The Dunciad*, edited by James Sutherland (London: Methuen, 1952). All subsequent references will be made parenthetically. The *Dunciad* will be identifed with an "A" and "B" designating the 1729 *Dunciad Variorum* and the 1743 *Dunciad in Four Books* respectively.

33 Susan Stanford Friedman, "Creativity and the Childbirth Metaphor: Gender Difference in Literary Discourse," in *Speaking of Gender*, edited by Elaine Showalter (New York: Routledge, 1984), 94.

34 Mary Douglas, *Purity and Danger: An Analysis of the Concepts of Pollution and Taboo* (1966; London: Ark Paperbacks, 1984), 98.

35 Pat Rogers, *An Introduction to Pope* (London: Methuen, 1975), 128, quoted in David Fairer, *Pope's Imagination* (Manchester University Press, 1984), 129.

36 Bakhtin, *Rabelais and His World*, 19.

37 Friedman, "Creativity and the Childbirth Metaphor," 85. In her discussion of the eighteenth-century use of birth imagery as a metaphor for literary production, she notes that with the "gynophobic ethos" of the time, "the childbirth metaphor became the ultimate insult to a male artist's creativity" (85).

38 Irvin Ehrenpreis, *Acts of Implication* (Berkeley: University of California Press, 1980), 87.

39 Susan Gubar, "'The Blank Page' and Issues of Female Creativity," in *The New Feminist Criticism: Essays on Women, Literature, and Theory*, edited by Elaine Showalter (New York: Pantheon Books, 1985), 295.

40 Paul-Gabriel Boucé, "Women, Monsters, and Imagination," in *Sexual Underworlds of the Enlightenment* (Chapel Hill: University of North Carolina Press, 1988), 88. For further discussion of this idea, see Boucé's "Some Sexual Beliefs and Myths in Eighteenth-Century Britain," in *Sexuality in Eighteenth-Century Britain*, edited by Paul-Gabriel Boucé (Manchester University Press, 1982).

41 Turner, as quoted in Boucé, "Women, Monsters, and Imagination," 90.

42 Roy Porter, "'The Secrets of Generation Displayed': *Aristotle's Masterpiece* in Eighteenth-Century England," *Eighteenth-Century Life* 9 (1985): 11.

43 David Hume, "On Essay Writing," in *Essays: Moral, Political and Literary* (Indianapolis: Liberty Classics, 1985), 537.

44 And, as Claudia Thomas describes, he designed aspects of his translation of Homer specifically for women. See *Alexander Pope and His Eighteenth-Century Women Readers*, chapter 1.

45 By the time Pope published the 1743 edition of the *Dunciad*, even the sciences had become popularized, if not "feminized." The increasing availability of the microscope, for example, allowed women to use it for various "domestic" experiences. In *The Female Spectator*, Eliza Haywood urges her readers to carry a microscope with them when they walk so they can more closely examine the flora and fauna they encounter. Also in 1739 Elizabeth Carter translated from Italian *Sir Isaac Newton's Philosophy Explained for the Use of Ladies in Six Dialogues on Light and Colours*, which presented the concepts of attraction and light in "domesticated" terms offering home experiments for women. For a further discussion see Gerald Dennis Meyer, *The Scientific Lady in England, 1650–1760: An Account of Her Rise, with Emphasis on the Major Roles of the Telescope and Microscope* (Berkeley: University of California Press, 1959), especially chapter 6: " The Scientific Lady Comes of Age."

46 *The Compact Edition of the Oxford English Dictionary*, vol. II (New York: Oxford University Press, 1973), 292–93.

47 *The Complete Poems of John Wilmot, Earl of Rochester*, edited by David M. Vieth (New Haven: Yale University Press, 1973), 11–12.

48 Robert Ness, "The *Dunciad* and Italian Opera in England," *Eighteenth-Century Studies* 20 (Winter 1986/87): 172–94.

49 Elias F. Mengel, Jr. suggests that Pope also subtly attacks bookseller Ann Dodd (d. 1750?) by attributing the London reprinting of the *Dunciad* to her, a suggestion with which I strongly agree. The imprint identifies the location of the first prints as Dublin to suggest that the poem is from "the hand of an Irish dunce, one more Mac Flecknoe." And, since Dodd published "trivial poems, tales and miscellaneous pieces she might well be expected to reprint an Irish poem" ("The *Dunciad* Illustrations," *Eighteenth-Century Studies* 7.2 [1973]: 164). Reginal Harvey Griffith cautions that "what precise meaning was attached to the appearance of a bookseller's name on the title-page, we do not know" (*Alexander Pope: A Bibliography, Vol. I. Part II: Pope's Own Writings 1735–1751* [Austin: University of Texas Press, 1927], xliv). The "Bibliographical Appendix" to the Twickenham Edition of the *Dunciad* (*TE* v, p. 438) identifies Dodd, the wife of stationer William Dodd, as the keeper of a pamphlet shop at the Peacock near Temple Bar. She printed a variety of pieces "either separately or (more frequently) in collaboration with other publishers, such as Curll." In fact, subsequent to the publication of the *Dunciad*, she apparently began selling many of the published attacks on Pope, including Curll's *Key to the Dunciad*. She seems to have also functioned as a mercury (see Vander Meulen, *Pope's Dunciad of 1728*). In June 1744, Dodd published *The Last Will and Testament of Alexander Pope of Twickenham, Esq.* Herbert Atherton describes Ann Dodd as "one of the many women in the pamphlet selling trade . . . [and] a major distributor of

some of the more scurrilous material of the day: bawdy tales and allegedly seditious material (*Political Prints in the Age of Hogarth: A Study of the Ideographic Representation of Politics* [Oxford: Clarendon Press, 1974], 32). Dodd had numerous encounters with governmental authorities. The list of all the seditious libels prosecuted since Queen Anne indicates Dodd was brought up on charges three times between 1728 and 1745 (Public Record Office, London KB 15/54 fos. 152, 154, 156).

50 Thomas was primarily self-educated, reading and writing poetry in her youth and corresponding with Dryden, who dubbed her "Corinna." She had a sixteen-year courtship with Richardson Gwinnett, and was the friend but not lover of Henry Cromwell. Her life changed rapidly after 1718 and, according to the *Dictionary of American and British Women Writers*, "her last dozen years were filled with horrors: litigation, sickness, solitude, imprisonment for debt . . . and death in poverty." Her published works included *Miscellany Poems on Several Subjects* (1722), *Codrus* (1728), *The Metamorphoses of the Town: or a View of the Present Fashion* (1733, published posthumously) and *Pylades and Corinna* (1731), the published correspondence between Thomas and Gwinnett. See also Anne McWhir, "Elizabeth Thomas and the Two Corinnas: Giving the Woman Writer a Bad Name," *ELH* 62 (1995): 105–19.

51 The full title was *Mr. Pope's Familiar Letters written to Henry Cromwell Esq. Between 1707 and 1712, with original Poems by Mr. Pope, Mr. Cromwell, and Sappho* (London, 1726).

52 T. R. Steiner, "The Misrepresentation of Elizabeth Thomas, 'Curll's Corinna'," *Notes and Queries* n.s. 30 (1983): 506–08.

53 *Pylades and Corinna: Or Memoirs of the Lives, Amours, and Writings of Richard Gwinnett, Esq. and Mrs. Elizabeth Thomas* (London, 1731–32), 95.

54 Jerry C. Beasley, *Novels of the 1740s* (Athens: University of Georgia Press, 1982), 162. For a general biographical introduction to Haywood see Jerry C. Beasley, "Eliza Haywood," *Dictionary of Literary Biography*, vol. 39, edited by Martin C. Battestin (Detroit: Gale Research Company, 1985); *The Dictionary of National Biography*, vol. 9, edited by Leslie Stephen and Sidney Lee (Oxford University Press, 1917; rpt. 1921–22), 313–12; *A Dictionary of British and American Women Writers 1660–1800*, edited by Janet Todd (Totowa, NJ: Rowman and Littlefield, 1987); or Mary Anne Schofield, *Eliza Haywood* (Boston: Twayne Publishers, 1985). These sources all perpetuate inaccurate information about Haywood which Christine Blouch corrects in "Eliza Haywood and the Romance of Obscurity," *Studies in English Literature* 31 (1991): 535–52. For more detailed bibliographic references to Haywood's body of work and role in the development of the English novel, see the next two chapters.

55 Maynard Mack, *Collected in Himself*, 388.

56 An author, projector, and very much a man of the new literary world, Hill had a volatile relationship with Pope which subsequent editions of the *Dunciad* illustrates.

57 Patricia Crawford, "Women's Published Writing 1600–1700," in *Women in English Society 1500–1800*, edited by Mary Prior (London: Methuen, 1985), 216.

58 Both of these episodes are well known and well documented. See, especially, Maynard Mack, *Alexander Pope: A Life* (New York: W. W. Norton and Co., 1985), 296, and George Sherburn, *The Early Career of Alexander Pope* (Oxford University Press, 1934), especially chapters 4, 5, and 6.

59 The observation occurs in Rose's discussion of Pope's 1741 lawsuit against Curll over the 1735 publication of his letters (*Authors and Owners*, 62).

60 Shef Rogers, "Pope, Publishing, and Popular Interpretations of the *Dunciad Variorum*," *Philological Quarterly* 74 (1995): 279–95.

61 Eve Kosofsky Sedgwick, *Between Men: English Literature and Male Homosocial Desire* (New York: Columbia University Press, 1985), 21. For further discussion of traffic in women see also Luce Irigaray, *This Sex Which is Not One*, trans. by Catherine Porter (Ithaca: Cornell University Press, 1977), especially chapter 8, "Women on the Market"; Gayle Rubin, "The Traffic in Women: Notes toward a Political Economy of Sex," in *Toward an Anthropology of Women*, edited by Rayma Ruter (New York: Monthly Review Press, 1975), 157–210. For a discussion of how this paradigm figures in Pope's later exchange with Colley Cibber (in very different ways) see Kristina Straub, *Sexual Suspects: Eighteenth-Century Players and Sexual Identity* (Princeton University Press, 1992).

62 Indeed, as Vander Meulen notes, many people in London, and certainly in the provinces, were confused by the initials and dashes Pope used in his poem and asked the poet for a key to the work (*Pope's Dunciad of 1728*, 20).

63 Bakhtin, *Rabelais and His World*, 19.

64 Stallybrass and White, *The Politics and Poetics of Transgression*, 9.

65 *The Compleat Key to the Dunciad* (London, 1728). For a complete listing of the pamphlets published in response to the *Dunciad*, see J. V. Guerinot, *Pamphlet Attacks on Alexander Pope 1711–1744: A Descriptive Bibliography* (London: Methuen and Co., 1969).

66 *Codrus: Or, the Dunciad Dissected Being the Finishing Stroke* (London, 1728).

67 *The Compleat Key to the Dunciad*, 18.

68 *The Female Dunciad* (London, 1728), 44.

69 Terry Eagleton, *The Rape of Clarissa: Writing, Sexuality and Class Struggle in Samuel Richardson* (Minneapolis: University of Minnesota Press, 1982), 20–21.

70 Maynard Mack, *Collected in Himself*, Appendix A, 395–461.

71 Samuel Johnson, *Lives of the English Poets*, iii, p. 188.

72 As Maynard Mack observes, "like every writer dependent on a public, Pope had to give as much consideration to what he was perceived to be as to what he was" (*Alexander Pope: A Life*, 655).

73 *The Female Dunciad*, 12.

74 *A Popp upon Pope: or, a True and Faithful Account of a Late Horrid and Barbarous Whipping, Committed on the Body of A. Pope, a Poet* (London, 1728).

75 Mack, *Alexander Pope: A Life*, 490.

76 *The Popiad* (London, 1728).

77 Bakhtin, *Rabelais and His World*, 21.

78 For a discussion of this theme in popular texts see David Kunzle, "World Upside Down: The Iconography of a European Broadsheet Type," in *The*

Reversible World: Symbolic Inversion in Art and Society, edited by Barbara Babcock (Ithaca: Cornell University Press, 1978), 39–94.

79 Wimsatt, *The Portraits of Alexander Pope*, 245.

80 *Mr. Pope's Literary Correspondence, Volume the Second* (London, 1735).

81 *The Curliad, A Hypercritic upon the Dunciad Variorum* (London, 1729).

82 *Mr. Pope's Literary Correspondence, Volume the Second*, xvi.

83 Mack addresses this episode in *Alexander Pope: A Life*, as does Winn in *A Window in the Bosom*.

84 *Mr. Pope's Literary Correspondence, Volume the Fourth* (London, 1736), 148–49.

3 HAYWOOD AND THE CULTURE OF PROFESSIONAL AUTHORSHIP

1 Barbara Babcock, "Introduction," *The Reversible World*, 32.

2 Indeed, Haywood seems to tacitly acknowledge this "paper credit" when her only response to the 1728 *Dunciad* was to contribute a novella, *Irish Artifice; or, The History of Clarina*, to Edmund Curll's attack on Pope, *The Female Dunciad* (see discussion in previous chapter).

3 Paul Langford, *A Polite and Commercial People: England 1727–1783* (Oxford at the Clarendon Press, 1989), 91.

4 Dedication, *The Fair Captive* (London, 1721), vi.

5 She self-consciously observes: "I have often thought the Authors made use of such Introductions more to swell the Bulk of their books than any other Reason" (*The Injur'd Husband: or, the Mistaken Resentment* [London, 1723], Dedication).

6 David Oakleaf, "Introduction," *Love in Excess or, The Fatal Enquiry* (Peterborough, Ontario: Broadview Literary Press, 1994), 7.

7 Turner, *Living By the Pen*, 39.

8 William Rufus Chetwood, *A General History of the Stage (More Particularly the Irish Theatre) from its Origin in Greece down to the present Time* (Dublin, 1749), 57.

9 David Erskine Baker, *Biographia Dramatica; or a Companion to the Playhouse containing historical and critical memoirs, and original anecdotes, of British and Irish dramatic writers, from the Commencement of our Theatrical exhibitions* (London, 1764), 321.

10 It also appeared in the 1724 collected works, *The Works of Mrs. Eliza Haywood* as well as the 1725 collection, *Secret Histories, Novels and Poems*.

11 James Raven, *Judging New Wealth: Popular Publishing and Responses to Commerce in England, 1750–1800* (Oxford at the Clarendon Press, 1992), 60.

12 Terry Belanger, "Publishers and Writers in Eighteenth-Century England," in *Books and Their Readers in Eighteenth-Century England*, 22 .

13 *Love in Excess; or the Fatal Enquiry* (London, 1719/20). The previously cited modern edition, edited by David Oakleaf, is also now available. John Richetti notes that *Love in Excess* was one of the three most popular works of fiction before *Pamela*; the other two were *Gulliver's Travels* and *Robinson Crusoe* (*Popular Fiction before Richardson*, 179).

14 Public Record Office (PRO), London; State Papers Domestic (SP) 35 22/54.

15 Haywood expressed a reluctance to do translations. In the preface to *Letters*, she

calls her translation a "paraphrase" and admits to "the liberty I have taken, in many places, of adding, and in others of diminishing (where I thought so doing would render the whole more entertaining)." Unwilling to be bound by somebody else's words, Haywood retained her own narrative voice. Her publication pattern suggests that she wrote translations at junctures in her career where she needed to produce a text fairly easily to get money quickly. After the May publication of the *Dunciad* in 1728, she translated *The Disguised Prince, Part One*. After the March failure of *Frederick of Lunenbergh* in 1729, *The Disguised Prince, Part Two* appeared. When she opened her print shop in 1741/42, she wrote and sold at least two translations, *The Busy Body* and *The Virtuous Villager*.

16 The subscription list also includes an "Ann Dodd," possibly referring to the bookseller by that name who also appears in the *Dunciad*.

17 Eliza Haywood, *The Female Spectator* in 4 vols. (London, 1744–46), 1, p. 14.

18 William Rufus Chetwood (d. 1766) was a bookseller and dramatist who was clearly part of the literary crowd in which Haywood circulated. The information about his time at Smock Alley comes largely from his own recollections in *The History of the Stage* (1749). When he arrived in London, he was an apprentice to Edmund Curll before opening his own shop. First, he operated a bookseller's shop at Tom's Coffee House, Covent Garden, and then (1721) at Cato's Head in Russell Street, Covent Garden. It appears that J. Roberts, who printed a number of Haywood's works in the 1720s, took over Chetwood's business as bookseller after Chetwood became prompter at Drury Lane in 1722, a position he would hold for nearly twenty years. It was through his time at Drury Lane that Chetwood would have encountered Anne Oldfield, who acted there in 1699–1706 and 1708–30. Other discussions of Chetwood (*Dictionary of National Biography*; *A Biographical Dictionary of Actors, Actresses, Musicians, Dancers, Managers and Other Stage Personnel in London, 1660–1800*) do not mention Chetwood's early tenure at Smock Alley. Indeed, *The Biographical Dictionary of Actors* cites a contemporary of Chetwood's, George Stevens, who claims he was "a measureless and bungling liar." *The Dictionary* tacitly concurs: "there seems to be enough evidence in what we know of the prompter's life to suggest that in many things he was somewhat irresponsible" (195). For a discussion of Haywood's time at the Smock Alley Theatre, see William Smith Clark, *The Early Irish Stage: The Beginnings to 1720* (Oxford at the Clarendon Press, 1955), 149–52.

19 This group would have included Richard Savage, Martha Fowke Sansom (the woman for whom Savage left Haywood; Haywood attacked her in *Memoirs of a Certain Island*), Susannah Centlivre, and David Mallet, among others. For discussions of this group see Clarence Tracy, *The Artificial Bastard: A Biography of Richard Savage* (University of Toronto Press, 1953); Dorothy Brewster, *Aaron Hill: Poet, Dramatist, Projector* (New York: Columbia University Press, 1913); John Wilson Bowyer, *The Celebrated Mrs. Centlivre* (Durham, NC: Duke University Press, 1952), and William McBurney, *Four before Richardson: Selected English Novels, 1720–1727* (Lincoln: University of Nebraska Press, 1963).

20 Whicher's assertion that Haywood left her clergyman husband, Valentine

Haywood, in 1719 has been repeated in nearly all discussions of Haywood after 1915. Christine Blouch disproves Whicher's inaccurate statements, but she does not determine to whom Haywood was married ("Eliza Haywood and the Romance of Obscurity"). Haywood refers to herself as a widow in letters from the 1720s, and parish registers from the 1740s refer to her as "widow Haywood." In his discussion of her 1714 theatrical experience, Clark describes her as a woman "recently abandoned by her husband," trying "the stage as a means of livelihood" (149). He does not cite a source for this information, although other scholars have suggested that scenario as well. For a discussion of Haywood's relationships with Savage and Hatchett, see Brewster, Tracy, Blouch, and Tom Lockwood, "Eliza Haywood in 1749: *Dalinda*, and Her Pamphlet on the Pretender," *Notes and Queries* n.s. 36 (1989): 475–77 and "William Hatchett, *A Rehearsal of Kings* (1737), and the Panton Street Puppet Show (1748)," *Philological Quarterly* 68.3 (1989): 315–23.

21 Ros Ballaster observes that, more than any of her contemporaries, Haywood's "textual production was most consistently identified with sexual promiscuity" (*Seductive Forms*, 158). Similarly, Jacqueline Pearson, discussing women dramatists, claims "a woman writer was almost by definition sexually immoral" (*The Prostituted Muse: Images of Women and Women Dramatists, 1642–1737* [London: Harvester Wheatsheaf, 1988], 9).

22 Paula McDowell, "Consuming Women: The Life of the 'Literary Ladies' as Popular Culture in Eighteenth-Century England, " *Genre* 26 (1993): 227.

23 *A Spy on the Conjurer; or, A Collection of Surprising and diverting stories, with merry and ingenious letters. By way of memoirs of the famous Mr. Duncan Campbell, demonstrating the astonishing foresight of that wonderful deaf and dumb man* (London, 1725), 1.

24 *The Memoirs of the Baron de Bosse* (London, 1725), v. For a discussion of Haywood's prefaces, see Joseph Bartolomeo, *A New Species of Criticism: Eighteenth-Century Discourse on the Novel* (Newark: University of Delaware Press, 1994), 33–35.

25 Laura Runge, "Gendered Strategies in the Criticism of Early Fiction," *Eighteenth-Century Studies* 28.4 (1995): 365. Ros Ballaster observes that "Writing a work of fiction in search of public fame entails the same risks for a woman as entering into a criminal 'conversation' with a man" (*Seductive Forms*, 169).

26 Gallagher, *Nobody's Story*, xvii, n. 8.

27 Hunter, *Before Novels*, 76.

28 *The Life of Madam De Villesache* (London, 1727), 1. She offers similar justifications in many other prefaces. For example, in the preface to *The Fair Hebrew, or, a True but Secret History of Two Jewish Ladies* (London, 1729) she writes: "If among all who shall read the following sheets, any one Person may reap so much Advantage as to avoid the Misfortunes the subject of them fell into by his Inadvertency and giving a Loose to Passion; the Little Pains I have been at, will be infinitely recompens'd."

29 Critics like Mary Anne Schofield seem too quick to compare uncritically readers of Haywood's novels to readers of twentieth-century romances as configured by Janice A. Radway in *Reading the Romance: Women, Patriarchy and Popular Literature* (Chapel Hill: University of North Carolina Press, 1984). See,

for example, Schofield's discussion in *Masking and Unmasking the Female Mind: Disguising Romances in Feminine Fiction, 1713–1799* (Newark: University of Delaware Press, 1990). Toni Bowers makes a similar gesture in "Sex, Lies and Invisibility: Amatory Fiction from the Restoration to Mid-Century," in *Columbia History of the Novel* (New York: Columbia University Press, 1994), 50–72.

30 *L'Entretien des Beaux Esprits. Conversations Comprising a great variety of Remarkable Adventures, Serious, Comic and Moral* (London, 1734), 1.

31 *Dalinda: or, the Double Marriage* (London, 1749), x. Despite the later date of this text, it is consistent with the prefaces and parameters Haywood sets up in her earlier texts as well.

32 *The Disguised Prince; or, the Beautiful Parisian* (London, 1733), 1.

33 Stallybrass and White, *The Politics and Poetics of Transgression*, 35.

34 *The Fatal Secret; or, Constancy in Distress* (London, 1724), Dedication.

35 *The Fair Captive* (London, 1721), Dedication.

36 *The Fatal Secret*, Dedication.

37 *Love in Excess*, 149–50.

38 Ibid., 84–85.

39 *The City Widow; or, Love in a Butt, A Novel* (London, 1729), 8.

40 The feminist criticism that discusses this cultural practice is multiple, well known, and detailed in chapter 2, n. 58.

41 He continues by noting "Inconstant love is a figure for the instability of exchange value" (McKeon, *The Origins of the English Novel*, 262).

42 *The Mercenary Lover: Or, The Unfortunate Heiresses. Being a True, Secret History of a City Amour* (London, 1726), 37. All subsequent references will be made parenthetically.

43 *The City Jilt: or, The Alderman Turn'd Beau; a Secret History* (London, 1726). A modern edition is also available in *Three Novellas: The Distress'd Orphan, The City Jilt, and The Double Marriage*, edited by Earla A. Wilputte (East Lansing: Colleagues Press, 1995). All subsequent references will be made parenthetically to the modern edition.

44 Catherine Craft-Fairchild suggests that "Glicera's error is in not understanding that her position in the patriarchal economy is one of an object of barter, a commodity equivalent to the money that was supposed to change hands." While that statement may be true at the beginning of the text, as the narrative continues, Glicera profoundly alters the "economy" in which she participates (*Masquerade and Gender: Disguise and Female Identity in Eighteenth-Century Fictions by Women* [University Park: Pennsylvania University Press, 1993], 68–69).

45 When Glicera writes Melladore after they have consummated their relationship, she laments, "how infinitely inferior was my Unhappiness in being deprived of Wealth, when compared to those more valuable Treasures thy fatal Passion has robb'd me of " (12).

46 Addison and Steele, *The Spectator*, IV, p. 121.

47 A white Perriwig with a huge Fore-top, Clothes trim'd with Silver, a long Sword with a brocaded Ribband hanging to it, and every Implement of the most perfect Beau, which,

join'd to a diminutive Stature, small Face and Limbs, made him look exactly like one of those little Imitators of Humanity, which are carried about Streets to make Sport for Children. (81–82)

48 By demonstrating Helena's extravagance, Haywood tapped into a well-known concern during this period. Susan Staves observes that "Anxiety over ruin at the hands of a spendthrift wife is a common eighteenth-century theme" (*Married Women's Separate Property*, 169–70).

49 McKeon, *Origins*, 262.

50 For discussions of the clitoris and its associations with female sexuality see Lynne Friedli, "'Passing Women': A Study of Gender Boundaries in the Eighteenth Century," *Sexual Underworlds of the Enlightenment*, edited by G. S. Rousseau and Roy Porter (Chapel Hill: University of North Carolina Press, 1988), 234–60; Tom Laquer, *Making Sex: Body and Gender from the Greeks to Freud* (Cambridge, MA and London: Harvard University Press, 1990); and Valerie Traub, "The Psychomorphology of the Clitoris," *Gay and Lesbian Quarterly* 2 (1995): 81–113.

51 At one point he even acts like a poet with a fit of tormented imagination: "he went from Coffee-house to Coffee-house, endeavouring but in Vain, some Cessation of his perplex'd Imagination" (60).

52 Haywood continues, "Those who believ'd themselves, and were by all believ'd to be in a State of the most fixed Tranquillity that could be, were in Effect on the Brink, and ready to plunge into a Gulph of Destruction, as much to be trembled at, as their imaginary Comfort was before to be desir'd and coveted" (15).

4   THE (GENDER) POLITICS OF THE LITERARY MARKETPLACE

1 *Selected Letters of Samuel Richardson*, ed. John Carroll (Oxford: Clarendon Press, 1964), 46–47.

2 Gallagher, *Nobody's Story*, xxii.

3 These letters (B.M. Add. MS. 4293 f. 81 and f. 82) date probably from April 1728 (not long after the *Dunciad*), as Blouch has persuasively suggested in "Eliza Haywood and the Romance of Obscurity."

4 B.M. Add. MS 4293 f. 81. The British Museum Sloane collection also contains an undated letter to Hans Sloane from Haywood in which she seeks his sub-scription to a collection of poems by someone other than herself. She describes the volume as "the productions of the best Genius's of the present Age; and that . . . become the closet of the philosopher and Divine, [or] the fine gentle-man" (B.M. Sl. 4059 f. 144). She may be referring to the 1729 miscellany published by Joseph Mitchell, *Poems on Several Occasions*. The text includes work by Aaron Hill, Richard Savage, and Haywood, as well as other members of her literary circle. For a brief discussion of this volume, see Dorothy Brewster, *Aaron Hill*, pp. 170–73. Were this the volume, the letter would date from approxi-mately the same time as the two quoted in the main text.

5 B.M. Add. MS. 4293 f. 92. Although there is still much to be learned about Haywood's personal life, it increasingly appears that she did not abandon her

husband (as previously and repeatedly suggested), that she had two children, and, most important, that she was a widow.

6 In *Living by the Pen*, Cheryl Turner claims that writing was one of the few legitimate and potentially profitable professions open to women at this point in the eighteenth century, giving credence to Haywood's plea.

7 B.M. Add. MS 4293 f. 82. *Frederick, Duke of Brunswick-Lunenbergh* appeared at the Lincoln's Inn Fields on Tuesday March 4, 1729 with receipts of £42 18s 6d, and on Thursday March 6, 1729 with receipts of £57 8s 6d. Its total receipts were below those of contemporaneous plays also running at Lincoln's Inn Fields. For example, the March 3 performance of *The Country Wife* took in £73 19s and the March 18 *The Provoked Wife* £92 18s.

8 John R. Elwood, "The Stage Career of Eliza Haywood," *Theatre Survey* 5.2 (1964): 110. See also Maria Heinemann, "Eliza Haywood's Career in the Theatre," *Notes and Queries* n.s. 20.1 (1973): 12–13.

9 The second example is from the advertisement for the May 23, 1737 performance of *The Historical Register* and *Eurydice Hiss'd*, which was a benefit performance for Haywood.

10 Robert Hume also suggests that Haywood's *A Wife to be Lett* (1723) was the precedent for Fielding's *The Modern Husband* (Robert Hume, *Henry Fielding and the London Theatre, 1728–1737* [Oxford at the Clarendon Press, 1988], 123). For a discussion of Haywood's animosity toward Fielding, see John R. Elwood, "Henry Fielding and Eliza Haywood: A Twenty Year War," *Albion* 5.3 (1973): 184–92.

11 Charles B. Woods, ed., *The Author's Farce* (Lincoln: University of Nebraska Press, 1966), 103. See also Arthur C. Scouten, *The London Stage 1660–1800*; Part 3: 1729–1747 (Carbondale: Southern Illinois University Press, 1960), for the detailed listing of performances.

12 Hume, *Henry Fielding and the London Theatre*, p. 86, n. 98.

13 *The London Stage*, Part 3, lxvi. He additionally notes that "productions did not resume until 12 July and then curtain time was set back to seven o'clock."

14 *The London Stage*, Part 3, clxiv. Battestin and Hume both suggest that Haywood remained connected with Little Haymarket and played a role on and off the stage, possibly writing some of the unattributed scripts between 1733 and 1737 and also acting regularly with the company (Hume, *Henry Fielding and the London Theatre*, 233; Martin C. Battestin with Ruthe R. Battestin, *Henry Fielding: A Life* [London and New York: Routledge, 1989], 215, 233ff. See also Thomas Lockwood, "Fielding and the Licensing Act," *Huntington Library Quarterly* 50.4 [1987]: 379–93). Haywood's theatrical activities were extensive enough to warrant a single charitable benefit performance of a double bill of *The Historical Register* with *Eurydice Hissed* given for her on Monday May 23, 1737 which was attended by the Dowager Duchess of Marlborough. "Benefit Mrs. Haywood the Muse, Author of Love in Excess, and many other entertaining pieces, 6:30 p.m. *Daily Advertiser* 23 May 1737: 'We hear that her Grace the Dutchess Dowager of Marlborough will be at the theatre in the Hay-Market this Night'" (*The London Stage*, Part 3, 674). Haywood had previously sought

support from the Dowager Duchess, dedicating her 1736 political satire, *The Adventures of Eovaii,* to her as well.

15 In the 1736/37 season Hume suggests that "Fielding was running a company genuinely devoted to contemporary plays. Nothing of the sort had ever been tried in the modern history of the London theatre ... Anyone who wanted variety and experimentation would have to seek it from Fielding's company" (*Henry Fielding and the London Theatre,* 229).

16 *The London Stage,* Part 3, clxv.

17 Richard Savage, "Authors of The Town; a Satire: Inscribed to the Author of the Universal Passion," in *The Poetical Works of Richard Savage,* edited by Clarence Tracy (Cambridge University Press, 1962) 73, lines 157–60. During the 1730s when she was trying to succeed in the theatre, Haywood also wrote *The Companion for the Theatre,* in which, suggests Christine Blouch ("Eliza Haywood and the Romance of Obscurity"), she "accomplishes a series of mediations through her representational function so that the plays, representations themselves, are recontextualized" (543) in a way that attempts to influence interpretation.

18 Henry Atherton describes the shop as follows: "in the Piazza [of Covent Garden] and perhaps under one of the arcades on the north or east side lived Elizabeth Haywood 'at the sign of fame.' She was an author as well as publisher. Haywood published (c1742) *The Ghost of Eustace Budgel Esq. To the Men in Blue . . . a satire on Robert Walpole*" (Atherton, *Political Prints in the Age of Hogarth,* 17).

19 *The Female Spectator,* for T. Gardner (London, 1745). The periodical was published monthly from April 1744 to May 1746.

20 For example, when asked "whether he keeps a shop and in what manner he supports himself," hawker David Lynch describes how "he has a Hawker's Lisence and gets his living by selling Books and pamphlets in the Coffe houses and other places in this Town" (PRO SP 36/111 47).

21 David Foxon, *Libertine Literature in England 1669–1745* (New Hyde Park, NY: University Books, 1965), 7.

22 Langford, *A Polite and Commercial People,* 92.

23 C. J. Mitchell, "Women in the Eighteenth-Century Book Trade," in *Writers, Books and Trade: An Eighteenth-Century English Miscellany for William B. Todd,* edited by O. M. Brack, Jr. (New York: AMS Press, 1994), 37.

24 A fully developed comparison of Fielding's *Shamela* and *Anti-Pamela,* worthy further discussion, is not my purpose here. But I would like to point briefly to the differing nature of their critiques. Fielding's *Shamela* parodies Richardson's novel rather than examining the generic conventions it establishes. Fielding's elaborate framing device situates his parodic and Richardson's legitimate text within the commercialized *Pamela* craze and Richardson's own self-promoting techniques. Fielding highlights the tension Haywood notes between pleasure and interest – or in the parlance of his text, between "love" which satisfies desire and "necessity" which supplies conveniences. He similarly empties "vartue" of its value, demonstrating its function as a primarily, if not exclusively, performative signifier. He indicates Shamela's inability to practice any sort of "economy" with her excessive spending immediately after the wedding. He

endows Shamela with specific sexual desires (left unfulfilled by Booby) that force her, like Syrena Tricksy, to satisfy sexual and financial interests that are at cross-purposes. While his satire is obviously successful in its own terms, its treatment of gender differs greatly from Haywood's in both nature and degree.

25 Eliza Haywood, *Anti-Pamela; or Feigned Innocence detected* (London, 1742), 261. All subsequent references will be made parenthetically. For a brief discussion of *Anti-Pamela* see Bernard Kreissman, *Pamela–Shamela: A Study of the Criticisms, Burlesques, Parodies and Adaptations of Richardson's "Pamela"* (Lincoln: University of Nebraska Studies, 1960), 24–27.

26 Thompson, *Models of Value*, 137.

27 For example, between 1741 and 1756, she published at least sixteen texts, including four periodicals, a translation, two conduct books, and six novels. As McKillop notes, "evidently the opportunist Mrs. Haywood was making the most of both sides; even while she was writing and publishing her *Anti-Pamela*, she was taking advantage of the popularity of Richardson's book by getting out such works as *A Present for a Serving Maid*" (*Samuel Richardson: Printer and Novelist* [Chapel Hill: University of North Carolina Press, 1936], 80).

28 *The Monthly Review. A Periodical Work, Giving An Account, with proper abstracts of, and Extracts from, the New Books, Pamphlets, &c. as they come out*, vol. II (London, January 1750), 167. *The Monthly Review* also observes that Haywood's arrest, and the confiscation of all copies of the text, caused them to "be rescued from a fate they might otherwise have undergone, that of being turned into wastepaper." The quotation continues:

> For, it seems, the custom is to purge this species of literature from the offensive matter they are supposed to contain, by the famous fiery nostrum formerly practiced by the physicians of the soul in Smithfield, and elsewhere; and now as successfully used in treasonable as then in heretical cases: with this happy difference, however, in the method of treatment; that in the one case the bodies, in the other only the books, of the patient, are destroyed. (167)

29 *The Penny London Post*, no. 1197. Haywood clearly knew Carrington and his professional responsibilities as one of the King's messengers since she also mentions him in *The Parrot*: "Mr. Carrington, one of his Majesty's messengers is gone down with his Prisoner to Preston who are to be evidence against the Rebels tried there." Such mentions by both Haywood and *The Penny Post* were often a coded way to alert other members of the print trade to increased governmental scrutiny or activity.

30 PRO SP 36/111 204–12. In "Eliza Haywood in 1749: *Dalinda* and the Pamphlet on the Pretender," *Notes and Queries* n.s. 36 (December 1989) 4: 475–77, Tom Lockwood mentions the arrest but, surprisingly, does not discuss the examination of Haywood herself, which occurred almost a month after these (SP 36/112 24) or that of Haywood's servant, Hannah Stredden. Both of these depositions provide important new information that significantly illuminates our understanding of the event.

31 There are a number of ways to determine whether a seditious libel has been prosecuted, including PRO KB 15/54, which is a list of all prosecutions for

seditious libels since the reign of Queen Anne. The prosecution of Haywood does not appear. Additionally, all the other locations in which evidence of Haywood's case should appear if it were prosecuted offer nothing. While only "negative evidence" is available, it strongly suggests that Haywood was never brought to trial.

32 The full title is *A Letter From H— G—g, Esq.; One of the Gentlemen of the Bed-Chamber to the young Chevalier, and the only Person of his own Retinue that attended him from Avignon, in his late Journey through Germany, and elsewhere: containing Many remarkable and affecting occurrences which happened to the P— during the Course of his Mysterious Progress. To a Particular Friend* (London, 1750). Significantly, there is no printer imprint. The presumed authorial persona is Henry Goring, who traveled with the Pretender after Culloden.

33 Carretta, *The Snarling Muse*, 23.

34 The Pretender's expansive rhetoric (as written by Haywood) appeared at a time when the King was using similarly exuberant language. In a speech he made to the House of Lords on November 16, 1749, reprinted in *The London Gazette*, the King proclaims: "I shall always look upon the True Greatness of my Crown, and the Stability of my Government, as inseparably united with the Happiness and Prosperity of my People."

35 PRO SP 36/111 f. 207.

36 Ibid. f. 206.

37 Ibid. f. 210.

38 Ibid. f. 213.

39 Haywood's failure to sustain her shop certainly suggests the increasingly limited opportunities for women in the material and production aspects of the trade as the century progressed. But it is also indicative of the difficulties that anyone would encounter in entering the trade at this point in the century. For discussions of the (typically unequal) relationship between author and publisher and the printing industry generally, see (for example) A. S. Collins, *Authorship in the Days of Johnson* (London: Robert Holden and Co., 1927); John Feather, *A History of British Publishing* (London: Routledge, 1988); Isabel Rivers, ed., *Books and Their Readers in Eighteenth-Century England*; Robin Myers, *The British Book Trade from Caxton to the Present Day* (London: Andre Deutsch Ltd., 1973).

40 PRO SP 36 112/24. In the examination, Haywood is named as Elizabeth Haywood, of Durham Yard in the Strand, Widow. Parish registers from this period complicate what we know about Haywood. During the period following her arrest, there is no Haywood recorded as living at Durham Yard which is in St. Martin in the Fields parish. There are, however, many anonymous assessments there (all very low) and Haywood could easily be one of them. The June/November 1749 assessments for New Street and Bedfordbury Wards in St. Martin in the Fields list a "Widow Haywood" at Castle Court Lane (F523 E 17). She also appears in the 1748 rate book. In 1749 she was assessed 11s 8d at the first and second rate, but her column was never totaled. This failure to pay could indicate that she moved (possibly to Durham Yard?) or could not pay. The 1750 rate book for St. Martin in the Fields, New Street Ward, lists a "Haywood,

Widw" at Little St. Martin's Lane. Again the assessment is low (12s 0d) for both rates and again the column is not totaled out (F525 f. 99). Since assessments were typically done in June and November, it is possible that Haywood lived at Durham Yard for only a few months between her Castle Lane and St. Martin's Lane address. If so, that would suggest a very peripatetic (and none too prosperous) existence for her during this time. Another explanation is, of course, that neither "widow Haywood" is Eliza Haywood.

41 In the *Key to the Dunciad*, Curll claims Haywood's children are by a "poet and a bookseller," often thought to be Savage and Hatchett, respectively. If Curll really is referring to Hatchett, it would suggest that *his* bookselling activities predate Haywood's and that he may have been instrumental in either introducing her or sustaining her in the business. Thomas Lockwood describes Hatchett as "an author and actor of sorts" who swam in the "shallows of the London entertainment industry, between print shop and play house" (Lockwood, "William Hatchett, *A Rehearsal of Kings* [1737], and the Panton Street Puppet Show [1748]," 316). Erskine Baker describes Hatchett as "Mr. Hatchett, a gentleman with whom she appears to have had a close literary intimacy" (216).

42 PRO SP 36/111 147. Lynch was taken up for selling "A Dialogue between a Married Woman and a Maid" and "Venus in the Cloister." Of course Lynch's situation might also have been improved by his offer that if "discharged he could and would be of great service in discovering the Authors, Printers, and Publishers of Obscene books and prints." He also claims to have sold three thousand prints of the royal family during the late rebellion.

43 Jerry C. Beasley, "Portraits of a Monster: Robert Walpole and Early English Prose Fiction," *Eighteenth-Century Studies* 14 (1981): 405–31.

44 The full title is *The Parrot, with a Compendium of the Times. By the Authors of the Female Spectator*. The imprint is: London: Printed and published by T. Garner, at Cowley's Head, 1746.

45 Ballaster, *Seductive Forms*, 156.

46 For a discussion of the news–novel nexus, see Lennard J. Davis, *Factual Fictions: The Origins of the English Novel* (New York: Columbia University Press, 1983).

47 PRO SP 36/111 f. 39.

48 KB 10/29 Part 1 Hilary 23 George II. The item described appeared in *The London Evening Post*, no. 3430 from Saturday November 11 to Tuesday November 14, 1749.

49 The initial mention of the indictment appears in the secretary's letter book, PRO SP 44/133 f. 9. The indictment appears in crown-side affidavit, KB 1/10 Part I Hilary 23 George II.

50 PRO SP 44/134 f. 28; cf. PRO KB 15/54; Meres indictment in KB 10/29 Part 1 Hilary 23 George II.

51 SP 36/112 f.34 January 18, 1749/50.

52 Belanger, "Publishers and Writers in Eighteenth-Century England," 15.

53 *The History of Miss Betsy Thoughtless* (London, 1751). All subsequent references will be made parenthetically to the modern edition of this text, edited by Beth Fowkes Tobin (Oxford and New York: Oxford University Press, 1997).

54 William B. Warner, "The Elevation of the Novel in England: Hegemony and Literary History," *ELH* 59 (1992): 580. This important essay, which has informed my discussion of *Betsy Thoughtless*, explores the ways Richardson and Fielding "hegemonize" the culture's practice of reading by defining themselves against the earlier popular forms of fiction (such as Haywood's). The "fathers" of the novel "overwrite" these previous texts, simultaneously incorporating and obscuring the more objectionable aspects of earlier texts. Warner rightly suggests that we need to read these texts in tandem to recognize the antagonistic competition for cultural space implicit in the later forms of the novel.

55 A novel like *Clarissa* departs from this loose generalization in obvious ways, but it retains the didacticism and tone of high moral rigor consistent with other texts during this decade. The most significant work done on the history of the novel, discussed in the Introduction, would include that by Ian Watt, Michael McKeon, J. Paul Hunter, Nancy Armstrong, and John Bender. For a recent discussion of *Betsy Thoughtless*, see Deborah J. Nestor, "Virtue Rarely Rewarded: Ideological Subversion and Narrative Form in Haywood's Later Fiction," *Studies in English Literature* 34.3 (Summer 1994): 579–98.

56 See, for example, Nancy Armstrong, *Desire and Domestic Fiction: A Political History of the Novel* (New York: Oxford University Press, 1987).

57 The quotation continues in a way that highlights Haywood's familiarity with the commercial value of political discourse and, perhaps, her professional jealousy at Fielding's success in that pursuit:

> in doing which it appears extremely probable, that he had two views; the one to get money, which he very much wanted, from such as delighted in low humour, and could not distinguish true satire from scurrility; and the other, in the hope of having some post given him by those whom he had abused, in order to silence his dramatic talent. But it is not my business to point out either the merit of that gentleman's performances, or the motives he had for writing them, as the town is perfectly acquainted both with his abilities and success; and has since seen him, with astonishment, wriggle himself into favour, by pretending to cajole those he had not the power to intimidate. (45–46)

58 For example, someone suggests to Mr. Goodman that he complain "to the court of Chancery of the imposition practiced on you, and procure a *Ne exeat regnum*" (227).

59 Betsy's actions implicitly contrast with those of Miss Forward, who is willing to pay too much and too often for the obligations her "suitors" place on her.

60 Hysom also notes the time spent actually getting to Betsy's residence: "you should consider I live a great way off: – 'tis a long walk from Mile End to St. James's" (119).

5   RICHARDSON AND THE DOMESTICATION OF PAPER CREDIT

1 *Pamela; or, Virtue Rewarded*, edited by T. C. Duncan Eaves and Ben D. Kimpel (first published 1740; rpt. Boston: Houghton Mifflin Co., 1971). All subsequent references will be made parenthetically.

2 James Cruise, "Pamela and the Commerce of Authority," *Journal of English and*

Germanic Philology 87 (1988): 342–88. Readers of Richardson's novel (beginning with Henry Fielding and Eliza Haywood) have recognized Pamela's pre-occupation with money. For example, Ian Watt, in *The Rise of the Novel*, places Pamela and her connection with B in a relationship defined by the powers of capitalism, though not necessarily speculative investment. Terry Eagleton's *The Rape of Clarissa* discusses the class anxiety *Pamela* mediates, an anxiety certainly connected to the larger financial issues discussed here. Eagleton's more broadly based concerns differ from my own in his pursuit of class struggle rather than specific economic practices. I agree with some of the larger claims Eagleton makes for *Pamela*'s significance as a novel in terms of its role as an agent, not just an account, of a bourgeois attempt to wrestle ideological hegemony (3–4). Yet his preoccupation with *Clarissa* causes him to underestimate the significance of *Pamela*, which he calls at one point "a cartoon version of *Clarissa*" (37). By focusing on what he views as *Pamela*'s comic or utopian nature, he limits the depth of his engagement with the text. In *Origins of the English Novel*, Michael McKeon identifies *Pamela* as a narrative of progressive ideology (as defined within his schema) and rightly suggests that "Mr. B is, in short, as transitional a figure as Pamela is, and they are equally and symmetrically representative of that complex social phenomenon which their posterity learned to call the rise of the middle class" (366). Though I agree with McKeon's suggestion about the novel's ideological concerns, I think he ignores some of the more subtle kinds of powers and interactions, also located very much in middle-class culture, that inform the novel. For example, my discussion certainly runs counter to his claim that "Pamela's essential power [is] that of being virtuous" (364). Mona Sheuermann attempts to dismantle the "perception" that women were not interested or involved in wealth in her study of the eighteenth-century novel, *Her Bread to Earn*. In her conclusion, she mentions Pamela's accounting abilities and asserts "her awareness of money ... defines her character" (245–46). However, her study, which engages a critical perspective different from my own, does not offer a sustained discussion of *Pamela* or explore women's involvement with speculative investment. Other recent discussions of class, economy, and *Pamela* include Christopher Flint, "Anxiety of Affluence: Family and Class (Dis)order in *Pamela; or, Virtue Rewarded*," *Studies in English Literature* 29 (1989): 489–524; and Ann Louise Kibbie, "Sentimental Properties: *Pamela* and *Memoirs of a Woman of Pleasure*," *ELH* 58.3 (1991): 561–77, among others. My own concern is with Pamela as an actor in an economy specifically marked by speculative investment and the new financial instruments, rather than as a subject more generally concerned with commerce, money, and accounting in a manner consistent with the middle classes during this period. While the latter is certainly an accurate characterization of Pamela, her motivations, as I suggest, are more complicated than that.

3 McKeon, *The Origins of the English Novel*, 375.

4 For a list of works discussing the financial revolution, see the Introduction, n. 10.

5 In his recent and compelling study, *Models of Value*, James Thompson discusses how the "interrelation between the development of the novel and economic change" must be understood as "mediated by the concurrent development of political economy as a discourse and the novel as a discourse" (8). Chapters 1 and 2, on political economy and monetary theory respectively, lay the groundwork for his provocative model. He does not discuss *Pamela*, though he claims "similar arguments can be mounted about Samuel Richardson" (8).

6 Pocock, discussing this deferral in terms of the repayment of government stock, observes: "Government stock is a promise to repay at a future date; from the inception and development of the National Debt, it is known that this date will in reality never be reached ... Government is therefore maintained by the investor's imagination concerning a moment which will never exist in reality" ("The Mobility of Property and the Rise of Eighteenth-Century Sociology," 112).

7 J. G. A. Pocock, "Early Modern Capitalism: The Augustan Perception," in *Feudalism, Capitalism and Beyond*, edited by Eugene Kamenka and R. S. Neale (Canberra: Australian University Press, 1975), 79.

8 I am referring here to the argument made by Hirschman in *The Passions and the Interests*. Hirschman suggests that, during the eighteenth century, the "passions" that drive men to acquisitive self-interest are, through a process of recuperation, harnessed and redirected into "interests" that benefit the general welfare of the nation. While he does not explore the gender implications of the passions or transformation he details, his work implicitly suggests how the impulses characterized as "feminized" are also made more "manly" or "masculine" when transformed into interests.

9 Obviously, there were members of the aristocracy who invested speculatively, beginning in the late seventeenth century (indeed, in 1720 members of the House of Lords were pressured to buy South Sea Company stock to increase the project's appearance of stability – 177 peers and 401 MPs subscribed [Dickson, *The Financial Revolution*, table 10, p. 108]). Others, of course, resisted such financial developments throughout the eighteenth century. I certainly don't mean to characterize a social group's financial activities in a monolithic or reductive way. What is apparent is that an increasing acceptance of these financial practices, and to a certain extent their stabilization and regulation following the South Sea Bubble, made them more appealing generally.

10 Pocock, *Machiavellian Moment*, 456.

11 Caroll Smith-Rosenberg, "Domesticating 'Virtue': Coquettes and Revolutionaries in Young America," in *Literature and the Body: Essays on Populations and Persons* (Baltimore: Johns Hopkins University Press, 1988), 164. An important discussion of the transformation of the concept of virtue can be found in Shelley Burtt's *Virtue Transformed* (Cambridge University Press, 1992) which asserts that civic virtue is transformed rather than eclipsed, details the "varieties of virtue" (12) circulating in eighteenth-century culture, and explores the "politics of the politics of virtue" (37). For her specific response to Pocock's work, see pp. 32–37.

12 Isaac Kramnick, "Republican Revisionism Revisited," *The American Historical Review* 87.3 (1982): 662.

13 Richardson also noted that "Twenty years ago I was the most obscure man in Great Britain, and now I am admitted to the company of the first characters of the Kingdom" (*Selected Letters of Samuel Richardson*, 179, 14).

14 Although the paucity of Richardson's personal papers limits our knowledge of his specific investment activities, what little we know clearly indicates Richardson's active involvement in a variety of financial schemes. For discussions of Richardson's business activities see T. C. Eaves and Ben D. Kimpel, *Samuel Richardson: A Biography* (Oxford at the Clarendon Press, 1971), 41–45, 498–510, and, especially, chapter 8, and Alan D. McKillop, *Samuel Richardson: Printer and Novelist* (Chapel Hill: University of North Carolina Press, 1936), Appendix, "Records of Richardson's Life and Business." William M. Sale, *Samuel Richardson: A Bibliographical Record of His Literary Career with Historical Notes* (New Haven: Yale University Press, 1936) and *Samuel Richardson: Master Printer* (Ithaca: Cornell University Press, 1950), focuses (usefully) on Richardson's career as a printer, but not his personal finances.

15 Eaves and Kimpel, *Samuel Richardson*, 45.

16 Sale (1950), *Samuel Richardson: Master Printer*, 59.

17 Not much work has been done on the English Stock. It is briefly discussed by Sale, McKillop, and Eaves and Kimpel in their studies of Richardson. For more extensive treatment see Cyprian Blagden, *The Stationers' Company: A History, 1403–1959* (London: George Allen and Unwin Ltd., 1960); John Feather, *A History of British Publishing* (London and New York: Routledge, 1988); and Marjorie Plant, *The English Book Trade: An Economic History of the Making and Sale of Books* (London: George Allen and Unwin Ltd., 1939).

18 Blagden, *The Stationers' Company*, 100.

19 The distribution of shares increased steadily between 1729 and 1770 to enable more liverymen to participate in and profit from the English Stock. Four "denominations" of shares existed: £320, £160, £80, £40. Between 1729 and 1750, the number of £40 shares increased from 40 to 60; £80 shares increased from 40 to 50; £160 shares from 30 to 40; and £320 shares from 15 to 20. This change was enabled by the commensurate rise in the amount of capital, and thus dividend, available as a result of the interest. In 1729 the capital funding the English Stock stood at £14,400 with a dividend, at $12\frac{1}{2}$%, or £1,800. By 1756 the capital had grown to £19,200 generating a dividend of £2,280.

20 "Though partners could not normally assign their shares (because this might cut across the pattern of seniority to which the Court adhered), they could use them as securities for loans" (Blagden, *The Stationers' Company*, 95).

21 It is important to note that this structure applies to the authorized print trade as defined by the Stationers' Company and members of the livery. An individual like Haywood, when operating as a "bookseller," obviously would not have been a member of the livery for she, like many individuals operating in Grub Street, was an "unauthorized" part of the print trade. While the previous chapters suggest the ways in which those sites of literary and cultural

production demanded a similar belief and investment in narratives, it is significant the institutional underpinning of the authorizing agent of the print trade operated under similar demands.

22 In 1736 Richardson purchased a yeomanry or £80 share. In December 1741 he was elected to the ruling body of the Stationers' Company, the Court of Assistants, and in 1746 he was voted a livery or £160 share of stock. Finally, in 1751, he acquired the largest denomination share, £320. His status in the company remained high and he served as the Master of the Company in 1754. For details on Richardson's livery activities see Eaves and Kimpel (*Samuel Richardson*, 42) and William Sale (*Samuel Richardson: Master Printer*, 31). As Sale notes, a liveryman was required to "turn over to another member his share of a lesser value when he was voted a share of larger denomination. Consequently no member could hold more than £320 of the stock. Even with these provisions, however, there was no period in Richardson's lifetime when all members of the livery were enabled to profit by the company's monopoly rights" (31).

23 Quoted in McKillop, *Samuel Richardson: Printer and Novelist*, 8. Richardson also printed a series of pamphlets by Archibald Hutcheson in 1720 relating to the South Sea crises (including "Some Calculations relating to the South Sea Company," "An Estimate of the Value of the South-Sea Stock," "A Collection of Calculations and Remarks," and "A Letter relating to South-Sea Stock") suggesting his conversance with the event.

24 Richardson had a "considerable amount of money invested in copyrights," and, in his will, listed them as one of his chief assets (Sale, *Samuel Richardson: Master Printer*, 89). Copyright has become an important and increasingly extensive area of scholarship in terms of the legal and ideological construction of authorship. Most recently the work of Mark Rose and Martha Woodmansee has introduced the significant implications of copyright into discussions of authorship. See, for example, Mark Rose, *Authors and Owners*; Martha Woodmansee, *The Author, Art, and the Market: Rereading the History of Aesthetics* (New York: Columbia University Press, 1994), and editor with Peter Jaszi, *The Construction of Authorship: Textual Appropriation in Law and Literature* (Durham, NC: Duke University Press, 1994). But copyright, *per se*, is really not in my purview here. Rather I want to suggest what Richardson's treatment of copyrights as a type of intangible, indeed speculative, property reveals about his immersion in a culture increasingly defined by credit and speculative investment.

25 "We can take him as a kind of emblem," suggests Mark Rose, "of the link between the book trade, concerned with property, and the discourse of originality." He operated at a time when the contestations over copyright law highlighted the difference between literary property as material object and as imaginative (and intangible) creation (*Authors and Owners*, 117). See also chapter 4, "The Author in Court," for a discussion of the changing understanding following Pope v. Curll.

26 Sale, *Samuel Richardson: Master Printer*, 91. There were actually two types of bookselling congers – wholesaling congers and copy-owning congers – and

together they dominated the activities of the book market, were instrumental in securing profitable copyright legislation with the Copyright Act of 1710, and in some ways determined the value of certain texts. The history of the congers is complex and addressed in Feather, *A History of British Publishing*, chapter 6, and Terry Belanger, "Publishers and Writers," among others.

27 *Samuel Richardson*, 28.

28 An individual Richardson used in this manner was James Purser, one of his workmen whose name appeared on the colophon from 1728 to 1732 and "who presumably carried on the paper for Richardson in a house Richardson rented in 1728, across from his own dwelling" (Eaves and Kimpel, *Samuel Richardson*, 45). As discussed in the previous chapter, a James Purser was later prosecuted for seditious libel after printing Cleland's *Fanny Hill*. It seems plausible that the same man is involved in both incidents. This initial episode with Richardson suggests how individuals who operate in the unauthorized cultural spaces were often unable to reposition themselves in the print trade.

29 McKillop, *Samuel Richardson: Printer and Novelist*, 14.

30 As quoted in Eaves and Kimpel, *Samuel Richardson*, 71. Richardson's ability to do this stemmed from his willingness to write prefaces and other supplementary materials for booksellers. As he described in his 1753 letter to Stinstra, "Some of them [booksellers], even thought fit to seek me, rather than I them, because of the Readiness I shewed to oblige them, with writing Indexes, Prefaces, and sometimes for their minor Authors, honest Dedications; abstracting, abridging, compiling, and giving my Opinion of Pieces offered them" (*The Richardson–Stinstra Correspondence and Stinstra's Prefaces to Clarissa*, edited by William C. Slattery [Carbondale and Edwardsville: Southern Illinois University Press, 1969], 26).

31 Sale, *Samuel Richardson: A Biographical Record*, 4.

32 Sale, *Samuel Richardson: Master Printer*, 96.

33 J. H. Plumb, "The Commercialization of Leisure in Eighteenth-Century England," in *The Birth of a Consumer Society*, 272.

34 Samuel Richardson, *Letters Written to and for Particular Friends, on the Most Important Occasions. Directing Not only the Requisite Style and Forms to be Observed in Writing Familiar Letters; But How to Think and Act Justly and Prudently, in the common concerns of Human Life* (London, 1741), xxvii. In a letter Richardson described this as "a little Volume of Letters, in a common Style, on such Subjects as might be of use to those Country Readers who were unable to indite for themselves" (Carroll, *Selected Letters*, 232).

35 Samuel Richardson, *The Apprentice's Vade Mecum; or, the Young Man's Pocket-Companion* (London, 1734), xii; a facsimile reproduction with an introduction by James E. Evans (Delmar, NY: Scholars' Facsimiles and Reprints, 1980).

36 Plumb, "The Acceptance of Modernity," in *The Birth of a Consumer Society*, 316. "Both commercial activity and the consumer response to it were feverish," writes Neil McKendrick. "Uncontrolled by any sense of commercial decorum, men advertised in unprecedented numbers – whole newspapers were taken over by advertisements, and a very large proportion of all newspapers were

filled with advertising" ("The Consumer Revolution of Eighteenth-Century England," in *The Birth of a Consumer Society*, 11).

37 Carroll, *Selected Letters*, 41.

38 Doody, *A Natural Passion*, chapter 6, "*Clarissa* and Earlier Novels of Love and Seduction," 128–50. Doody devotes pages to illustrating language, settings, and fictional situations originally found in Haywood and subsequently used by Richardson in *Pamela* and *Clarissa*. While William Warner correctly notes that "Richardson does not have to read Haywood to have his text receive the shaping force of the 'influenza' of her popularity" ("The Elevation of the Novel in England," 588), Doody's case makes it overwhelmingly apparent that Richardson did know of and read Haywood. Additionally, in 1735 Richardson printed Haywood's play, *A Wife to be Lett*, produced in 1723, indicating his knowledge (however limited) of her in a professional capacity. See Sale, *Samuel Richardson: Master Printer*, 173.

39 Warner, "The Elevation of the Novel in England," 582.

40 Interestingly, Warner's language underscores (but he does not elaborate upon) the symbolic cultural economy in which both authors circulated when he describes the "sudden violent shift in the cultural credit from an earlier species of writing to one proclaimed to be an-other" (ibid., 581). He also notes that "Richardson and Fielding disavowed rather than assumed their debt to those popular novels whose cultural space they would redefine and whose narrative resources they incorporate" (583).

41 As Doody describes, "Richardson combines the world of the bourgeois novel of courtship with the fantastic world of the novel of rape and seduction" (*A Natural Passion*, 149).

42 Richardson retains the specificity of physical description when Lovelace recounts his attempt to seduce Clarissa: "My cheek reclined on her shoulder – kissing her hands by turns . . . I put one arm around her waist; I imprinted a kiss on her sweet lips . . . and then with my other hand drew aside the handkerchief that concealed the beauty of beauties, and pressed with my burning lips the charmingest breast that ever my ravished eyes beheld." But Clarissa's rejection of Lovelace removes her from the physical realm and demonstrates her unshakable virtue (*Clarissa, or the History of a Young Lady* [originally published London, 1747–48; first edition reprinted New York: Penguin Books, 1985] edited by Angus Ross, 705).

43 Richardson's gesture feminizes his male characters (and his novels) by making them so overtly emotional and sentimental. Mr. B and Lovelace resemble the man of feeling and anticipate the cult of sensibility's reliance on theatrical and self-perpetuating sentimentality. Mr. B and especially Lovelace savor the extreme emotions stirred by Pamela and Clarissa. When Clarissa briefly considers marrying Lovelace, he is moved to tears. In a letter to Belford, Lovelace writes first of the feeling and then of his aestheticizing of the experience (see 695ff.). The emotionalism, the inarticulateness, and the use of dashes to convey extremity of experience anticipate the descriptions of the sentimental male, the so-called "man of feeling," while imitating the discourse of Haywood's

impassioned women. Richardson also sanctifies the emotionalism – finely drawn by the seemingly unmediated style of the epistolary novel – consistently associated simultaneously with hacks and stock-jobbers.

44 Really the only example of unbridled female passion in Richardson's fiction is Clementina in *Sir Charles Grandison*. From the beginning of that novel, however, Clementina's marginalized and slightly "abnormal" status as both an Italian and an emotionally troubled woman is emphasized.

45 *Pamela* became the subject of a poem, a play, an opera, a hundred miniature figure waxworks, and, later, Joseph Highmore's twelve oil paintings and subsequent plates. There was also the Pamela fan, "for the Entertainment of the Ladies, more especially those who have the Book, representing the principal Adventures of her Life, in Servitude, Love, and Marriage" (*Daily Advertiser*, April 28, 1741, quoted in Sale, *Samuel Richardson: A Biographical Record*, 11). As Edward Cave describes in *Gentleman's Magazine*, it was "judged in Town as great a Sign of Want of Curiosity not to have read Pamela, as not to have seen the French and Italian dancers" (xi [January 1741] 56).

46 As McKillop notes, though the alleged incident may have happened after the text's publication, he suggests its significance lies in its demonstration of "how Pamela took hold of what we may call the folk-imagination" (*Samuel Richardson: Printer and Novelist*, 45). While I agree with the power of imagination, I am obviously attributing it to a slightly different cultural temper. For another discussion, see also Alan Dugald McKillop, "Wedding Bells for Pamela," *Philological Quarterly* 28 (1949): 323–25.

47 See my discussion of Eagleton's study, n. 2.

48 Carroll, *Selected Letters*, 39. Also, in *The Apprentice's Vade Mecum*, in a section that "cautions against suretiship," Richardson warns of the "pernicious consequence, suretiship, and other engagements flowing often from" early and ill-advised friendships (44).

49 This quotation appears in the revised 1801 text, but not the first edition. It has been quoted from *Pamela*, edited by Peter Sabor (New York: Penguin, 1980), 113.

50 Throughout the early eighteenth century, particularly during the time of the South Sea Company's introduction, the term "project" typically referred to an (often dubious) economic scheme for earning money and attracting investors. For discussions of Pamela's clothing see Carey McIntosh, "Pamela's Clothes," in *Twentieth-Century Interpretations of Pamela*, edited by Rosemary Cowler (Englewood Cliffs, NJ: Prentice-Hall, Inc., 1969) and Caryn Chaden, "Pamela's Identity Sewn in Clothes," in *Eighteenth-Century Women and the Arts*, edited by Frederick M. Keener and Susan E. Lorsch (New York: Greenwood Press, 1988). See also Doody's brief discussion, *A Natural Passion*, 40–42.

51 Pamela later terms herself "a mere tennis-ball of fortune" (280).

52 Pocock traces the virtue–fortune polarity throughout the civic humanist tradition, from Boethius's configuration to its neo-Harringtonian manifestation. Though discussed at multiple points in *The Machiavellian Moment*, see particularly pp. 36–41, 84–97, and 349–75.

53 Terry Castle observes that Pamela introduces a carnivalesque element to B—
Hall as she penetrates the upper reaches of the society. "*Pamela* remains one
could argue one of the greatest carnivalesque plots in literature. It has to do
with the violation of taxonomic boundaries, with unprecedented (and gratifying) couplings of things that should remain apart: high and low, masters and
servant, rake and virgins" (*Masquerade and Civilization*, 135–36).

54 Armstrong, *Desire and Domestic Fiction*, 115. Armstrong's discussion of *Pamela*
(108–34) focuses on the political implications of the novel; she is concerned
with the way Richardson empowers Pamela, locating that power within
her female subjectivity and self-possession. It is, she suggests, a text that
"repackages political resistance as the subjectivity of a woman" (132).
Armstrong places it within a broader cultural and discursive transformation
that results in the "feminization" of the novel and the reorganization of
political power within the domestic household and in specifically gendered
terms. While Armstrong's significant study has influenced subsequent scholarship, her discussion of *Pamela*, though persuasive on some issues, ignores the
material and symbolic economy that, to my mind, pervades the novel. Like
Armstrong, I think Richardson endows Pamela with a great deal of power and
value. But, unlike Armstrong, I think Pamela constructs her value within an
imaginative and speculative domestic economy dependent on her letters,
journals, and other forms of paper credit. When Armstrong does discuss
economics, in the broadest sense of the term, she suggests that Pamela's "will
... poses an alternative moral economy to that of the dominant class" (114).
Certainly Pamela's actions, like the credit economy generally, offer an alternative to the moral economy but they are profoundly informed by speculative
investment.

55 The 1801 edition continues, "My fortune is the more valuable to me, in the
world's eye, to do credit to your virtue" (367).

56 John Bender, *Imagining the Penitentiary: Fiction and the Architecture of the Mind in
Eighteenth-Century England* (University of Chicago Press, 1987), 7.

57 *Pamela* was first published in November 1740. A revised edition followed in
February 1741 and three further revised editions appeared that year. In 1742, a
deluxe octavo edition, which combined *Pamela I* and *II*, appeared. Two more
revised editions of *Pamela* were published in 1746 and 1754.

CONCLUSION: NEGOTIABLE PAPER

1 Carroll, *Selected Letters*, 43.

2 Ibid., 44.

3 In addition to the five editions of *Pamela* that appeared between 1741 and 1751,
as is well known, Richardson published three revised editions of *Clarissa*, in the
third adding extensive letters and annotations in an attempt to guide readers'
interpretation of the text. He also published the new letters separately as *Letters
and Passages Restored from the Original Manuscripts of the History of Clarissa* (1751), a
text described as "published for the Sake of doing Justice to the Purchasers of

the First Two Editions of the Work." In addition to these textual additions, Richardson also published supplementary texts such as *Clarissa's Meditations* and *A Collection of the Moral and Instructive Sentiments from Pamela, Clarissa and Sir Charles Grandison* (1755), attempts to further inculcate his didactic message and reap profits from the popularity of his texts.

4 The fact that the edition of letters, if published during his lifetime, would be published in German appealed to Richardson since it would eliminate the self-aggrandizing gesture (one for which Pope was criticized) of publishing one's letters during one's lifetime. As Carroll notes, "Reich's proposal led the novelist to believe that an edition of his correspondence would be called for after his death" (*Selected Letters*, 4).

5 May 23, 1758 (FC xi f. 242) as quoted in Carroll, ibid., 7.

6 The rapid appearance of the 1729 *Dunciad Variorum*, begun within a month of the *Dunciad*'s publication, underscores that text's role in a more protracted Grub Street exchange as discussed in chapter 2. Pope's footnotes, appendixes, and extensive reading apparatus preempted the information Curll attempted to provide in the various *Keys* to the *Dunciad*, allowing Pope to refine further the locus of his attack and enhance his financial profits.

7 Mack, *Alexander Pope*, 333.

8 *Corr.*, Introduction, 1, p. ix.

9 (January 19, 1743/44), Carroll, *Selected Letters*, 60.

10 Ibid., 100.

11 Ibid., 179–80.

12 Cheyne to Richardson, February 12, 1741, quoted in Eaves and Kimpel, *Samuel Richardson*, 124.

13 Richardson's friendships and professional relationships primarily included individuals Pope regarded as "dunces." Richardson printed Smedley's *Poems on Several Occasions* (1721), John Dennis's attack on *The Rape of the Lock* and *Remarks Upon Several Passages in the Preliminaries to the Dunciad* (1729), and a number of texts for Aaron Hill – including the *Plain Dealer* – with whom he maintained a close association. He published the work of quite a few female novelists. In addition to the previously mentioned Haywood texts, he also published Susanna Centlivre's *The Gamester* (1736), Sarah Fielding's *The Governess* (1749), and Charlotte Lennox's *The Female Quixote* (1752).

14 Terry Eagleton suggests that Richardson, by privileging sentiment in his novels and in his complicated relationship with his coterie of female readers, effectively makes what he terms "the bourgeois 'feminization of discourse' ... a more vitally constitutive part of the male public sphere" (*The Rape of Clarissa*, 13). While I agree, to a certain extent, with the impulse (and the terms he uses to describe it), as the previous chapters have demonstrated, the discourse of the feminization of culture with which I am concerned involves much more than the "pity, pathos, and the pacific, 'womanly' qualities suppressed by a warring nobility" (15) that Eagleton details.

15 Documents relating to Haywood's dealings with John Nourse in the 1730s and 1740s give an indication of the type of arrangement she might typically have

had with a bookseller and how limiting the financial relationship would be for an author in her position. In March 1734, she signed an agreement with Francis Cogan and John Nourse for a book called *The History of the British Theatre*. At that time, Haywood received £16 4s payment for the first volume and, as was customary, sold the copyright to this and future volumes: "at the Request of the Said Frank Cogan and J. Nourse . . . the said Eliza Haywood shall immediately assign over to them all her the said Eliza Haywood's right title Interest claim Demand or pretence whatsoever to the Copy and Copyright of the said Book for ever by such Instrument as they shall be advised is proper and sufficient for the purpose" (B.M. Add. MS 38,728 f. 112). Haywood received payment for the subsequent editions of these volumes in 1745, on September 26. She wrote other things for Nourse, receiving a total of more than £15 on two separate occasions between March 1746/47 and April 1747 for a translation entitled *Memoirs of a Man of Honour*.

Bibliography

PRIMARY SOURCES

Addison, Joseph and Richard Steele. *The Spectator*. Ed. Donald Bond. 5 vols. Oxford: Clarendon Press, 1965.

The Tatler. Ed. Donald Bond. 3 vols. Oxford: Clarendon Press, 1987.

Aislabie, John. *Mr. Aislabie's Second Speech on his Defence in the House of Lords, on Thursday, July 20, 1721*. London, 1721.

Mr. Aislabie's Two Speeches Considered; with his Tryal at Large in both Houses of Parliament. London, 1721.

Baker, David Erskine. *Biographia Dramatica: or, a Companion to the Playhouse*. London, 1764; rpt. 1812.

The Battle of the Bubbles. Shewing their Several Constitutions, Alliances, Policies, and Wars; from their First Sudden Rise to their Late Speedy Decay. London, 1720.

Bond, William. *The Progress of Dulness*. London, 1728.

The Supernatural Philosopher: or, the Mysteries of Magick, in all its Branches clearly unfolded. London, 1728.

Carter, Elizabeth. *Sir Isaac Newton's Philosophy Explained for the Use of Ladies in Six Dialogues on Light and Colour*. London, 1739.

The Case of the Borrowers on the South-Sea Loans, Stated. London, 1721.

Chetwood, William Rufus. *South-Sea; or, the biters bit. A Tragi-Comi-Pastoral Farce*. London, 1720.

The Stock-Jobbers: or, the Humours of Exchange-Alley. A Comedy in Three Acts. London, 1720.

Churchill, Sarah, Duchess of Marlborough. *The Letters of Sarah Duchess of Marlborough*. London: John Murray, 1875.

The Memoirs of Sarah, Duchess of Marlborough together with her Characters of her Contemporaries and her Opinions. Ed., with an Introduction, by William King. London: George Routledge & Sons Ltd., 1930.

Curll, Edmund. *The Compleat Key to the Dunciad*. London, 1728.

The Curliad. A Hypercritic Upon the Dunciad Variorum, with a farther Key to New Characters. London, 1729.

The Popiad. London, 1728.

Defoe, Daniel. *The Anatomy of Exchange-Alley: or, a System of Stock-Jobbing*. London, 1719.

The Dumb Philosopher; or, Great-Britain's Wonder. London, 1719.

An Essay Upon Publick Credit: Being an Inquiry How Publick Credit comes to Depend upon the Change or the Ministry, or the Dissolutions of Parliament: and whether it does so or no. London, 1710.

The History of the Life and Adventures of Mr. Duncan Campbell. London, 1720.

Secret Memoirs of the late Mr. Duncan Campbell. London, 1732.

Dennis, John. *An Essay upon Public Spirit; Being a Satyr in Prose upon the Manners and Luxury of the Times, the chief Sources of our present Parties and Divisions.* London, 1711.

D'Urfey, Thomas. *New Opera's, with Comical Stories, and Poems, on Several Occasions, Never Before Printed.* London, 1721.

An Essay on the South-Sea Trade. With an Enquiry into the Grounds and Reasons of the Present Dislike and Complaint against the Settlement of a South-Sea Company. London, 1712.

An Examination and Explanation of the South-Sea Company's Scheme. London, 1720.

Exchange-Alley: or, the Stock-jobber turn'd Gentleman; with the Humours of our Modern Projectors. London, 1720.

A Farther Examination and Explanation of the South-Sea Company's Scheme. London, 1720.

Gay, John. *Letters.* Ed. C. F. Burgess. Oxford: Clarendon Press, 1966.

Haywood, Eliza. *Adventures of Eovaii, Princess of Ijaveo.* London, 1736.

The Adventures of Natura: or, Life's Progress through the Passions. London, 1748.

The Agreeable Caledonian: or, Memoirs of Signora di Morella, a Roman Lady. London, 1728.

Anti-Pamela: or, Feigned Innocence detected; In a Series of Syrena's Adventures. London, 1742.

The Arragonian Queen: a Secret History. London, 1734.

Bath-Intrigues: in Four Letters to a Friend in London. London, 1725.

The British Recluse: or, Secret History of Cleomira, supposed dead. A Novel. London, 1722.

The Capricious Lover: or, No Trifling with a Woman. London, 1727.

The City Jilt: or, the Alderman turned Beau: A Secret History. London, 1726.

The City Widow: or, Love in a Butt, A Novel. London, 1729.

Cleomelia: or, the Generous Mistress. Being the Secret History of a Lady Lately arriv'd from Bengall, a Kingdom in the East-Indies. London, 1727.

Dalinda: or, the Double Marriage. Being the Genuine History of a very recent, and interesting Adventure. London, 1749.

The Disguised Prince; or, the Beautiful Parisian. London, 1733.

The Distressed Orphan, or Love in a Madhouse. London, 1726.

The Double Marriage: or, the Fatal Release. A True Secret History. London, 1726.

The Dumb Projector: Being a Surprizing Account of a Trip to Holland Made by Duncan Campbell. London, 1725.

Epistles for the Ladies. London, 1749.

The Fair Captive: A Tragedy. As it is Acted by His Majesty's Servants. London, 1721.

The Fair Hebrew: or, a True, but Secret History of Two Jewish Ladies. London, 1729.

Fantomina: Or, Love in a Maze. London, 1725.

The Fatal Secret: or, Constancy in Distress. London, 1724.

The Female Spectator. London, 1744–46.

The Force of Nature: or, the Lucky Disappointment. London, 1725.

The Fortunate Foundlings: Being the Genuine History of Colonel M—rs, and his Sister, Madam DUP—y. London, 1744.

Frederick, Duke of Brunswick-Lunenbergh. A Tragedy. London, 1729.

The Fruitless Enquiry: Being a Collection of Several Entertaining Histories and Occurrences. London, 1727.

The History of Miss Betsy Thoughtless. Ed. Beth Fowkes Tobin. Oxford and New York: Oxford University Press, 1997.

The Husband. In Answer to the Wife. London, 1751.

Idalia: or, the Unfortunate Mistress, a Novel. London, 1723.

The Injur'd Husband: or, the Mistaken Resentment. London, 1723.

The Irish Artifice; or, the History of Clarina. A Novel. In *The Female Dunciad.* London, 1728.

La Belle Assemblee: Being a Curious Collection of Some Very Remarkable Incidents which Happened to Persons of the First Quality in France. London, 1736.

The Lady's Philosopher Stone: or, The Caprices of Love and Destiny: An Historical Novel. London, 1725.

Lasselia: or, the Self-Abandoned. A Novel. London, 1724.

L'Entretien des Beaux Esprits. Conversations, comprising a great variety of Remarkable Adventures, Serious, Comic and Moral. London, 1734.

A Letter from H— G—g, Esq.; One of the Gentlemen of the Bed-Chamber to the Young Chevalier . . . to a Particular Friend. London, 1749.

Letters from a Lady of Quality to a Chevalier. London, 1721.

The Life of Madam De Villesache. Written by a Lady, who was an eye-witness of the greatest part of her adventures. London, 1727.

Life's Progress through the Passions; or, the Adventures of Natura. London, 1748.

Love in Excess: or the Fatal Enquiry. London, 1719.

Love in its Variety: Being a Collection of Select Novels. London, 1727.

Love Letters on All Occasions lately passed between Persons of Distinction. London, 1730.

The Lucky Rape: Or, Fate the Best Disposer. London, 1727.

Mary Stuart, Queen of Scots: being the secret history of her life, and the real cause of all her misfortunes. London, 1725.

The Masqueraders: or, the Fatal Curiosity; being the Secret History of a Late Amour. London, 1724.

Memoirs of a Certain Island Adjacent to the Kingdom of Utopia. London, 1726.

The Mercenary Lover: Or, The Unfortunate Heiresses. Being a True Secret History of a City Amour. London, 1726.

Modern Characters: Illustrated by Histories in Real Life, And Address'd to the Polite World. London, 1753.

The Parrot, with a Compendium to the Times. By the Authors of the Female Spectator. London, 1746.

The Perplex'd Dutchess: or, Treachery Rewarded. London, 1728.

Persecuted Virtue: or, the Cruel Lover. A True Secret History. Writ at the Request of a Lady of Quality. London, 1729.

Philidore and Placentia: or, L'Amour trop Delicat. London, 1727.

The Rash Resolve: or, the Untimely Discovery. A Novel. London, 1724.

Reflections on the Various Effects of Love, according to the Contrary Dispositions of the Persons on Whom it Operates. London, 1726.

A Spy on the Conjurer; or, A Collection of Surprising and diverting stories, with merry and ingenious letters. By way of memoirs of the famous Mr. Duncan Campbell, demonstrating the astonishing foresight of that wonderful deaf and dumb man. London, 1725.

The Surprise; or, Constancy Rewarded. London, 1724.

The Tea-Table: or, a Conversation between some polite Persons of both Sexes at a Lady's visiting Day. London, 1725.

The Unequal Conflict; or, Nature Triumphant: A Novel. London, 1725.

The Unfortunate Princess: or, the Life and Surprising Adventures of The Princess of Ijaveo. London, 1741.

The Virtuous Villager, or Virgin's Victory: Being the Memoirs of a very Great Lady at the Court of France. London, 1742.

The Wife. London, 1756.

A Wife to be Lett: A Comedy. London, 1735.

Haywood, Eliza, and William Hatchett. *The Opera of Operas; or, Tom Thumb the Great. Altered from the Life and Death of Tom Thumb the Great and Set to Musick after the Italian-Manner.* London, 1733.

Howard, Henrietta, Countess of Suffolk. *Letters to and from Henrietta, Countess of Suffolk, and her second husband, the Hon. George Berkeley: 1712–1767.* 2 vols. Ed. J. W. Croker. London, 1824.

Hume, David. *Essays: Moral, Political and Literary.* Indianapolis: Liberty Classics, 1985.

Johnson, Samuel. *Lives of the English Poets.* 3 vols. Ed. George Birkbeck Hill. Oxford: Clarendon Press, 1945.

Jones, Erasmus. *Luxury, Pride, and Vanity, The Bane of the British Nation.* 3rd edition. London, 1736.

A Letter to a Conscientious Man: Concerning the Use and the Abuse of Riches, and the Right and The Wrong Ways of Acquiring them: Shewing that Stock-jobbing is an unfair Way of Dealing; and particularly demonstrating the Fallaciousness of the South-Sea Scheme. London, 1720.

A Letter to a Member of Parliament, concerning the South-Sea Company: with Proposals for settling a certain annual dividend. London, 1720.

Mackworth, Sir Humphrey. *A Proposal for Payment of the Publick Debts, for Relief of the South-Sea Company. And for Easing the Nation of the Land and Malt Taxes.* London, n.d.

Milner, James. *Three Letters Relating to the South-Sea Company and the Bank. The First Written in March, 1719–1720. The Second in April 1720. The Third in September, 1720. Now First Published.* London, 1720.

Montagu, Lady Mary Wortley. *Complete Letters.* Ed. Robert Halsband. 3 vols. Oxford: Clarendon Press, 1965–67.

Pope, Alexander. *The Correspondence of Alexander Pope.* 5 vols. Ed. George Sherburn. Oxford: Oxford University Press, 1956.

The Twickenham Edition of the Poems of Alexander Pope. 11 vols. Gen. ed. John Butt. London: Methuen, 1938–68.

A Popp Upon Pope: or, a True and Faithful Account of a Late Horrid and Barbarous Whipping Committed on the Body of A. Pope, a Poet. London, 1728.

Publick Securities: or, the Parliamentary Funds established for Paying the Annuities. Extracted from all the Acts of Parliament relating there unto. London, 1712.

Ramsey, Alexander. *A Poem on the South-Sea, to which is Prefixed, a Familiar Epistle to Anthony Hammond, Esq.* London, 1720.

Remarks upon the Bank of England, with Regard more especially to our Trade and Government. Occasion'd by the present Discourse concerning the intended Prolongation of the Bank. London, 1705.

Richardson, Samuel. *Selected Letters of Samuel Richardson.* Ed., with an Introduction, by John Carroll. Oxford: Clarendon Press, 1964.

The Richardson–Stinstra Correspondence and Stinstra's Prefaces to Clarissa. Ed. William C. Slattery. Carbondale and Edwardsville: Southern Illinois University Press, 1969.

Savage, Richard. *The Poetical Works of Richard Savage.* Ed. Clarence Tracy. Cambridge University Press, 1962.

Some Considerations on the late Mismanagement of the South-Sea Stock; on the New Scheme propos'd for Redress; and likewise on Trade. London, n.d.

Some Observations upon the Bill now depending on Parliament, for Relief of the Unhappy Sufferers in the South-Sea Company. London, n.d.

Some Observations upon a Late Pamphlet, intitled, A Modest Representation of the Past and Present State of Great Britain, occasioned by the Late Change in the Administration. London, 1711.

A Speech upon the Consolidated Bill. London, 1721.

Swift, Jonathan. *The Complete Poems.* Ed. Pat Rogers. New Haven: Yale University Press, 1983.

Thomas, Elizabeth. *Codrus; Or, the Dunciad Dissected Being the Finishing Stroke.* London, 1728.

The Metamorphoses of the Town: or, a View of the Present Fashion. London, 1733.

Miscellany Poems on Several Subjects. London, 1722.

Pylades and Corinna: or Memoirs of the Lives, Amours and Writings of Richard Gwinnett, Esq. . . . and Mrs. Elizabeth Thomas. London, 1731–32.

Thomas, Gordon. *A Learned Dissertation upon Old Women.* London, 1720.

Trick for Trick; or, the Hasty Cuckold. London, 1714.

Wilmot, John, Earl of Rochester. *The Complete Poems.* Ed. David M. Vieth. New Haven: Yale University Press, 1968.

SECONDARY SOURCES

Agnew, Jean-Christophe. *Worlds Apart: The Market and the Theatre in Anglo-American Thought, 1550–1750.* Cambridge University Press, 1986.

Alsop, J. D. "Defoe and His Whig Paymasters." *Notes and Queries* 28 (1981): 225–26.

"New Light on Nathaniel Mist and Daniel Defoe." *Papers of the Bibliographical Society of America* 75 (1981): 57–60.

Appleby, Joyce Oldham. *Economic Thought and Ideology in Seventeenth-Century England.* Princeton University Press, 1978.

Armstrong, Nancy. *Desire and Domestic Fiction: A Political History of the Novel.* New York: Oxford University Press, 1987.

Armstrong, Nancy and Leonard Tennenhouse, eds. *The Ideology of Conduct: Essays on Literature and the History of Sexuality.* New York: Methuen, 1987.

Ashton, T. S. *An Economic History of England: The Eighteenth Century.* New York: Barnes and Noble, Inc., 1954.

Atherton, Herbert M. *Political Prints in the Age of Hogarth: A Study of the Ideographic Representation of Politics.* Oxford: Clarendon Press, 1974.

Atkins, G. Douglas. *Quests of Difference: Reading Pope's Poems.* Lexington: University Press of Kentucky, 1986.

Babcock, Barbara, ed. *The Reversible World: Symbolic Inversion in Art and Society.* Ithaca: Cornell University Press, 1979.

Backscheider, Paula R. *Daniel Defoe: His Life.* Baltimore: Johns Hopkins University Press, 1989.

"Defoe's Lady Credit." *Huntington Library Quarterly* 44 (1981): 89–100.

Spectacular Politics: Theatrical Power and Mass Culture in Early Modern England. Baltimore and London: Johns Hopkins University Press, 1993.

Bakhtin, Mikhail M. *The Dialogic Imagination: Four Essays.* Ed. Michael Holquist. Trans. Caryl Emerson and Michael Holquist. Austin: University of Texas Press, 1981.

Rabelais and His World. Trans. Helene Iswolsky. Bloomington: Indiana University Press, 1984.

Ballaster, Ros. *Seductive Forms: Women's Amatory Fiction from 1684 to 1740.* Oxford: Clarendon Press, 1992.

Barrett, Michele. *Women's Oppression Today: The Marxist/Feminist Encounter.* London: Verso, 1980. Revised edition, 1988.

Bartolomeo, Joseph. *A New Species of Criticism: Eighteenth-Century Discourse on the Novel.* Newark: University of Delaware Press, 1994.

Baym, Nina. "Melodramas of Beset Manhood: How Theories of American Fiction Exclude Women Authors." *American Quarterly* 33 (1981): 123–39.

Beasley, Jerry C. "Eliza Haywood." *Dictionary of Literary Biography.* Ed. Martin C. Battestin. 251–59. Detroit: Gale Research Co., 39.

Novels of the 1740s. Athens: University of Georgia Press, 1982.

"Portraits of a Monster: Robert Walpole and Early English Prose Fiction." *Eighteenth-Century Studies* 14 (1981): 406–31.

Beauvoir, Simone de. *The Second Sex.* Trans. and ed. H. M. Parshley. New York: Vintage Books. 1952; rpt. 1974.

Belanger, Terry. "Publishers and Writers in Eighteenth-Century England." *Books and Their Readers in Eighteenth-Century England.* Ed. Isabel Rivers. 5–25. Leicester University Press, 1982.

Bender, John. *Imagining the Penitentiary: Fiction and the Architecture of Mind in Eighteenth-Century England.* University of Chicago Press, 1987.

Berry, Reginald. *A Pope Chronology.* Boston: G. K. Hall and Co., 1988.

Besant, Sir Walter. *London in the Eighteenth Century.* London: Adam and Charles Black, 1903.

Black, Jeremy. *The English Press in the Eighteenth Century*. Philadelphia: University of Pennsylvania Press, 1987.

Blagden, Cyprian. *The Stationers' Company: A History, 1403–1959*. London: George Allen and Unwin Ltd., 1960.

Blewett, David. "Changing Attitudes toward Marriage in the Time of Defoe: The Case of Moll Flanders." *Huntington Library Quarterly* 44 (1981): 77–88.

Bogel, Fredric. "Johnson and the Role of Authority." *The New Eighteenth Century: Theory, Politics, English Literature*. Ed. Felicity Nussbaum and Laura Brown. 189–209. New York: Methuen, Inc. 1987.

Bond, Richard. "The Lottery: A Note for the Year 1710." *The South Atlantic Quarterly* 70 (1971): 135–48.

Boucé, Paul-Gabriel, ed. *Sexuality in Eighteenth-Century Britain*. Manchester University Press, 1982.

Bowyer, John Wilson. *The Celebrated Mrs. Centlivre*. Durham, NC: Duke University Press, 1952.

Brewer, John. *The Sinews of Power: War, Money and the English State. 1688–1783*. New York: Alfred A. Knopf, 1989.

Brewer, John and Roy Porter, eds. *Consumption and the World of Goods*. London and New York: Routledge, 1993.

Brewer, John and Susan Staves. *Early Modern Conceptions of Property*. London and New York: Routledge, 1995.

Brewster, Dorothy. *Aaron Hill: Poet, Dramatist, Projector*. New York: Columbia University Press, 1913.

Brissenden, R. F. *Virtue in Distress: Studies in the Novel of Sentiment from Richardson to Sade*. London: Macmillan, 1974.

Brophy, Elizabeth Bergen. *Women's Lives and the Eighteenth-Century Novel*. Tampa: University of South Florida Press, 1991.

Brown, Irene Q. "Domesticity, Feminism and Friendship: Female Aristocratic Culture and Marriage in England, 1660–1760." *The Journal of Family History* 7 (1982): 406–24.

Brown, Laura. *Alexander Pope*. Oxford: Basil Blackwell, 1985.

Ends of Empire: Women and Ideology in Early Eighteenth-Century English Literature. Ithaca: Cornell University Press, 1993.

"Reading Race and Gender: Jonathan Swift." *Eighteenth-Century Studies* 23 (1990): 424–43.

Brown, Norman O. *Life against Death: The Psychoanalytical Meaning of History*. Middletown, CT: Wesleyan University Press, 1959.

Butler, Judith. *Gender Trouble: Feminism and the Subversion of Identity*. New York: Routledge, 1990.

Carretta, Vincent. *George III and the Satirists from Hogarth to Byron*. Athens: University of Georgia Press, 1990.

The Snarling Muse: Verbal and Visual Political Satire from Pope to Churchill. Philadelphia: University of Pennsylvania Press, 1983.

Carswell, John. *The South Sea Bubble*. Stanford University Press, 1960.

Castle, Terry. *Clarissa's Ciphers: Meaning and Disruption in Richardson's Clarissa.* Ithaca: Cornell University Press, 1982.

Masquerade and Civilization: The Carnivalesque in Eighteenth-Century English Culture and Fiction. Stanford University Press, 1986.

Clark, William Smith. *The Early Irish Stage: The Beginnings to 1720.* Oxford: Clarendon Press, 1955.

Cockerell, Douglas. *Bookbindings and the Care of Books: A Textbook for Bookbinders and Librarians.* London: Sir Isaac Pitman and Sons, Ltd., 1957.

Cole, Arthur H. *The Great Mirror of Folly (Het Groote Tafereel der Dwaasheid): An Economic-Bibliographical Study.* Boston: Harvard University Press, 1949.

Collins, A. S. *Authorship in the Days of Johnson.* London: Robert Holden and Co., 1927.

The Profession of Letters: A Study of the Relation of Author to Patron, Publisher and Public, 1780–1832. London: George Routledge and Sons, Ltd., 1928.

Cotton, Nancy. *Women Playwrights in England c. 1363–1750.* Lewisburg: Bucknell University Press, 1980.

Cowles, Virginia. *The Great Swindle: The Story of the South Sea Bubble.* London: Collins Press, 1960.

Craft-Fairchild, Catherine. *Masquerade and Gender: Disguise and Female Identity in Eighteenth-Century Fictions by Women.* University Park: Pennsylvania State University Press, 1993.

Crawford, Patricia. "Women's Published Writing 1600–1700." In *Women in English Society 1500–1800.* Ed. Mary Prior. London: Methuen, 1985.

Cruise, James. "Fielding, Authority and the New Commercialism in *Joseph Andrews*." *ELH* 54 (1987): 253–76.

"Pamela and the Commerce of Authority." *Journal of English and Germanic Philology* 87 (1988): 342–88.

Cunningham, William. *The Growth of English Industry and Commerce in Modern Times: Volume Two, The Mercantile System.* New York: Augustus M. Kelley, 1968.

Damrosch, Leopold, Jr. *The Imaginative World of Alexander Pope.* Berkeley: University of California Press, 1987.

Davis, Lennard J. *Factual Fictions: The Origins of the English Novel.* New York: Columbia University Press, 1983.

Dickson, P. G. M. *The Financial Revolution in England: A Study in the Development of Public Credit 1688–1756.* New York: St. Martin's Press, 1967.

Diehl, Edith. *Bookbinding: Its Background and Technique.* New York: Rinehart and Co., Inc., 1946.

Doody, Margaret Anne. *A Natural Passion: A Study of the Novels of Samuel Richardson.* Oxford University Press, 1974.

Doody, Margaret Anne and Peter Sabor, eds. *Samuel Richardson: Tercentenary Essays.* Cambridge University Press, 1989.

Douglas, Mary. *Purity and Danger: An Analysis of the Concepts of Pollution and Taboo.* London: Ark Paperbacks. First published 1966; rpt. 1984.

Eagleton, Terry. *Criticism and Ideology: A Study in Marxist Literary Theory.* London: Verso, 1978.

Marxism and Literary Criticism. Berkeley and Los Angeles: University of California Press, 1976.
The Rape of Clarissa: Writing, Sexuality and Class Struggle in Samuel Richardson. Minneapolis: University of Minnesota Press, 1982.

Earle, Peter. *The Making of the English Middle Class: Business, Society and Family Life in London, 1660–1730.* Berkeley and Los Angeles: University of California Press, 1989.

Eaves, T. C. and Ben D. Kimpel. *Samuel Richardson: A Biography.* Oxford: Clarendon Press, 1971.

Ehrenpreis, Irvin. *Acts of Implication: Suggestion and Covert Meaning in the Works of Dryden, Swift, Pope, and Austen.* Berkeley: University of California Press, 1980.

Elwood, John. "Swift's Corinna." *Notes and Queries* 12 (1955): 529–30.

Erskine-Hill, Howard. "Pope and the Financial Revolution." In *Writers and Their Backgrounds: Alexander Pope.* Ed. Peter Dixon. 203–29. Athens: Ohio University Press, 1972.
The Social Milieu of Alexander Pope: Lives, Examples and the Poetic Response. New Haven: Yale University Press, 1975.

Ezell, Margaret J. M. *Writing Women's Literary History.* Baltimore and London: Johns Hopkins University Press, 1993.

Fairer, David. *Pope's Imagination.* Manchester University Press, 1984.

Faulkner, Thomas C. and Rhonda L. Blair. "The Classical and Mythographic Sources of Pope's Dulness." *Huntington Library Quarterly* 43 (1980): 213–46.

Flint, Christopher. "Anxiety of Affluence: Family and Class (Dis)order in *Pamela; or, Virtue Rewarded*." *Studies in English Literature* 29 (1989): 489–513.

Flynn, Carol Houlihan. *Samuel Richardson: A Man of Letters.* Princeton University Press, 1982.

Foxon, David. *Libertine Literature in England 1669–1745.* New Hyde Park, NY: University Books, 1965.
Pope and the Early Eighteenth-Century Book Trade. Revised and ed. James McLaverty. Oxford: Clarendon Press, 1991.

Friedli, Lynne. "'Passing Women': A Study of Gender Boundaries in the Eighteenth Century." In *Sexual Underworlds of the Enlightenment.* Ed. G. S. Rousseau and Roy Porter. 234–60. Chapel Hill: University of North Carolina Press, 1988.

Gallagher, Catherine. *Nobody's Story: The Vanishing Acts of Women Writers in the Marketplace, 1670–1820.* Berkeley and Los Angeles: University of California Press, 1994.
"Political Crimes and Fictional Alibis: The Case of Delariviere Manley." *Eighteenth-Century Studies* 23 (1990): 502–21.
"Raymond Williams and Cultural Studies." *Social Text* 30 (1992): 79–89.

Gardiner, Judith Kegan. "The First English Novel: Aphra Behn's *Love Letters*, the Canon, and Women's Tastes." *Tulsa Studies in Women's Literature* 8 (1989): 201–22.

George, Mary Dorothy. *London Life in the Eighteenth Century.* London: Kegan, Paul, Trench, Trubner and Co. Ltd., 1930.

Gilbert, Sandra M. and Susan Gubar. *The Madwoman in the Attic: The Woman Writer and the Nineteenth-Century Literary Imagination*. New Haven: Yale University Press, 1979.

Goldberg, Rita. *Sex and Enlightenment: Women in Richardson and Diderot*. Cambridge University Press, 1984.

Goldgar, Bertrand A. *Walpole and the Wits: The Relation of Politics to Literature, 1722–1742*. Lincoln: University of Nebraska Press, 1976.

Goldsmith, Elizabeth C., ed. *Writing the Female Voice: Essays on Epistolary Literature*. Boston: Northeastern University Press, 1989.

Goux, Jean-Joseph. *Symbolic Economies after Marx and Freud*. Trans. Jennifer Curtiss Gage. Ithaca: Cornell University Press, 1990.

Griffin, Dustin H. *Alexander Pope: The Poet in the Poems*. Princeton University Press, 1978.

Griffin, R. H. *Alexander Pope: A Bibliography, Vol. I, Part II: Pope's Own Writings 1735–1751*. Austin: University of Texas Press, 1927.

Gubar, Susan. "The Female Monster in Augustan Satire." *Signs* 3 (1977): 380–94.

Guerinot, Joseph V. *Pamphlet Attacks on Alexander Pope 1711–1744: A Descriptive Bibliography*. New York University Press, 1969.

Guest, Harriet. "A Double Lustre: Femininity and Sociable Commerce." *Eighteenth-Century Studies* 23 (1990): 479–501.

Gwilliam, Tassie. "Pamela and the Duplicitous Body of Femininity." *Representations* 34 (1991): 104–33.

Hagstrum, Jean H. *Sex and Sensibility: Ideal and Erotic Love from Milton to Mozart*. University of Chicago Press, 1980.

Halsband, Robert. *The Life of Lady Mary Wortley Montagu*. Oxford at the Clarendon Press, 1956.

Handover, P. M. *Printing in London from 1476 to Modern Times: Competitive Practice and Technical Invention in the Trade of Book and Bible Printing, Periodical Production, Jobbing & c.* London: George Allen and Unwin Ltd., 1960.

Harris, Frances. *A Passion for Government: The Life of Sarah, Duchess of Marlborough*. Oxford: Clarendon Press, 1991.

Harris, Jocelyn. *Samuel Richardson*. Cambridge University Press, 1987.

Heinemann, Marcia. "Eliza Haywood's Career in the Theatre." *Notes and Queries* 20 (1973): 9–13.

Highfill, Philip H., Jr., Kalman A. Burnim, and Edward A. Langhans. *A Biographical Dictionary of Actors, Actresses, Musicians, Dancers, Managers and Other Stage Personnel in London, 1660–1800*. Carbondale and Edwardsville: Southern Illinois University Press, 1982.

Hill, Christopher. *The Century of Revolution: 1603–1714*. New York: W. W. Norton and Co., 1961.

"Clarissa Harlowe and Her Times." *Essays in Criticism* 5 (1955): 313–56.

Hillhouse, James T. *The Grub Street Journal*. New York: Benjamin Blom. Originally published, 1928; rpt. 1967.

Hirschman, Albert O. *The Passions and the Interests: Political Arguments for Capitalism before Its Triumph*. Princeton University Press, 1977.

Hoppit, Julian. "The Use and Abuse of Credit in Eighteenth-Century England." In *Business Life and Public Policy: Essays in Honour of D. C. Coleman.* Ed. Neil McKendrick and R. B. Outhwaite. 67–78. Cambridge University Press, 1986.

Hume, Robert D. *Henry Fielding and the London Theatre 1728–1737.* Oxford: Clarendon Press, 1988.

Hunter, J. Paul. *Before Novels: The Cultural Contexts of Eighteenth-Century English Fiction.* New York: W. W. Norton and Co., 1990.

Huyssen, Andreas. *After the Great Divide: Modernism, Mass Culture, Postmodernism.* Bloomington: Indiana University Press, 1986.

Irigaray, Luce. *This Sex Which Is Not One.* Trans. Catherine Porter. Ithaca: Cornell University Press, 1985.

Jameson, Fredric. *The Political Unconscious: Narrative as a Socially Symbolic Act.* Ithaca: Cornell University Press, 1981.

Jerrold, Walter, C. and Clare Jerrold. *Five Queer Women.* London: Brentano's Ltd., 1929.

Jones, Vivien, ed. *Women in the Eighteenth Century: Constructions of Femininity.* New York: Routledge, 1990.

Kahn, Madeleine. *Narrative Transvestism: Rhetoric and Gender in the Eighteenth-Century English Novel.* Ithaca: Cornell University Press, 1991.

Kinkead-Weekes, Mark. *Samuel Richardson: Dramatic Novelist.* London: Methuen and Co. Ltd., 1973.

Kramnick, Isaac. *Bolingbroke and His Circle: The Politics of Nostalgia in the Age of Walpole.* Originally published 1968; rpt. Ithaca: Cornell University Press, 1992.

    ed. *Lord Bolingbroke: Historical Writings.* University of Chicago Press, 1972.

Langford, Paul. *A Polite and Commercial People: England 1727–1783.* Oxford: Clarendon Press, 1989.

    Public Life and the Propertied Englishman 1689–1798. Oxford: Clarendon Press, 1991.

Laquer, Thomas. *Making Sex: Body and Gender from the Greeks to Freud.* Cambridge, MA and London: Harvard University Press, 1990.

Laslett, Peter. *The World We Have Lost.* London: Methuen and Co., 1965.

Lévi-Strauss, Claude. *The Elementary Structures of Kinship.* Boston: Beacon Press, 1969.

Lockwood, Thomas. "Eliza Haywood in 1749: *Dalinda,* and Her Pamphlet on the Pretender." *Notes and Queries* n.s. 36 (1989): 475–77.

    "William Hatchett, *A Rehearsal of Kings* (1737), and the Panton Street Puppet Show (1748)." *Philological Quarterly* 68 (1989): 315–23.

Lovell, Terry. *Consuming Fiction.* London: Verso, 1987.

McBurney, William H. *A Check List of English Prose Fiction 1700–1739.* Cambridge, MA: Harvard University Press, 1960.

    "Edmund Curll, Mrs. Jane Barker, and the English Novel." *Philological Quarterly* 37 (1958): 385–99.

    Four before Richardson: Selected English Novels, 1720–1727. Lincoln: University of Nebraska Press, 1963.

MacDermott, Kathy. "Literature and the Grub Street Myth." In *Popular Fictions: Essays in Literature and History*. Ed. Peter Humm, Paul Stigant, and Peter Widdowson. 16–28. New York: Methuen, 1986.

MacDonald, W. L. *Pope and His Critics: A Study in Eighteenth-Century Personalities*. London: J. M. Dent and Sons, Ltd., 1951.

MacFarlane, Alan. *The Culture of Capitalism*. New York: Blackwell, 1987.
  Marriage and Love in England: Modes of Reproduction, 1300–1840. Oxford: Basil Blackwell, 1986.

Mack, Maynard. *Alexander Pope: A Life*. New York: W. W. Norton and Co., 1985.
  Collected in Himself: Essays Critical, Biographical and Bibliographical on Pope and Some of His Contemporaries. Newark: University of Delaware Press, 1982.
  Essential Articles for the Study of Alexander Pope. Hamden, CT: Archon Books, 1964.
  The Garden and the City: Retirement and Politics in the Later Poetry of Pope, 1731–1743. University of Toronto Press, 1969.

McDowell, Paula. *The Women of Grub Street: Press, Politics and Gender in the London Literary Marketplace, 1676–1730*. Oxford at the Clarendon Press, 1998.

McKendrick, Neil, John Brewer, and J. H. Plumb. *The Birth of a Consumer Society: The Commercialization of Eighteenth-Century England*. Bloomington: Indiana University Press, 1982.

McKenzie, Alan T. *Certain Lively Episodes: The Articulation of Passion in Eighteenth-Century Prose*. Athens: University of Georgia Press, 1990.

McKeon, Michael. *The Origins of the English Novel 1600–1740*. Baltimore: Johns Hopkins University Press, 1987.

McKillop, Alan D. "Letters from Aaron Hill to Richard Savage." *Notes and Queries* 199 (1954): 388–91.
  Samuel Richardson: Printer and Novelist. Chapel Hill: The University of North Carolina Press, 1936.

Malcolmson, Robert W. *Popular Recreations in English Society 1700–1850*. Cambridge University Press, 1973.

Marks, Sylvia Kasey. *Sir Charles Grandison: The Compleat Conduct Book*. Lewisburg: Bucknell University Press, 1986.

Maxted, Ian. *The London Book Trades 1775–1800: A Preliminary Checklist of Members*. Folkestone: William Dawson and Sons, 1977.

Mengel, Elias F., Jr. "The *Dunciad* Illustrations." *Eighteenth-Century Studies* 7 (1973/74): 161–78.

Messenger, Ann. *His and Hers: Essays in Restoration and Eighteenth-Century Literature*. Lexington: University Press of Kentucky, 1986.

Meyer, Gerald Dennis. *The Scientific Lady in England 1650–1760: An Account of Her Rise, with Emphasis on the Major Roles of the Telescope and Microscope*. Berkeley: University of California Press, 1959.

Miller, Nancy K. "Emphasis Added: Plots and Plausibilities in Women's Fiction." *Publication of the Modern Language Association* 96 (1981): 36–48.

Mish, Charles C. "Early Eighteenth-Century Best Sellers in English Prose Fiction." *The Papers of the Bibliographical Society of America* 75 (1981): 413–18.

Mitchell, C. J. "Women in the Eighteenth-Century Book Trade." In *Writers, Books and Trade: An Eighteenth-Century English Miscellany for William B. Todd.* Ed. O. M. Brack, Jr. 25–76. New York: AMS Press, 1994.

Modleski, Tania. *Loving with a Vengeance: Mass-Produced Fantasies for Women.* New York: Methuen, 1982.

Moi, Toril. *Sexual/Textual Politics: Feminist Literary Theory.* New York: Methuen, 1985.

Moore, C. A. "A Note on the Biography of Mrs. Eliza Haywood." *Modern Language Notes* 33 (1918): 248–50.

Mumby, Frank Arthur. *Publishing and Book Selling, Part One: From the Earliest Times to 1870.* London: Jonathan Cape, Ltd., 1930.

Myers, Robin. *The British Book Trade: From Caxton to the Present Day.* London: André Deutsch, 1973.

Ness, Robert. "The *Dunciad* and Italian Opera in England." *Eighteenth-Century Studies* 20 (1986/87): 172–94.

Neuburg, Victor E. *Chapbooks: A Bibliography of References to English and American Chapbook Literature of the Eighteenth and Nineteenth Centuries.* London: Vine Press, 1964.

Nicholson, Colin. *Writing and the Rise of Finance: Capital Satires of the Early Eighteenth Century.* Cambridge University Press, 1994.

Novak, Maximillian. *Economics and the Fiction of Daniel Defoe.* Berkeley: University of California Press, 1962.

    ed. *English Literature in the Age of Disguise.* Berkeley: University of California Press, 1977.

Nussbaum, Felicity. *The Brink of All We Hate: English Satires on Women, 1660–1750.* Lexington: University Press of Kentucky, 1984.

Nussbaum, Felicity and Laura Brown, eds. *The New Eighteenth Century: Theory, Politics, English Literature.* New York: Methuen, Inc., 1987.

Okin, Susan Moller. "Patriarchy and Married Women's Property in England: Questions on Some Current Views." *Eighteenth-Century Studies* 17 (1983/84): 121–38.

Paulson, Ronald. *Breaking and Remaking: Aesthetic Practice in England, 1700–1820.* New Brunswick: Rutgers University Press, 1989.

    Emblem and Expression: Meaning in English Art of the Eighteenth Century. London: Thames and Hudson, 1975.

    Hogarth: "The Modern Moral Subject" 1697–1732. New Brunswick: Rutgers University Press, 1991.

    Popular and Polite Art in the Age of Hogarth and Fielding. University of Notre Dame Press, 1979.

Pearson, Jacqueline. *The Prostituted Muse: Images of Women and Women Dramatists 1642–1737.* London: Harvester Wheatsheaf, 1988.

Plant, Marjorie. *The English Book Trade: An Economic History of the Making and Sale of Books.* London: George Allen and Unwin Ltd., 1939.

Plomer, Henry Robert. *A Dictionary of the Printers and Booksellers Who Were at Work in England, Scotland and Ireland from 1668–1725.* Oxford University Press, 1922.

Plumb, J. H. *England in the Eighteenth Century (1714–1815)*. Baltimore: Penguin Books, 1960.

Pocock, J. G. A. *The Machiavellian Moment: Florentine Political Thought and the Atlantic Republican Tradition*. Princeton University Press, 1975.

ed. *The Political Works of James Harrington*. Cambridge University Press, 1977.

Politics, Language and Time: Essays on Political Thought and History. New York: Atheneum, 1971.

Virtue, Commerce and History: Essays on Political Thought and History, Chiefly in the Eighteenth Century. Cambridge University Press, 1985.

Pohli, Carol Virginia. "'The Point Where Sense and Dulness Meet': What Pope Knows about Knowing and about Women." *Eighteenth-Century Studies* 19 (1985/86): 206–34.

Pollak, Ellen. *The Poetics of Sexual Myth: Gender and Ideology in the Verse of Swift and Pope*. University of Chicago Press, 1985.

Porter, Roy. *English Society in the Eighteenth Century*. New York: Penguin Books, 1982.

Probyn, Clive T. *English Fiction of the Eighteenth Century 1700–1789*. London: Longman, 1987.

Radway, Janice A. *Reading the Romance: Women, Patriarchy and Popular Culture*. Chapel Hill: University of North Carolina Press, 1984.

Raven, James. *Judging New Wealth: Popular Publishing and Responses to Commerce in England, 1750–1800*. New York: Oxford University Press, 1992.

Richetti, John. *Popular Fiction before Richardson: Narrative Patterns 1700–1739*. Oxford: Clarendon Press, 1969.

"Popular Narrative in the Early Eighteenth Century: Formats and Formulas." In *The First English Novelists: Essays in Understanding*. Ed. J. M. Armistead. 3–39. Tennessee Studies in Literature. Knoxville: University of Tennessee Press, 1985.

"Voice and Gender in Eighteenth-Century Fiction: Haywood to Burney." *Studies in the Novel* 19 (1987): 263–72.

Rogers, Pat, ed. *The Eighteenth Century*. New York: Holmes and Meier, 1978.

Grub Street: Studies in a Subculture. London: Methuen and Company, Ltd., 1972.

Literature and Popular Culture in Eighteenth-Century England. Totowa, NJ: Barnes and Noble Books, 1985.

Rose, Mark. "The Author as Proprietor: *Donaldson vs. Becket* and the Genealogy of Modern Authorship." *Representations* 23 (1988): 51–85.

Authors and Owners: The Invention of Copyright. Cambridge, MA: Harvard University Press, 1993.

Rosslyn, Felicity. "'Dipt in the Rainbow': Pope on Women." *Parnassus* 12/13 (1985): 179–93.

Rousseau, G. S. "Threshold and Explanation: The Social Anthropologist and the Critic of Eighteenth-Century Literature." *The Eighteenth Century: Theory and Interpretation* 22 (1981): 127–52.

Rousseau, G. S. and Marjorie Nicolson. *"This Long Disease, My Life": Alexander Pope and the Sciences*. Princeton University Press, 1968.

Rousseau, G. S. and Roy Porter, eds. *Sexual Underworlds of the Enlightenment.* Chapel Hill: University of North Carolina Press, 1988.

Rousseau, G. S. and Pat Rogers, eds. *The Enduring Legacy: Alexander Pope Tercentenary Essays.* Cambridge University Press, 1988.

Rubin, Gayle. "The Traffic in Women: Notes toward a Political Economy of Sex." In *Toward an Anthropology of Women.* Ed. Rayma Ruter. 157–210. New York: Monthly Review Press, 1975.

Rumbold, Valerie. *Women's Place in Pope's World.* Cambridge University Press, 1989.

Runge, Laura. "Gendered Strategies in the Criticism of Early Fiction." *Eighteenth-Century Studies* 28 (1995): 363–78.

Sale, William M. *Samuel Richardson: A Bibliographical Record of His Literary Career with Historical Notes.* New Haven: Yale University Press, 1936.

Samuel Richardson: Master Printer. Ithaca: Cornell University Press, 1950.

Schofield, Mary Anne. *Eliza Haywood.* Boston: Twayne Publishers, 1985.

Masking and Unmasking the Female Mind: Disguising Romances in Feminine Fiction, 1713–1799. Newark: University of Delaware Press, 1990.

Quiet Rebellion: The Fictional Heroines of Eliza Fowler Haywood. Washington DC: University Press of America, 1982.

Schofield, Mary Anne and Cecilia Macheski, eds. *Fetter'd or Free? British Women Novelists, 1670–1815.* Athens: Ohio University Press, 1986.

Schultz, Dieter. " 'Novel,' 'Romance,' and Popular Fiction in the First Half of the Eighteenth Century." *Studies in Philology* 70 (1973): 77–91.

Sedgwick, Eve Kosofsky. *Between Men: English Literature and Male Homosocial Desire.* New York: Columbia University Press, 1985.

Sekora, John. *Luxury: The Concept in Western Thought, Eden to Smollett.* Baltimore: Johns Hopkins University Press, 1977.

Shell, Marc. *Money, Language, and Thought: Literary and Philosophic Economies from the Medieval to the Modern Era.* Baltimore: Johns Hopkins University Press, 1982.

Sherburn, George. *The Early Career of Alexander Pope.* Oxford : Clarendon Press, 1934.

Shesgreen, Sean, ed. *Engravings by Hogarth.* New York: Dover Publications, Inc., 1973.

Shevelow, Kathryn. *Women and Print Culture: The Construction of Femininity in the Early Periodical.* London: Routledge, 1989.

Showalter, Elaine. *The Literature of Their Own: British Women Novelists from Bronte to Lessing.* Princeton University Press, 1977.

ed. *The New Feminist Criticism: Essays on Women, Literature and Theory.* New York: Pantheon Books, 1985.

ed. *Speaking of Gender.* New York: Routledge, 1989.

Smallwood, Angela J. *Fielding and the Woman Question: The Novels of Henry Fielding and Feminist Debate, 1700–1750.* New York: St. Martin's Press, 1989.

Smith, Barbara Herrnstein. "The Contingencies of Value." *Critical Inquiry* 10 (1983): 1–35.

Spacks, Patricia Meyer. *Desire and Truth: Functions of Plot in Eighteenth-Century English Novels.* University of Chicago Press, 1990.

"Imaginations Warm and Tender: Pope and Lady Mary." *South Atlantic Quarterly* 83 (1984): 207–27.

Imagining a Self: Autobiography and Novel in Eighteenth-Century England. Cambridge, MA: Harvard University Press, 1976.

Speck W. A. " Politicians, Peers and Publication by Subscription 1700–50." In *Books and their Readers in Eighteenth-Century England*. Ed. Isabel Rivers, 47–68. Leicester University Press, 1982.

Spencer, Jane. *The Rise of the Woman Novelist: From Aphra Behn to Jane Austen*. Oxford: Basil Blackwell, 1986.

Spender, Dale. *Mothers of the Novel: 100 Good Writers before Jane Austen*. New York: Pandora, 1986.

Sperling, John G. *The South Sea Company: An Historical Essay and Bibliographical Finding List*. Cambridge, MA: Harvard University Press, 1962.

Stallybrass, Peter and Allon White. *The Politics and Poetics of Transgression*. London: Methuen, 1986.

Staves, Susan. *Married Women's Separate Property in England, 1660–1833*. Cambridge, MA: Harvard University Press, 1990.

Steiner, T. R. "The Misrepresentation of Elizabeth Thomas, 'Curll's Corinna'." *Notes and Queries* 30 (1983): 506–08.

Stevens, Frederick George, ed. *Catalogue of Political and Personal Satires Preserved in the Department of Prints and Drawings in the British Museum Volume Two: 1689–1783*. London: British Museum Publications, Ltd. Originally published 1873; rpt. 1978.

Straub, Kristina. "Men from Boys: Cibber, Pope, and the Schoolboy." *The Eighteenth Century: Theory and Interpretation* 32 (1991): 219–39.

Sexual Suspects: Eighteenth-Century Players and Sexual Ideology. Princeton University Press, 1992.

Thomas, Claudia N. *Alexander Pope and His Eighteenth-Century Women Readers*. Carbondale and Edwardsville: Southern Illinois University Press, 1994.

Thompson, E. P. *Customs in Common*. London: Penguin Books. 1991.

"The Moral Economy of the English Crowd in the Eighteenth Century." *Past and Present* 50 (1971): 76–136.

Whigs and Hunters: The Origin of the Black Act. New York: Pantheon Books, 1975.

Thompson, James. *Models of Value: Eighteenth-Century Political Economy and the Novel*. Durham, NC: Duke University Press, 1996.

Todd, Dennis. "The 'Blunted Arms' of Dulness: The Problems of Power in the *Dunciad*." *Studies in Philology* 79 (1982): 177–204.

Imagining Monsters: Miscreations of the Self in Eighteenth-Century England. University of Chicago Press, 1995.

Todd, Janet. *The Sign of Angellica: Women, Writing and Fiction, 1660–1800*. New York: Columbia University Press, 1989.

Turner, Cheryl. *Living by the Pen: Women Writers in the Eighteenth Century*. London and New York: Routledge, 1992.

Turner, James Grantham. "Pope's Libertine Self-Fashioning." *The Eighteenth Century: Theory and Interpretation* 29 (1988): 123–44.

Vander Meulen, David L. *Pope's Dunciad of 1728: A History and Facsimile*. Charlottesville and London: University Press of Virginia, 1991.

Veeser, H. Aram, ed. *The New Historicism*. New York and London: Routledge, 1989.

Warner, William Beatty. "The Elevation of the Novel in England: Hegemony and Literary History." *ELH* 59 (1992): 577–96.

    Reading Clarissa : The Struggles of Interpretation. New Haven: Yale University Press, 1979.

Watt, Ian. *The Rise of the Novel: Studies in Defoe, Richardson and Fielding*. Berkeley: University of California Press, 1957.

Whicher, George Frisbie. *The Life and Romances of Mrs. Eliza Haywood*. New York: Columbia University Press, 1915.

Williams, Raymond. *The Country and the City*. New York: Oxford University Press, 1973.

    Keywords: A Vocabulary of Culture and Society. New York: Oxford University Press, 1976.

    Marxism and Literature. Oxford and New York: Oxford University Press, 1977.

Wilson, Penelope. "Feminism and the Augustans: Some Readings and Problems." *Critical Inquiry* 28 (1984): 80–92.

Wimsatt, William. *The Portraits of Alexander Pope*. New Haven: Yale University Press, 1965.

Winn, James. "On Pope, Printers, and Publishers." *Eighteenth-Century Life* 6 (1981): 93–102.

    A Window in the Bosom: The Letters of Alexander Pope. Hamden: Archon Books, 1977.

Woodmansee, Martha. *The Author, Art and the Market: Rereading the History of Aesthetics*. New York: Columbia University Press, 1994.

    "The Genius and the Copyright: Economic and Legal Conditions of the Emergence of the Author." *Eighteenth-Century Studies* 17 (1984): 425–48.

Woodmansee, Martha and Peter Jaszi, eds. *The Construction of Authorship: Textual Appropriation in Law and Literature*. Durham, NC: Duke University Press, 1994.

Index

Aislabie, John, South Sea Company and, 19, 21, 25–26, 178 n. 2, 178–79 n. 7

Anti-Pamela, 109, 110, 111–16, 195–96 n. 24; bills of exchange in, 114; business and pleasure in, 111–14; consumerism and, 112–15; duty in, 114–15; economy in, 112, 114–15, 116; female desire in, 112–14

Armstrong, Nancy, 15, 159, 207 n. 54

"Augustan" ideology, constructions of, 8–9, 15, 39, 41–42, 43, 75, 171. *See also* Kramnick, Isaac

Authorship. *See* Professional authorship

Blount, Martha: Haywood and, 60; Pope and, 45, 53, 68, 183 n. 19

Bount, Teresa, 45–46, 68

"Business of Pleasure," for women, 20–21, 26, 33, 35–36, 37, 39, 87, 95, 111, 112–13, 140, 164. *See also* Women, as investors

Carnivalesque: *Dunciad* and, 50, 64; Grub Street and, 40–42; speculative investment and, 37–38; *Pamela* and, 207 n. 53

Chetwood, William Rufus, 19, 32, 190 n. 18; Haywood and 60, 79, 81; *The Stock-jobbers* and, 33, 34–36, 39

Churchill, Sarah, Duchess of Marlborough, 32

The City Jilt, 78, 89–95; consumerism and, 92–93; desire in, 90, 91, 93; property in, 92, 94; sexual-financial economy in, 89–90, 91, 93–94, 95, 192 n. 44; speculative investment in, 89, 90, 92–93, 94, 95

Civic humanism: paper credit and, 140–41; tradition of, 3–4, 21, 117–18; virtue and, 22, 140, 142, 201 n. 11

Clarissa, 118, 128, 147, 150, 164, 205 n. 42

Commerce. *See* Literary marketplace; Paper credit; Print trade; Speculative investment

Copyrights: Haywood and, 12, 169, 172, 208–09 n. 15; Pope and, 12, 169, 172; Richardson and, 12, 145–46, 169, 172, 203 n. 4

Credit, figure of, 2, 4, 23–25, 30, 40, 91, 180 n. 25; Defoe's representations of, 37, 179 n. 12

Cromwell, Henry: Pope's letters to 46, 66, 67–68, 69, 70; Thomas, Elizabeth, and, 58, 187 n. 50

Curll, Edmund: Haywood and, 60, 68, 69–70; in literary marketplace, 41, 67, 72–75, 76, 186 n. 49, 190 n. 18; Pope and, 47, 48, 63–76, 169; publication of Pope's letters, 73–74; Richardson and, 147; Thomas, Elizabeth, and, 58, 59–60. Works published by: *Codrus*, 71–72; *Compleat Key to the Dunciad*, 66–67; *Curliad*, 66, 73; *The Female Dunciad*, 68, 69–70; *Popiad*, 71; *A Popp upon Pope*, 70–71

Defoe, Daniel, 24, 146, 179 n. 12

Dennis, John, 35, 68, 75; Pope and, 63, 71; on stock-jobbing, 22; Richardson and, 208 n. 13

Dulness, figure of, 1, 5, 40; Belinda and, 51–53; carnivalesque and, 50; fecundity of, 1, 49, 50–51; feminine characteristics of, 1, 49–53, 54–55; feminization and, 48–50; paper credit and, 5; sway and, 55–56; women and, 54–55

Dunces, 21–22, 41, 49, 53–54, 55–56

Dunciad, 1, 48–62, 65, 171, 208 n. 6; carnivalesque in, 64; cultural categories in, 8–9, 10, 41–43, 45, 47–48, 50, 63–64, 87; Curll and, 58, 59–60, 65–66, 73; dunces and, 56; feminization and, 47–49; Haywood and, 11, 39, 60–62, 69, 72, 77, 87, 108, 137; hybridity of, 64; literary marketplace and, 41, 56, 62–65, 168; opera in, 56–57; paper credit and, 11, 43; Richardson's attitude toward, 169–70; sexuality in, 56, 57–58; Thomas, Elizabeth, and, 57–60, 72

227

Printed in the United States
40590LVS00006B/18

9 780521 023016

7270